A Theology of the Old Testament

A THEOLOGY OF THE OLD TESTAMENT

Cultural Memory, Communication, and Being Human

John W. Rogerson

Fortress Press
Minneapolis

To the Theological Faculties of the
Friedrich-Schiller-Universität, Jena, and
the Albert-Ludwigs-Universität, Freiburg im Breisgau,
in grateful acknowledgement of the conferral of the
degrees of Doktor der Theologie, honoris causa

A THEOLOGY OF THE OLD TESTAMENT
Cultural Memory, Communication, and Being Human
First Fortress Press edition 2010

Cover Image: *Crossing of the Red Sea*, from The Story of the Exodus suite, 1966 by Marc Chagall. Spaightwood Galleries. www.spaightwoodgalleries.com.
© ADAGP, Paris and DACS, London 2008.
Cover Design: Laurie Ingram

Library of Congress Cataloging-in-Publication Data
Rogerson, J. W. (John William), 1935-
  A theology of the Old Testament : cultural memory, communication, and being human / J.W. Rogerson.—1st Fortress Press ed.
    p. cm.
  Includes bibliographical references and indexes.
  ISBN 978-0-8006-9715-0 (alk. paper)
  1. Bible. O.T.—Theology. 2. Communication—Biblical teaching. I. Title.
  BS1192.5.R635 2010
  230'.0411—dc22   2009047597

The paper used in this publication meets the minimum requirements of American National Standard for Information Sciences—Permanence of Paper for Printed Library Materials, ANSI Z329.48-1984.
Manufactured in the U.S.A.

14   13   12   11   10   1   2   3   4   5   6   7   8   9   10

Contents

Preface

As this book goes to press in Great Britain with SPCK and in North America with Fortress Press, I would like to recount how the book came to be. More than twenty years have passed since Judith Longman, then of SPCK, suggested that I should write an Old Testament Theology, and gave me a contract to do this, with a deadline considerably shorter than twenty years later! There are various reasons why it has taken the project so long to be completed, and completed in a way quite different from how I originally envisaged it. My first priority was to complete the biography of W. M. L. de Wette on which I had begun serious work in 1985. This took me until early 1991, although the task of dealing with proofs, indexes and lists of de Wette's publications and letters, prior to the publication of the book in 1992, was also very time-consuming. I then had invitations to deliver special series of lectures – the F. D. Maurice Lectures in London in 1992, six Gifford Lectures in Aberdeen in 1994, and the Prideaux Lectures in the University of Essex in 1998. I suppose that I could have declined these invitations on the grounds that completing my Theology was more important, but apart from not being very good at saying 'no', there was the fact that I had no clear idea in my mind of how I was going to tackle the task of writing an Old Testament Theology. This was in spite of (or perhaps, because of) the fact that I had spent three months at the end of 1994 in Göttingen reading all the Old Testament theologies or their equivalents that I could find that had been published in German in the nineteenth century.

To cut short what could be a long story, I felt that the time to stop prevaricating had come when, in 2004, I received an invitation to deliver the 2006 Thomas Burns Lectures at the University of Otago in Dunedin, New Zealand. There were six lectures to be delivered over the course of two weeks in the August of that year, and I decided that they must become the basis for the Theology. It would also be an opportunity to get the reactions of colleagues to what I was trying to do. The lectures were delivered under the title 'A Communicative Theology of the Old Testament' and I should like to record my thanks to Professor Paul Trebilco and his colleagues for the invitation and for making the time in Dunedin so enjoyable and profitable.

The present work is a complete rewriting and enlargement of the lectures, although following their basic scheme. Something should be said, first, about the term 'communicative'. This term was key to the lectures and remains key throughout this book. It has, as reviewers may wish to point out, been used in the present work in a somewhat elastic way. It is a slippery term in any case, as Luhmann has pointed out.[1] My use of it is eclectic, owing something to Habermas's idea of communicative action,[2] as well as to my reading of Luhmann, and his use of systems theory. But its main thrust in the present work is twofold. First, it helps to emphasize that the purpose of the book is not to try to reconstruct the religious ideas that may have been held in ancient Israel and which were expressed in the Old Testament. Although an Old Testament Theology cannot avoid dealing with the past as the matrix from which the Old Testament emerged, the present work is concerned above all with today's world. It is an attempt to let parts of the Old Testament speak to the concerns of present-day readers. The term 'communicative' is meant to try to convey this. Second, 'communicative' serves as a theme around which certain topics can be organized, most notably in the chapters about disrupted communication in social relationships and divine–human relationships.

One of the most helpful observations made (by Dr M. E. Andrew) on the lectures in Dunedin was that they dealt extensively with actual passages from the Old Testament as opposed to relegating it to numerous references to the subjects being discussed. It was always my intention to try to let the texts 'speak', so to say, and I was thus glad of the encouragement given to me by Dr Andrew on this score. In the present work the space devoted to the exegesis of passages from the Old Testament has been considerably expanded. The translations are my own, and readers will notice that I have accepted many scholarly suggestions about emending the traditional Hebrew text. I hope that experts in Hebrew will be able to understand my transliterations. When I see transliterated Hebrew it often takes me some time to work out what the underlying Hebrew in fact is! I am also aware that extremely sophisticated transcriptions of the Hebrew have been undertaken by members of the 'Richter' school, based upon modern linguistics.[3] What I have tried to do is to give an 'oral' version of the Hebrew as it would be pronounced, roughly, in modern Israeli Hebrew pronunciation, and given that modern word-processors do not have all the diacritical marks that one would like. I hope that Hebraists will be able to see what I have done, whether or not they agree with my conclusions.

The various dynamics that have come together in the genesis of this book – the Burns Lectures, the stress on communication (in its various

---

[1] N. Luhmann, *Soziale Systeme: Grundriß einer allgemeinen Theorie*, Frankfurt a.M.: Suhrkamp, 1987, pp. 193–200.

[2] J. Habermas, *Theorie des kommunikativen Handelns*, 2 vols, Frankfurt a.M.: Suhrkamp, 1981.

[3] W. Richter (ed.), *Biblia Hebraica transcripta* (ATSAT 33.1–33.13), St Ottilien: Eos, 1991–3.

senses), the importance of exegesis – have resulted in a very different, and considerably shorter, work than I previously envisaged. At one stage, I thought of reviewing all the theologies that had been written in the nineteenth and twentieth centuries. It has also occurred to me that I have devoted no space to my work on Old Testament ethics, especially discourse ethics, which would fit well into the communicative scheme. All this is because my thinking tends to move on all the time, and I do not like to repeat myself more than is absolutely necessary. Another point that may well strike readers and reviewers is the lack of reference to other writers in the field, including Brueggemann, Barr, Childs, Rendtorff, Kaiser and Janowski, to mention only some of the most recent. It goes without saying that I have learned much from these, and many other, writers. If they are not, or hardly, mentioned, it is because I am trying to do things in a particular way that leads me along different paths. Also, I did not want to overload the book with footnotes for the sake of it. The book represents what I want to say now, not what I might have written twenty years ago, or even at some time in the future.

My friend and colleague Philip Davies has read and commented upon the drafts of the chapters as they have emerged, and as always, I have greatly appreciated the discussions that have ensued. My wife Rosalind has, as ever, typed from my longhand – first the lectures, then their revised version with, I fear, too many footnotes in German. I do not need to say how much I have appreciated her help and support.

J. W. Rogerson

Abbreviations

AB	Anchor Bible
ANET	*Ancient Near Eastern Texts relating to the Old Testament*, 2nd edn (ed. J. B. Pritchard), Princeton: Princeton University Press, 1955
ATD	Das Alte Testament Deutsch
ATSAT	Arbeiten zu Text und Sprache im Alten Testament
BDB	*A Hebrew and English Lexicon of the Old Testament* (F. Brown, S. R. Driver and C. A. Briggs), Oxford: Clarendon Press, 1907
BE	Biblische Enzyklopädie
BHK	Biblia Hebraica, ed. Rudolf Kittel
BHS	Biblia Hebraica Stuttgartensia
BKAT	Biblischer Kommentar Altes Testament
BWANT	Beiträge zur Wissenschaft vom Alten und Neuen Testament
BZAW	Beihefte zur Zeitschrift für die alttestamentliche Wissenschaft
CBOT	Coniectanea biblica – Old Testament Series
ET	English translation
EU	*Einheitsübersetzung der Bibel*
FAT	Forschungen zum Alten Testament
FGLP	Forschungen zur Geschichte und Lehre des Protestantismus
FRLANT	Forschungen zur Religion und Literatur des Alten und Neuen Testaments
GHAT	Göttinger Handkommentar zum Alten Testament
GNB	Good News Bible
HAT	Handbuch zum Alten Testament
ICC	International Critical Commentary
KuD	*Kerygma und Dogma*
JSOT	*Journal for the Study of the Old Testament*
JSOTSS	Journal for the Study of the Old Testament, Supplement Series
LXX	Septuagint
NBL	*Neues Bibel-Lexikon* (ed. M. Görg and B. Lang), Zürich: Benziger, 1988–2001
NCB	New Century Bible
NEB	New English Bible
NF	Neue Folge
NIV	New International Version of the Bible

NRSV	New Revised Standard Version of the Bible
OBO	Orbis biblicus et orientalis
OTG	Old Testament Guides
OTL	Old Testament Library
REB	Revised English Bible
RGG	*Religion in Geschichte und Gegenwart* (ed. H. D. Betz), 4th edn, Tübingen: Mohr, 1998
RSV	Revised Standard Version of the Bible
SBS	Stuttgarter Bibelstudien
SBT	Studies in Biblical Theology
SDCH	*Sheffield Dictionary of Classical Hebrew* (ed. D. J. A. Clines), Sheffield: Sheffield Academic Press, vol. 2, 1995
SVT	Supplements to Vetus Testamentum
SWBA	Social World of Biblical Antiquity
TB or ThB	Theologische Bücherei
TRE	*Theologische Realenzyklopädie*
TW	Theologische Wissenschaft
UF	*Ugarit-Forschungen*
WMANT	Wissenschaftliche Monographien zum Alten und Neuen Testament
ZThK	*Zeitschrift für Theologie und Kirche*

Introduction

What form will your 'theology' take? What will be its organizing principle? I have often been asked these questions in recent years when colleagues have learned that I was planning to write a Theology of the Old Testament. My usual answer has been that I was not sure, and that every time I thought about the subject I came up with a different answer! Of one thing I was always sure, however, and that was that my 'theology' would attempt to address today's world, and would not be an exercise in trying to reconstruct what people may or may not once have believed in ancient Israel.[1]

Ever since I came upon the Epilegomena to Rudolf Bultmann's *Theologie des Neuen Testaments* I felt that it issued a challenge that I wanted to take on. In my translation it reads as follows:

> Because the New Testament is a document of history, and in particular, of the history of religion, its interpretation requires the work of historical investigation, whose methods were developed from the time of the Enlightenment, and which bore fruit in the investigation of early Christianity and the interpretation of the New Testament. Such work can only be carried out from two standpoints, either from that of reconstruction or that of interpretation. Reconstruction is concerned with past history, interpretation with the writings of the New Testament; and clearly, one cannot be done without the other. They always work mutually together. But the important question is which of the two is the servant of the other. Either the writings of the New Testament can be treated as 'sources' which the historian uses in order to reconstruct early Christianity as a phenomenon of the historical past, or the reconstruction serves the need of the interpretation of the New

---

[1] In this respect the enterprise resembles the view of writers such as Walter Benjamin and Ernst Bloch, that philosophy and history should assist our understanding of today's world. See H.-E. Schiller, *Bloch-Konstellationen: Utopien der Philosophie*, Lüneburg: zu Klampen, 1991, the essays 'Philosophie als Optativ: Ernst Blochs *Leipziger Vorlesungen zur Geschichte der Philosophie*', pp. 11–24, and 'Jetztzeit und Entwicklung: Geschichte bei Ernst Bloch und Walter Benjamin', pp. 25–50. See especially p. 22, 'Walter Benjamin hat in seinem Passagenwerk "die wahre Methode der Dinge sich gegenwärtig zu machen" durch die Aufgabe bestimmt, "sie in unserm Raum (nicht uns in ihrem) vorzustellen"': The reference is to Benjamin's *Das Passagen-Werk*, in *Gesammelte Schriften* V, Frankfurt a.M.: Suhrkamp, 1982, p. 1014; ET *The Arcades Project* (trans. H. Eiland and K. McLaughlin), Cambridge, Mass.: Harvard University Press, 1999, p. 846: 'The true method of making things present is: to represent them into our space (not to represent ourselves in their space.')

Testament writings, on the assumption that these writings have something to say to the present. The historical investigation involved in the picture that is presented here is put at the service of the latter view.[2]

What caught my attention was the statement that the historical reconstruction would serve the needs of the interpretation of the New Testament, on the assumption that its writings had something to say to the present. It is my hope that what follows in this work will enable the writings of the Old Testament to say something to the present, however one understands 'the present'.

Before I proceed I want to reflect further on Bultmann's statement, because doing so will enable me to clarify exactly what I hope the present 'theology' will achieve. Bultmann presents two alternatives: either the biblical texts are used as 'sources' for the reconstruction of beliefs (early Christianity) as a phenomenon of the historical past, or the reconstruction serves the need of the interpretation of the biblical texts on the assumption that they have something to say to the present. The reality is probably more complex than this, but the alternatives are a useful starting-point for reflection upon the genre of Old Testament theologies and their purposes.

Old Testament theology in its modern form is an invention of Protestant, mainly Lutheran, German scholarship of the nineteenth century. It owed its rise to the emancipation of biblical studies from subservience to dogmatic and systematic theology, an emancipation that happened gradually from the time of the Reformation and which accelerated in the seventeenth and eighteenth centuries. Basically, this involved a recognition that the thought-worlds of the Old Testament writers differed so fundamentally from those of Enlightenment Europe that it was no longer possible for the Old Testament to support uncritically the use that had traditionally been made of it in dogmatic and systematic theology.

In some cases, the recognition of the distance between Old Testament and modern thought-worlds could be easily accommodated to traditional Christian belief. For example, as it became clear, from voyages of exploration around the world, that the Table of the Nations in Genesis 10 did not include places such as North and South America, the conclusion, that Genesis 10 portrayed the world as it was known to the biblical writers, not the world as it was in its entirety, was a conclusion that did not in any way threaten traditional Christian belief. In other cases, the ancient principle of accommodation could be invoked in order to deal with problems

---

[2] R. Bultmann, *Theologie des Neuen Testaments*, 9th edn, Tübingen: J. C. B. Mohr (Paul Siebeck), 1984, p. 600.

arising from the difference between the biblical and modern thought-worlds.[3]

Accommodation had its origins in attempts to explain biblical statements about God that seemed to contradict traditional beliefs about the nature and being of God. A good example was found at Genesis 6.6, which states that God was sorry that he had created humankind. The older translations had, 'it repented the LORD' and earlier exegetes were agreed that 'repentance' was something of which God was not capable, since he knew all things in advance.[4] Genesis 6.6 was therefore a statement that was accommodated to human understanding. God did not, in fact, repent or feel grieved about having created humankind. The verse had a rhetorical function, which was to underline the seriousness of the wickedness of the human race prior to the Flood.

The principle of accommodation could be adapted and extended to cover the ways in which God had made himself and his will known to people whose scientific understanding of the world was, to put it mildly, rudimentary in comparison with the scientific knowledge of the seventeenth and eighteenth centuries.

An obvious strategy was to say that for ancient Israelites, phenomena of nature that we can explain in terms of scientific causality were seen by them in terms of divine speaking and acting. Thus, it was a thunderstorm that caused Adam and Eve to flee from the Garden of Eden, and the lightning of that storm that was understood by them to be a flaming sword guarding the way to the tree of life. The thunder was for them the voice of God expressing his anger, because they had disobeyed him. This kind of strategy made it possible for interpreters, especially in the eighteenth century, to 'de-supernaturalize' the Old Testament; to rid it of its worldview of angels, miracles and divine interventions. All these had been the interpretations of natural occurrences by a people with little knowledge of scientific explanations. Modern interpreters could make use of the biblical text by 'de-supernaturalizing' it.[5]

This approach could deal not only with the scientific difficulties that the text contained for modern European readers; it could also deal with moral difficulties. These had long been recognized by Christian interpreters,

---

[3] K. Scholder, *Ursprünge und Probleme der Bibelkritik im 17. Jahrhundert* (FGLP 10/33), Munich: Kaiser, 1966.

[4] See J. Calvin, *Genesis* (trans. J. King), Edinburgh: Banner of Truth, 1965, pp. 248–9, 'The repentance which is here ascribed to God does not properly belong to him, but has reference to our understanding of him . . . the Spirit accommodates himself to our capacity.'

[5] See further J. W. Rogerson, *Myth in Old Testament Interpretation* (BZAW 134), Berlin: de Gruyter, 1974, ch. 1.

and a variety of methods had been developed in order to deal with them. Augustine, in the *City of God* (*c.* 412 CE), had recognized that Abraham violated the rule of monogamy by having a child, Ishmael, by his wife's servant Hagar (Genesis 16).[6] Augustine excused Abraham on the ground that what he did was without lust or sexual gratification, and designed to do what his wife, Sarah, was unable to do at the time, to provide him with offspring. Joshua's slaughter of the Canaanites during the occupation of Canaan was excused on the ground that the Canaanites were excessively wicked and that Joshua was carrying out God's sentence of judgement on this wickedness. David's adultery with Bathsheba and the subsequent elimination of her husband, Uriah, by placing him in the front line of battle (2 Samuel 11) was dealt with by distinguishing between David in his office as king, and David as a private individual. In his office as king, David was truly the man after God's own heart (cf. 1 Samuel 13.14); as a private individual his behaviour was wicked and justly punished by God (2 Samuel 12).[7]

These explanations became increasingly unacceptable from the seventeenth century onwards, although some survived well into the nineteenth century in some orthodox circles. Where they were rejected, they were replaced by another type of accommodation. This assumed that the moral understanding of ancient Israelites was much inferior to that of modern Europeans, and that actions that we would regard as immoral were not regarded in this way in ancient Israel. A test case was God's command to Abraham to offer his son Isaac in sacrifice (Genesis 22). How could someone believe that God was commanding him to do something as immoral as sacrificing another human being? The answer was that this was only possible in a situation in which people did not value highly the life of individuals, a situation where morality operated at a lower level compared with modern European societies. This led in turn to the view that the Old Testament was, among other things, the record of the process by which God had led the Israelites from crude religious and moral ideas to higher and more sophisticated notions.[8] All this was the background to the rise, in the nineteenth century, of theologies of the Old Testament, and it is not

---

[6] Augustine, *The City of God against Pagans* (Loeb Classical Library, trans. E. M. Sanford and W. M. Green), London: Heinemann; Cambridge, Mass.: Harvard University Press, 1965, Book 16, XXV (pp. 120–3).

[7] See generally the section entitled 'Seeming Contradictions to Morality' in T. H. Horne, *An Introduction to the Critical Study and Knowledge of the Holy Scriptures*, 5th edn, London, 1825, vol. 1, pp. 562–78.

[8] See J. W. Rogerson, *Old Testament Criticism in the Nineteenth Century: England and Germany*, London: SPCK, 1984, pp. 246–7.

surprising that the earliest practitioners saw their task in descriptive and historical terms. L. F. O. Baumgarten-Crusius, writing in 1828, saw the task of Old Testament theology as that of giving an account of the historical development of the ideas of the biblical writers, as opposed to how the texts had been used in the Church and in dogmatics. It was an exercise 'without prior views to which it must conform, and without regarding it [i.e. the Old Testament] as a supernatural unity, or containing a double (spiritual) sense through divine inspiration'.[9] According to J. C. F. Steudel Old Testament theology was 'the systematic overview of the religious ideas which are to be found in the books of the Old Testament, including the Apocrypha'.[10] However, scholars such as Steudel did not see their task as purely descriptive. There was a theological purpose, which was to bring to expression the divine process that was at work behind and within the development of human religious ideas.

If we look back to the alternatives stated by Bultmann, those of using the Bible as a source to reconstruct past religious beliefs, or using historical reconstruction to assist the interpretation of the Bible for the present day, we have to say that these Old Testament theologies were firmly on the side of the first alternative. The Old Testament was a source for reconstructing the beliefs that had been held at differing times in ancient Israel. This was not surprising. The recognition that there was a significant gap between the world-views of the biblical writers and modern Europeans had brought a reluctance to cite biblical texts as though they conveyed direct information from God. On the other hand, there was a growing interest in history as a process through which God worked and revealed his will. In 1811–12, B. G. Niebuhr had published a *History of Rome* in which he argued that the hand of God could be seen to be at work in particular times of crisis in that nation's history.[11] The idea that history was a process guided by God seemed also to be a view found in the Old Testament. In the climax of the story of Joseph, when Joseph finally discloses his identity to his brothers, he says,

> do not be distressed, or reproach yourselves for having sold me here; it was
> in order to preserve life that God sent me before you . . . it was not you who
> sent me here, but God.   (Genesis 45.5, 8)

---

[9] L. F. O. Baumgarten-Crusius, *Grundzüge der biblischen Theologie*, Jena: F. Fromann, 1828, p. 7, my translation.

[10] J. C. F. Steudel, *Vorlesungen über die Theologie des Alten Testaments*, Berlin: G. Reimer, 1840, p. 1, my translation.

[11] B. G. Niebuhr, *Römische Geschichte*, 1–2, Berlin: G. Reimer, 1811–12; ET by J. C. Hare and C. Thirlwall, *The History of Rome*, London: Taylor & Walton, 1847.

A classical statement of the position that was to determine the writing of Old Testament theologies well into the twentieth century was made by Heinrich Ewald in 1843 at the beginning of his *History of Israel*:

> The history of this ancient people is in reality the history of the growth of true religion, rising through all stages to perfection . . . finally revealing itself in full glory and power, in order to spread irresistibly from this centre, never again to be lost, but to become the eternal possession and blessing of all nations.[12]

At this point it is necessary to make an observation which is of critical importance not only for Old Testament theologies in general, but for what will follow in the present work. The historical reconstruction of which Bultmann spoke; the historical survey of beliefs to be found in the Old Testament as envisaged by Baumgarten-Crusius, Steudel and others, and the history of Israel as written by Ewald was not a simple retelling of the story of Israelite religion as found in the Old Testament. It was a scholarly reconstruction of history using, as Bultmann observed, methods of historical investigation developed from the time of the Enlightenment.

As I have sought to demonstrate elsewhere, it was W. M. L. de Wette who pioneered a breakthrough in the critical reconstruction of ancient Israelite history that set an agenda with which all subsequent scholarship has had to come to terms.[13] In his doctoral dissertation on Deuteronomy (1805) and his *Beiträge zur Einleitung in das Alte Testament* (1806–7) de Wette argued that the Old Testament's own account of its history of religion and sacrifice did not agree with what could be established by historical research. According to the Old Testament, Moses established a fully fledged system of priesthood and sacrifice at Mount Sinai following the Israelite exodus from Egypt (see Exodus 19—24 and the material in Leviticus and Numbers). According to de Wette this fully fledged system was not given once-for-all at an early point in Israel's history. It developed gradually over many centuries, and did not reach the form in which it is now presented in the Old Testament until many centuries after the time of Moses.

There is no point in rehearsing here the reasons adduced by de Wette for this radical position.[14] What is important for present purposes is a consideration of the implications of his work. De Wette himself did not

---

[12] H. Ewald, *Geschichte des Volkes Israel*, Göttingen: Dietrichs Buchhandlung, 1843, vol. 1, p. 9; ET *History of Israel*, London: Longmans, Green & Co., 1876, vol. 1, p. 5.

[13] See J. W. Rogerson, *W. M. L. de Wette, Founder of Modern Biblical Criticism: An Intellectual Biography* (JSOTSS 126), Sheffield: Sheffield Academic Press, 1992.

[14] See my *Old Testament Criticism*, pp. 20–36, and *W. M. L. de Wette*, pp. 39–61.

see scholarly reconstructed history as something in which the divine will could be discerned. He wrote a *Biblical Dogmatics* that drew upon the post-Kantian philosophy of his friend Jakob Friedrich Fries. Old Testament texts were valuable to the extent that they resonated with insights about the nature of truth and reality that were discerned by means of Fries's philosophy. But if de Wette did not view history in this way, others did; and we have seen above how Ewald understood and expressed the matter. However, de Wette's work posed the following dilemma: either one had to accept the Old Testament's own view of the history of Israelite religion or one had to reject it and replace it with a version reconstructed by biblical scholarship. There was no other possibility.

In conservative and traditional circles in Germany, elsewhere in Europe, and in North America, de Wette's rejection of the Old Testament's view of the history of its religion was seen as a rationalist attack on the inspiration of the Bible and a potential denial of fundamental Christian doctrines. A vigorous defence of the Old Testament picture was mounted by scholars such as E. W. Hengstenberg and J. C. K. von Hofmann in Germany, to name only two, while in Britain attempts to stem what was seen as the German rationalist tide were largely successful until the 1860s.[15]

Mention has already been made of Heinrich Ewald, and it is to him that attention must now be given. Ewald is important because he was the first scholar to publish a full-scale scholarly History of Israel. While he was immensely critical of de Wette's position (he also disagreed with almost every other contemporary scholar working in the field!), he accepted the basic premise of the de Wette position, which was that the Old Testament's own view of its religious history did not agree with that of modern critical scholarship. In the event, Ewald's reconstruction was much less radical than that of de Wette and had the effect of enabling some scholars to accept the results of critical scholarship, while adhering to a view of the history of Israelite religion that was closer to the biblical account than de Wette's version. However, the fundamental point became, and continued to be this: if de Wette's basic premise was correct, then the history of Israelite religion as reconstructed by critical scholarship would always necessarily be provisional. It would be affected by new discoveries, for example in the field of archaeology, new methods, for example in sociology and anthropology, and the theological or anti-theological agendas held by scholars from time to time.

From the perspective of the twenty-first century it seems strange that eminent and thoughtful scholars could accept the basic premise of de

---

[15] See my *Old Testament Criticism*, pp. 79–90, 104–11.

Wette's position without realizing that it was certainly incompatible with the idea that 'history' was a process guided by God in which he revealed his will. De Wette himself did not claim this for history. Von Hofmann squared the circle by exempting biblical history from critical reconstruction while subjecting all other history to its rigours. Even such a brilliant and perceptive scholar as William Robertson Smith towards the end of the nineteenth century could believe that the history of Israel, as reconstructed by critical investigation, was a history of divine grace.[16]

It is now necessary to return to Bultmann's formulation to see how it is affected by the immediately preceding discussion. His statement, that historical reconstruction must assist the interpretation of the New Testament, implies an acceptance of the de Wette either/or in terms of the indispensability of critical historical investigation as it was developed from the time of the Enlightenment in Europe (roughly, from the seventeenth century). This means that the background or context for biblical interpretation (the reconstruction) must be ever changing, for the reasons given above. Even in the present writer's short time of encounter with biblical scholarship, the scholarly understanding of the history of Israel's religion has changed out of all recognition. In my student days in the late 1950s, the text book recommended as 'modern scholarship at its best' was G. E. Wright's *Biblical Archaeology*, a book which began with pre-biblical times and proceeded serenely through the biblical periods as contained in the Old Testament: the Patriarchs, the Exodus, the Conquest of Canaan, the Period of the Judges, and so on. Although Wright's account was critical, it was also thoroughly traditional. The general outline of Israel's history as given in the Old Testament was reliable and could be backed up by archaeology.[17] Wright's position was repeated in much greater detail by J. Bright's *A History of Israel*, which was published in 1960.[18] It was therefore something of a shock as a student to have to come to terms with the English translation of Martin Noth's *The History of Israel*, which appeared in 1958.[19]

Noth's history began not with the Patriarchs, the Exodus and the Conquest of Canaan, but with the settlement of the Israelites in Canaan and the formation of a tribal league called the 'amphictyony'. The Old Testament narratives of the Patriarchs and the Exodus were treated as the

---

[16] W. R. Smith, *The Old Testament in the Jewish Church*, Edinburgh: A. & C. Black, 1881, pp. 15–16.

[17] G. E. Wright, *Biblical Archaeology*, revised and expanded edition, Philadelphia: Westminster Press, 1962.

[18] J. Bright, *A History of Israel* (OTL), London: SCM Press, 1960.

[19] M. Noth, *The History of Israel*, London: A. & C. Black, 1958, translated from *Geschichte Israels*, 2nd edn, Göttingen: Vandenhoeck & Ruprecht, 1955.

traditions of the tribal league, not as historical events that could be backed up by archaeology. This was all very disturbing for students, and they could hardly be expected to know that Noth's history was simply drawing together positions that had been advocated and worked out by German scholarship in the 1930s. In the period since the publication of Noth's history, the scholarly view of ancient Israel's history has moved in such a radical direction that Noth's work looks distinctly conservative! Scholars labelled 'minimalists' doubt whether very much can be known about ancient Israel in the pre-exilic period (i.e. before 587 BCE), while even 'maximalists' such as W. G. Dever have abandoned any attempt to begin their reconstructions with the Patriarchs and the Exodus.[20]

The effect of this on the writing of Old Testament theologies has been a strong affirmation of the first alternative of Bultmann's either/or: that the biblical texts should be used as sources for the reconstruction of religious beliefs in the past. Good examples of this are R. Albertz's *History of Israelite Religion* or E. Gerstenberger's *Theologies in the Old Testament*. Yet these works are just as subject to the ever-changing reconstructions of ancient Israelite history as any other study, although this is not to say that such work should not be undertaken.[21]

In the present book the nettle will be grasped by affirming Bultmann's second alternative, albeit in a modified form – that the reconstruction should serve the interpretation of the biblical texts in today's world. How is this to be done? The ugly ditch that supposedly separates the world of the Bible from our world(s)[22] will be bridged by concentration upon the necessary part played by modern interpreters and interpretations in bringing biblical texts to expression. This modern activity leaves no part of the interpretative process untouched. The forms and versions of the biblical texts that are interpreted are determined by modern scholarship. In the case of the Old Testament, although scholars work from the traditional, mediaeval Hebrew text, they do not hesitate to alter and correct it where it is considered to be corrupt, either on the basis of evidence from the Ancient Versions or, where that is lacking, by way of informed scholarly

---

[20] See P. R. Davies, *In Search of 'Ancient Israel'* (JSOTSS 148), Sheffield: Sheffield Academic Press, 1992; W. G. Dever, *Who Were the Early Israelites and Where Did They Come From?*, Grand Rapids: Eerdmans, 2003.

[21] R. Albertz, *Religionsgeschichte Israels in alttestamentlicher Zeit*, 2 vols (ATD Ergänzungsreihe 8), Göttingen: Vandenhoeck & Ruprecht, 1992; E. Gerstenberger, *Theologien im Alten Testament; Pluralität und Synkretismus alttestamentlichen Glaubens*, Stuttgart: Kohlhammer, 2001.

[22] It is well described by Mark Brett, *Biblical Criticism in Crisis? The Impact of the Canonical Approach on Old Testament Studies*, Cambridge: Cambridge University Press, 1991, pp. 86–100.

guesswork.[23] The study of the New Testament exhibits this problem even more sharply. The 'New Testament' that is studied by scholars and which is the basis for translations into modern European languages is entirely a modern, eclectic scholarly construct. This is in contrast to what happened for most of the history of Christianity where, prior to the invention of printing, churches had their own local texts. Even after the invention of printing, what emerged as the 'received text' was one based upon reception and use in churches, and not scholarly reconstruction.[24] Returning to the Old Testament, modern translations are affected by the modern study of comparative Semitic philology, as well as archaeological discoveries that shed light on obscure technical terms in biblical Hebrew.[25] Another factor that influences translation today is the rediscovery of the nature of Hebrew poetry, beginning in the eighteenth century. Any modern translation of the Old Testament will be made in the image of its translators, to a greater or lesser extent.

The same is true of theologies of the Old Testament. However hard scholars may strive for objectivity, however hard they may try not to read their own interests and assumptions into the way they organize their work, they will not be able to avoid the fact that they are situated in times and circumstances that inescapably affect and shape what they do. In the 1950s there was a debate between Walter Eichrodt and Gerhard von Rad about how a theology of the Old Testament should be organized.[26] Eichrodt had taken the theme of Covenant as his organizing principle. Von Rad objected that this was not as central to the Old Testament as Eichrodt

---

[23] An early, and influential, pioneer of this method in the eighteenth century was C. F. Houbigant. See my essay 'Charles-François Houbigant: His Background, Work and Importance for Lowth' in J. Jarick (ed.), *Sacred Conjectures: The Context and Legacy of Robert Lowth and Jean Astruc*, London: T. & T. Clark International, 2007, pp. 83–92.

[24] See the essay by D. Parker, 'The New Testament' in J. W. Rogerson (ed.), *The Oxford Illustrated History of the Bible*, Oxford: Oxford University Press, 2001, pp. 110–33, who notes (on p. 133) that a radical edition of the Greek text of the New Testament prepared by G. D. Kilpatrick was abandoned by the British and Foreign Bible Society in favour of a more traditional edition produced by the United Bible Societies.

[25] J. Emerton, 'The Hebrew Language' in A. D. H. Mayes (ed.), *Text in Context: Essays by Members of the Society for Old Testament Study*, Oxford: Oxford University Press, 2000, pp. 171–99, reviews recent developments in the study of biblical Hebrew. For the effect of archaeological discoveries, the Hebrew word *pim* or *payim* in 1 Samuel 13.21 was unknown until a weight inscribed with this word was discovered in Jerusalem. See Wright, *Biblical Archaeology*, pp. 91–2.

[26] For Eichrodt's account of this see W. Eichrodt, *Theology of the Old Testament*, vol. 1, London: SCM Press, 1961, pp. 512–20. See the summary by F. F. Bruce, 'The Theology and Interpretation of the Old Testament' in G. W. Anderson (ed.), *Tradition and Interpretation: Essays by Members of the Society for Old Testament Study*, Oxford: Clarendon Press, 1979, pp. 390–3.

claimed, and that in any case, it did not do justice to the way in which Israel confessed its faith through its historical traditions. Yet von Rad's magisterial and inspiring theology was fundamentally shaped by the dominating concerns of German Protestant Old Testament scholarship of the 1930s and 1940s, and it is also worth asking whether von Rad's stress on Israel's confession of its faith was in any way influenced by his opposition to National Socialism and his involvement with the Confessing Church.[27]

The same point needs to be made in connection with the various rigorous literary methods of Old Testament interpretation that have become a feature, particularly of German scholarship, since the pioneering work of Wolfgang Richter.[28] Any attempt to introduce rigour and objectivity into the exegesis of biblical texts must be welcomed. But again, it must be acknowledged that even this agenda is shaped by modern concerns, in these cases, ones grounded in the modern study of linguistics and reception criticism.

Taking these points into consideration, the present work will openly acknowledge that its agenda is set by the author's own concerns and interests. The writer is an active Anglican priest whose faith in its present form owes much to modern Lutheran German theology. He is also a humanist and a socialist, which is why writers such as Bloch, Benjamin, Adorno, Horkheimer and Habermas are referred to in the course of the work. The agenda will be set subjectively, not by themes drawn directly from the Old Testament, but from the author's intellectual predilections and his reflections on the plight of humanity living in today's world(s). The work will also assume, with Bultmann, that the Old Testament has something to say to today's world(s) when interrogated about problems that face these worlds. This does not mean that the Old Testament will be interpreted as though there were no such thing as biblical scholarship. On the contrary, this will be a scholarly exercise, with Old Testament texts being interrogated and expounded with the help of critical scholarship, but in accordance with an agenda set by one person's perception of the human condition in today's world(s). The work will not meet with the approval of

---

[27] See the essay by R. Smend, 'Gerhard von Rad' in R. Smend, *From Astruc to Zimmerli: Old Testament Scholarship in Three Centuries*, Tübingen: Mohr Siebeck, 2007, pp. 170–97.

[28] W. Richter, *Exegese als Literaturwissenschaft: Entwurf einer alttestamentlichen Literaturtheorie und Methodologie*, Göttingen: Vandenhoeck & Ruprecht, 1971; C. Hardmeier, *Erzähldiskurs und Redepragmatik im Alten Testament* (FAT 46), Tübingen: Mohr Siebeck, 2005; H. Utzschneider, *Gottes Vorstellung: Untersuchungen zur literarischen Ästhetik und ästhetischen Theologie des Alten Testaments* (BWANT 9.15), Stuttgart: Kohlhammer, 2007. For an overview see J. P. Floss, 'Form, Source and Redaction Criticism' in J. W. Rogerson and J. M. Lieu (eds), *The Oxford Handbook of Biblical Studies*, Oxford: Oxford University Press, 2006, pp. 591–614.

those committed to Radical Orthodoxy, or neo-Barthian Reformed theology,[29] or even adherents of canonical criticism. It if has models, they come from the nineteenth century in the shape of Wilhelm Vatke and W. M. L. de Wette, both of whom were courageous enough to approach the Old Testament from the standpoint, respectively, of Hegelian and post-Kantian philosophy.[30]

An observation that can be made, with some justice, is that a theology that does not deal explicitly with the nature of God and the world does not deserve the name 'theology'. I would reply by alluding to Friedrich Schiller's play *Wallensteins Lager*, the first of three plays about the tragic general on the Catholic side in the Thirty Years War in Europe.[31] The setting is Wallenstein's camp in Bohemia (his power base) at a time when this discredited general is seen by the Catholic rulers as a last resort in the face of the seemingly unstoppable military success of the Protestant Swedish ruler, Gustav Adolf. In *Wallensteins Lager* Wallenstein never appears at all. Yet he is the absent presence whose personality, and differing estimations of it by his followers, affects and penetrates every part of the play. The present work will deal with dilemmas that are integral to modern human existence, and will seek a dialogue in different ways with Old Testament texts from those standpoints. This does not mean that God will be any more absent from the work than Wallenstein is absent from *Wallensteins Lager*.

To conclude: *A Theology of the Old Testament* is a work which, to paraphrase Bultmann, will use the resources of historical criticism in the service of the interpretation of Old Testament texts, on the assumption that they have something to say to the present. It will be up to readers to decide whether the outcome is successful or not; whether the exercise enables them to understand themselves and today's world(s) in new ways.

---

[29] As represented by B. Brock, *Singing the Ethos of God: On the Place of Christian Ethics in Scripture*, Grand Rapids: Eerdmans, 2007.

[30] On Vatke, see my essay 'What is Religion? The Challenge of Wilhelm Vatke's *Biblische Theologie*' in C. Bultmann, W. Dietrich and C. Levin (eds), *Vergegenwärtigung des Alten Testaments: Beiträge zur biblischen Hermeneutik: Festschrift für Rudolf Smend zum 70. Geburtstag*, Göttingen: Vandenhoeck & Ruprecht, 2002, pp. 272–84. On de Wette, see my *W. M. L. de Wette*, pp. 96–120.

[31] F. Schiller, *Wallensteins Lager* in *Sämtliche Werke*, Darmstadt: Wissenschaftliche Buchgesellschaft, 1981, vol. 2, pp. 275–311. See also Schiller's account of the Thirty Years War: *Geschichte des Dreißigjährigen Kriegs* in *Sämtliche Werke*, vol. 4, pp. 363–745.

1

History and cultural memory

The history of the study of the Bible can be described in many ways. One possible description is that it is the story of the gradual discovery that the Bible does not contain infallible information upon every subject that concerns everyday human life. It was noted in the Introduction that voyages of discovery from the sixteenth century made it clear that Genesis 10 and the 'table of the nations' that it contains was not an exhaustive geographical description of the world. In the latter part of the seventeenth century the Reformed divine Richard Baxter warned against too broad a view of biblical infallibility and criticized those who 'feign it be instead of [i.e. hold it to contain infallible information about] all grammars, logic, philosophy, and all other arts and science, and to be a lawyer, physician, mariner, architect, husbandman, and tradesman, to do his work by'.[1]

Whether intentionally or not, Baxter did not mention history, and it is a fact that biblical interpreters have found this subject the most difficult to come to terms with in the light of modern knowledge. In the early part of the eighteenth century Humphrey Prideaux published a work which coordinated the history contained in the Bible with that known from classical sources about the history of the ancient world. Prideaux handled his non-biblical sources with critical skill and acumen, but where the biblical and non-biblical sources did not agree, preference was given to the former. 'The sacred writ, as being dictated by the holy spirit of God, must ever be of infallible truth.'[2] At the end of the eighteenth century Neologist scholars in Germany such as Johann Gottfried Eichhorn and Johann Philipp Gabler still regarded the opening chapters of Genesis as historical accounts of the beginnings of the human race. Their criticism was a scientific criticism, which stripped the stories of their supernatural elements on the grounds that the first humans, and those who recorded their experiences, had no knowledge of scientific causes, and therefore

---

[1] R. Baxter, *A Christian Directory* in *The Practical Works of Richard Baxter*, vol. 1, Morgan, Pa.: Soli Deo Gloria Publications, 2000, p. 724.

[2] H. Prideaux, *The Old and New Testament Connected in the History of the Jews and Neighbouring Nations*, London: Baynes & Son, 1716–18, vol. 1, p. 337.

attributed to divine agencies what modern science can explain naturally. With this proviso, Eichhorn and Gabler accepted the historical reliability of the opening chapters of Genesis, and of the other historical narratives of the Old Testament.[3]

The first scholar to mount a serious challenge to accepting the general accuracy of the historical narratives in the Old Testament was de Wette, in his *Beiträge* of 1806–7. He had very unusual reasons for wanting to do this. He had embraced a theory of myth from contemporary literary and Classical Greek and Roman studies, which regarded myths not as fabrications, but as attempts to express in poetic and narrative forms the intuitions of human beings about the nature of reality.[4] They were therefore of fundamental importance for philosophy and religion. The correct way to interpret them was not to strip off their supernatural trappings in order to arrive at a kernel of historical fact. The correct way was to use an aesthetic criticism that sought to uncover the intuitions (*Ahnungen*) of eternal reality to which they gave expression. Thus, for de Wette, the historical traditions of the Old Testament gave primarily an insight into the beliefs held at the time of writing by those who wrote them. It was not possible to get from them information about the historical Abraham, for example, but only about how Abraham had been seen by later generations as a man of model piety. The texts also had a reference beyond their time of composition in that they expressed timeless intuitions about the nature of humanity in relation to eternity and the contradictions of the present world.[5]

There was another reason why de Wette took the position that he did, and that was because he accepted the fragmentary view of the composition of the Pentateuch and other narratives.[6] The documentary view, that the Pentateuch had been put together from originally complete sources, allowed its advocates such as Eichhorn to argue that Moses was its author and that he had written, or had combined, ancient sources. This then enabled claims to be made for the historical reliability of the material.[7] The fragmentary view was that the biblical narratives had been put together from various types of source and that their narrative coherence was the work of their compilers rather than an accurate representation of actual sequences of events. De Wette thought that he was serving the interests

---

[3] See Rogerson, *Myth in Old Testament Interpretation*, ch. 1.

[4] See Rogerson, *W. M. L. de Wette*, pp. 47–9.

[5] See especially W. M. L. de Wette, 'Beytrag zur Charakteristik des Hebräismus', in *Studien*, vol. 3.2, (ed. C. Daub and F. Creuzer), Heidelberg, 1807, pp. 241–312 and the discussion in my *W. M. L. de Wette*, pp. 65–9.

[6] Rogerson, *W. M. L. de Wette*, p. 50.

[7] Rogerson, *Old Testament Criticism*, pp. 19–22.

of theology and religion by declaring many narratives to be 'mythical'. To most of his contemporaries and to subsequent generations, he appeared to be the advocate of an excessive and unnecessary historical scepticism.

The publication in 1878 and 1883 of Julius Wellhausen's *History of Israel* and *Prolegomena to the History of Israel* (the latter work being a second edition of the former) set the agenda for the remainder of the nineteenth century and for the twentieth century.[8] The issue was not whether the Old Testament contained accurate historical material, but how this material was to be used in a critical reconstruction of ancient Israel's history. Wellhausen's opponents believed that he had strayed too far from the overall picture of Israel's history, as it was presented in the Bible. One view was that he had taken insufficient account of the findings of the newly emerging discipline of Assyriology. In the first part of the twentieth century it was Palestinian archaeology that was held to have undermined Wellhausen's position fatally. There were also theological factors at work.

George Ernest Wright's monograph *God who Acts: Biblical Theology as Recital*, published in 1952, was based upon the conviction that 'history is the chief medium of revelation'.[9] The Bible was not so much the Word of God as the record of the Acts of God.[10] Wright was fully aware of the fact that historical events have to be interpreted if they are to have meaning, but in negotiating the matter of objectivity and subjectivity in understanding history, he came down firmly on the side of objectivity as guaranteeing the certainty and truth of divine revelation. History, and historical traditions were the primary sphere in which God revealed himself. Wright continued:

> To be sure, God also reveals himself and his will in various ways to the inner consciousness of man, as in other religions. Yet the nature and content of this inner revelation is determined by the outward, objective happenings of history in which individuals are called to participate. It is, therefore, the objectivity of God's historical acts which are the focus of attention, not the subjectivity of inner, emotional, diffuse and mystical experience.[11]

Wright believed that with the help of archaeology and the study of ancient Near Eastern history, the historicity of biblical 'events' such as the Exodus from Egypt could be verified, and that these 'events' were the objective basis for the traditions about them that testified to God. The nature of

---

[8] J. Wellhausen, *Prolegomena zur Geschichte Israels*, Berlin: Reimer, 1883.
[9] G. E. Wright, *God Who Acts: Biblical Theology as Recital* (SBT 8), London: SCM Press, 1952, p. 13.
[10] Wright, *God Who Acts*, p. 100.
[11] Wright, *God Who Acts*, p. 55.

God was disclosed by what he had done, as embodied in the traditions that commemorated these acts.[12]

Given such an important theological investment in the acts of God which the Bible was believed to witness to, it was no surprise that Wright and his colleagues, such as John Bright, defended a comparatively traditional reconstruction of Old Testament history. The surprising thing is that as this traditional reconstruction came more and more under attack, especially from the 1980s, there should have developed an attachment to the accuracy of Old Testament historical traditions that was hard to explain, unless it concealed strong religious motivations. For example, the clash between so-called minimalists and so-called maximalists in the 1990s about whether there had been a Davidic and Solomonic empire became so heated that it was difficult to remember that the discussion was supposed to be an academic exercise in which the participants would be willing to accept the force of the better argument, if necessary against their own interests. It appears that while scholars were willing to accept that the Old Testament was not an infallible authority on science and geography, or even on the origins of the human race, some were unwilling to extend that remit to its historical traditions, at any rate, those dealing with ancient Israel's history from the time of Saul and David.

It is now time to move away from this historical prologue to the chapter, and to address its primary aims. In the following sections I shall first outline and defend a narrative view of history, then discuss the importance of the concept of cultural memory, and third, argue that historical works in the Old Testament can be categorized as 'hot' or 'cold'.

A narrative view of history

It can be argued that the past does not exist; that when people talk or write about the past they are referring to memories or records of things said or done that are stored in many different ways, to which access in the present is possible, and which record only a tiny fragment of what has actually been said or done at any particular time in the inhabited world. The fact that what is recorded about past happenings is so limited, partly explains why it is possible for historians to produce different and sometimes divergent accounts of the past. This is also true of recent events such as the assassination by shooting of President John F. Kennedy in November 1963 or the death in a car accident of Diana, Princess of Wales, in Paris in August 1997. It might have been expected that an event such as Kennedy's

---

[12] Wright, *God Who Acts*, pp. 28, 50.

assassination, which was filmed, and witnessed by hundreds of people, would present no problems of reconstruction and interpretation, but this has not been the case. The death of Diana, Princess of Wales, has become the centre of conspiracy theories, such as that she was murdered on the orders of British secret intelligence. It is legitimate to raise the question as to how far it is possible to reconstruct happenings in the ancient world, if it is impossible to do so convincingly in the modern world.

Memories and records of things said and done in the past take many forms including, in today's world, electronic forms. Access to them in a meaningful way is possible only if they are embodied in a narrative. Suppose that a letter written in the nineteenth century is discovered in an attic. It will not make much sense unless it can be ascertained who wrote it, to whom, and in what circumstances. These details, if they can be discovered, will constitute a narrative in which the letter plays a role, and without which it may convey no useful information. That narrative will have been constructed by an investigator, and will have been shaped by the amount of information that it was possible to obtain, as well as by other narratives pertinent to its background. Suppose that the letter was a passionate declaration of love from a prominent statesman to his secretary, and revealed a relationship about which nothing was apparently otherwise known. Further investigation might then discover that the relationship was indeed known about in certain circles, but was kept secret. The scruples and considerations that kept the matter a secret in the nineteenth century would no longer apply in the twenty-first and the letter might then be the basis for an article which provided a new narrative about the persons concerned.

Switching to an entirely different matter, the modern discovery might not be that of a letter in an attic, but of an inscribed shard in the stratum of an ancient Israelite settlement. Again, of itself it would be meaningless unless a narrative could be constructed in which it could be embodied. How the narrative was constructed would depend on a number of variables, including presuppositions about the course of ancient Israelite history. The discovery of an Aramaic inscription at Tel Dan in 1993 produced narratives that varied between seeing it as a confirmation of certain events recorded in the Old Testament, and regarding it as a forgery.[13]

The view that in order to become available to the present, the past has to be narrated, is not new. It was hinted at by Walter Benjamin in his *Über den Begriff der Geschichte* and his essay on 'Eduard Fuchs, der Sammler

---

[13] See, for example, A. Lemaire, 'The Tel Dan Stela as a Piece of Royal Historiography', *JSOT* 81 (1998), pp. 3–14, and the bibliography to the article.

und der Historiker'.[14] It was set out explicitly by writers such as A. C. Danto in his *Analytical Philosophy of History* and Hans Michael Baumgarten in *Kontinuität und Geschichte*.[15] The claim of the narrative view of history is that while we do not invent the past, our narrative accounts of it are affected and shaped by factors such as our very limited knowledge of what happened in the past, and our situatednesses in nation, gender, class, political and religious commitment or lack of the same, and aims and interests in wanting to construct narratives about the past, in the first place. It becomes necessary to distinguish between at least two senses of the word 'history': history as the past, and history as narratives about the past. Danto posits the existence of a recording angel who notes down everything that happens and who therefore has complete knowledge of the past. As human beings we have only narratives about the past, narratives which have been constructed by human beings on the basis of limited knowledge, and shaped by various presuppositions. Even the distinction between a chronicler and a historian is not without problems. It might be argued that a chronicler lists events while a historian incorporates them into a narrative; but even the chronicler has to be selective in what is recorded, and by noting that a certain battle was fought on a certain date is giving a narrative form to what may have been a complex set of events. It used to be fashionable to describe history as fact plus interpretation. The reality is that no fact can become available in the present without being incorporated in some way into a narrative, which itself implies some form of interpretation.

The implication of what is being argued here is that declarations such as those of G. E. Wright referred to above, that God acts in history, that theology is a recital of what God has done in history, cannot be accepted. Their implication is that history is a 'thing' that can be recovered by scholarly investigation and that by means of such investigation God can be seen to have intervened actively in historical events. My objection to this is not that I do not believe that God can be active in human affairs, but that the view of history that Wright's claims imply is one that I cannot accept. On

---

[14] W. Benjamin, *Über den Begriff der Geschichte* in *Gesammelte Schriften* I.2, Frankfurt a.M.: Suhrkamp, 1991, pp. 691–704. See p. 701, 'Die Geschichte ist Gegenstand einer Konstruktion, deren Ort nicht die homogene und leere Zeit sondern die von Jetztzeit erfüllte bildet.' [History is the subject of a construction, whose place is formed not by homogeneous and empty time, but in fully developed present time]; 'Eduard Fuchs, der Sammler und der Historiker' in *Gesammelte Schriften*, II.2, pp. 465–505.

[15] A. C. Danto, *Analytical Philosophy of History*, Cambridge: Cambridge University Press, 1965; H. M. Baumgarten, *Kontinuität und Geschichte: Zur Kritik und Metakritik der historischen Vernunft*, Frankfurt a.M.: Suhrkamp, 1972.

the narrative view of history as I accept it, the value of the history-like traditions in the Old Testament lies not in their approximation to history as reconstructed by modern scholars (if, indeed, there is an approximation), but in their narrative witness to belief in God. As far as I am concerned, the scholarly view of the course of ancient Israel's history, which is a modern narrative constructed on the basis of limited knowledge and shaped by various interests, is something to be established by appeal to the force of the better argument, and nothing else. It will become possible to use the historical traditions in the Old Testament most positively for theology only when the attempt has been abandoned to maintain their historical veracity at all costs. The way forward is to approach them in terms of a theory of cultural memory.

Cultural memory

When we think of historians we instinctively think of individuals. There are, of course, collaborative works; one thinks of Oesterley and Robinson or Hayes and Miller in the field of Old Testament studies.[16] Yet even collaborative works are usually organized so that one writer deals with one particular period or topic, while the other is responsible for a different section. This tendency to ascribe history writing to individuals is taken back into how we think about the Old Testament. Standard works treat of the Yahwist or the Priestly Writer. The nearest we get to any corporate idea of the production of history is in discussions of the Deuteronomists or the Deuteronomistic School.

As over against this individualizing view of history (history as narratives about the past) the French sociologist Maurice Halbwachs, who was murdered in the concentration camp of Buchenwald in 1944, developed a theory of cultural memory. His work has been taken up and developed further by the German Egyptologist Jan Assmann. What follows next is indebted to Assmann's discussions, but developed in my own way.[17]

It was stated above that it can be argued that the past does not exist. It can also be argued that the present cannot exist without incorporating the past (in the sense of memories or narratives about the past) in some way, and that this incorporation has a communal dimension. Of course, all

---

[16] W. O. E. Oesterley and T. H. Robinson, *A History of Israel*, 2 vols, Oxford: Clarendon Press, 1932; J. H. Hayes and J. M. Miller, *Israelite and Judaean History* (OTL), London: SCM Press, 1977.

[17] See J. Assmann, *Das kulturelle Gedächtnis: Schrift, Erinnerung und politische Identität in frühen Hochkulturen*, Munich: C. H. Beck, 1999.

individuals have memories of the past as this affects them personally. These memories, however, have to be situated in a communal memory about the past, and if they are written down or told to other people they must take the form of a narrative. The particular communal narrative that is part of the biography of any individual will have been encountered and appropriated in many ways: through stories about the family told by parents and relatives, through what is learned at school, through allegiances to sporting teams or youth organizations or music groups. In today's world, television and the internet will also play a part. In countries that are ruled by totalitarian regimes, or where a particular religion officially shapes education and culture, the means whereby individuals encounter and appropriate communal memory will be more obviously controlled than in countries that are liberal democracies. However, it does not follow that the communal memories that are conveyed and preserved in liberal democracies will necessarily be more free from bias than in the other cases. All communal memories are selective, and shaped by special interests, whether these are transparent or not. Further, in today's world where it is no longer possible to isolate even a police state from ideas and information from other societies, there will always be dissidents who are dissatisfied with officially sponsored communal memories, and who will seek to challenge or subvert them.

In relation to the Old Testament, the notion of cultural memory raises some interesting questions. On the one hand, there are in the Old Testament features that fit well into the idea of cultural memory. Assmann has drawn attention to the importance of 'willed memory' ('gemachtes' Gedächtnis) conveyed by means of memorable slogans (he cites as an example 'Remember what Amalek did to you' in Deuteronomy 25.17) and reinforced by regular commemorative observances.[18] A modern British example would be the commemoration of those who died fighting for their country, held on 11 November each year and on the Sunday nearest to that date. The annual celebration of the Passover with its recollection of the exodus from Egypt would certainly count as an example of a 'willed memory'. Assmann draws attention to the injunctions in the book of Deuteronomy that parents should teach their children the sacred traditions:

> take care, and have respect for your lives, so that you do not forget the things your eyes have seen, and they do not slip from your mind as long as you live; teach them to your children and your children's children . . .
>
> (Deuteronomy 4.9)[19]

---

[18] J. Assmann, *Religion und kulturelles Gedächtnis*, Munich: C. H. Beck, 2000, pp. 18–19.
[19] Assmann, *Religion und kulturelles Gedächtnis*, pp. 20–31.

One could also cite Nehemiah 8 in this regard, according to which the law of Moses was read to the assembled people in Jerusalem by Ezra.[20]

It would be tempting to apply the idea of cultural memory to all the historical traditions in the Old Testament, but this must be resisted, for reasons that will be given below. There is no doubt that the notion can be usefully applied to parts of the Old Testament that most likely had their origins in oral tradition. The stories of Abraham and Jacob, of the so-called Judges, of Saul and Jonathan and David, of Samuel, Elijah and Elisha could well have once existed as cultural memories of groups at differing times and places in ancient Palestine. There are, however, two factors that should make us hesitate to subsume all Old Testament history under the category of cultural memory. They are, first, Assmann's observation that writing is primarily a medium of memory and storage and not a medium of communication[21] and, second, his notion of counter-present remembering (kontrapräsentische Erinnerung).[22]

To begin with the latter, there is a good deal of evidence in the Old Testament that ancient Israel was not characterized by a single, imposed, cultural memory. The story of Naboth's vineyard in 1 Kings 21 contains indications of arguably three versions of cultural memory. When King Ahab asks Naboth to exchange his vineyard for a better one that the king will give him or for its value in money, Naboth refuses, on the ground that the vineyard is 'the inheritance of his fathers' (cf. 1 Kings 21.3). Presumably, it would have been possible for Naboth to sell or exchange his vineyard had he wanted to. If he had exchanged it he would certainly have had what he got in exchange to pass on to his heirs. His reluctance to part with his vineyard was presumably based upon sentimental attachment, but also upon cultural memory in the sense of inherited traditions about his forebears and their connections with this piece of land. Ahab, although king, accepts Naboth's right not to part with his vineyard, a recognition presumably based upon cultural memory in the form of custom about these matters. The existence of an *explicit law* that stated that a man could not be forced to sell or exchange his property was about as likely as the notice that was alleged to say 'please do not throw stones at this notice'. Ahab's foreign wife Jezebel had other ideas, possibly derived from a different cultural memory that accorded to kings the right to do anything that they desired. Her response was, 'Is it you who now govern Israel?' or, in other words, what is the point of being king if you cannot get what you

---

[20] Cf. Assmann, *Religion und kulturelles Gedächtnis*, p. 90.
[21] Assmann, *Religion und kulturelles Gedächtnis*, p. 107.
[22] Assmann, *Religion und kulturelles Gedächtnis*, p. 28.

want? Jezebel arranges for Naboth to be convicted of blasphemy against God and the king, and when Naboth has been punished by being stoned to death, Ahab is able to take possession of the vineyard, presumably on the basis of legislation or customs that makes Naboth's property forfeit to the crown. At this point the prophet Elijah intervenes to reprove Ahab for what has been done in his name. Other examples that could be cited here include the judgements passed by the writers of the books of Kings on the rulers of Israel and Judah who did not abolish 'high places' and/or allowed the worship of other gods or sacred objects within their realms. Presumably, the rulers indicted did not think that they were doing anything out of the ordinary by not abolishing 'high places' and so forth. They may even have been guided by forms of cultural memory. After all, the Old Testament contains traditions about sanctuaries such as that in the land of Zuph where Samuel anointed Saul (1 Samuel 9.1—10.1), Gilgal where the kingdom was 'renewed' (1 Samuel 11.14–15), Shiloh where the boy Samuel grew up (1 Samuel 1—3), Mizpah where Samuel offered sacrifice in order to bring victory against the Philistines (1 Samuel 7.5–11) and Nob from which David sought succour after fleeing from Saul's court (1 Samuel 21.1–6). Presumably we would have no knowledge of these places as cult centres if there had not been cultural memories about them, and these, or some of them, may have been known to kings who did not abolish them but allowed them to continue as what the writers of the books of Kings regarded as 'high places'.

These, and other narratives, can be regarded as 'counter-present' memories, that is, written records that are critical of those centres of power which might have been expected to create and impose the cultural memories of the nation. One of the remarkable things about the Old Testament, given that writing was a craft that was primarily learned and practised in two centres in the ancient Near East including Israel and Judah – the royal court and the temple – is that so many of the narratives are highly critical of the court and temple! There might be two ways of accounting for this. First, there may have been within the royal circles of both Israel and Judah high officials and powerful families that secretly or openly opposed the established regime, perhaps because of sympathy with the ideals of prophetic groups. 1 Kings 18.3–16 introduces a certain Obadiah who was 'over the household', that is someone who held very high office in the administration. We are told that he hid and fed groups of prophets at a time when Jezebel 'cut them off' – presumably a euphemism for having them hunted down and killed. Obviously, Obadiah would not have done this personally, but would have deployed those under him to defy the wishes of the powerful queen. The narrative can be evaluated in two ways. It can be taken historically at its face value: there was a high official in the reign of Ahab named Obadiah who actively opposed official policy towards prophetic groups. If the narrative's historical accuracy is questioned it must still be allowed that it made sense to its original readers/ hearers and that it was making a statement about the legitimacy of action in support of prophetic groups against the wishes of royal houses.

We are possibly on firmer ground when the names of the members of the families that supported or opposed Jeremiah are analysed. The analysis appears to indicate that Jeremiah was supported and protected by members of the family of Shaphan, who was the 'secretary' during the reign of Josiah (2 Kings 22.3). Of Shaphan's sons, Elasa took Jeremiah's letter to the exiles in Babylon (Jeremiah 29.3), Gemariah provided a chamber in the temple from which Baruch read the scroll dictated by Jeremiah (Jeremiah 36.10) and Ahikam protected Jeremiah against the princes who wanted to put Jeremiah to death (Jeremiah 26.16–24). Ahikam's son, Gedaliah, was appointed by the Babylonians to govern Judah following the destruction of Jerusalem; Jeremiah was entrusted to his care (Jeremiah 39.13–14). When Gedaliah was assassinated the perpetrator was Ishmael son of Nathaniah son of Elishama, described as being 'of the royal family' (Jeremiah 41.1–3). If this Elishama is the person mentioned as 'secretary' in Jeremiah 36.12, at the time when Baruch read Jeremiah's scroll, there is indication of the existence of a powerful family opposing the family of Shaphan which supported Jeremiah. As with the narrative about Obadiah, two views might be taken, but even if it is argued that all these names and genealogies amount to nothing historically, it cannot be denied that the Jeremiah narrative taken as a whole is making a case for prophetic resistance to the policy of the royal house, and is advocating a course of action – submission to the Babylonians – that can be seen as treasonable.

So far, then, the possibility has been considered that the 'counter-present' narratives in the Old Testament owe their origin to the fact that families or groups within one of the centres in which there was a scribal culture, the royal court, actively opposed royal and national policies because of sympathy for the ideals of prophetic groups or individuals. These parties were able to use their access to scribes to record 'counter-present' narratives found in the Old Testament. The other possibility, not necessarily at odds with the first alternative, is that 'counter-present' narratives were written at a time when, because the royal house and its control of the state no longer existed, there was no danger in composing narratives that were critical of what had once been the royal establishment. The period of the so-called exile and restoration, from 587/6 onwards, would have been ideal for this, and there can be no doubt that some Old Testament historical narratives reached their final form during these periods.

Some readers may feel that the second alternative provides a completely satisfactory explanation for the existence of 'counter-present' narratives: that they owe their origin entirely to the situation after 587/6 when the loss of the state and independence could be blamed upon the kings, who could then be presented in a bad light without there being any danger of the scribes responsible being held to account. The view taken here is that while the period after 587/6 was favourable for the writing of 'counter-present' narratives, these narratives were based upon the memories of groups that had been active during the time of the monarchies in Israel and Judah. Even if one takes the view that the post-587/6 situation best accounts for the existence of the 'counter-present' narratives, it has to be admitted that they present a highly unusual account of a nation's history. One only has to compare the harsh criticisms of the kings of Israel and Judah in the books of Kings with the heroic accounts of the exploits of the Maccabean leaders in 1 and 2 Maccabees to get the point.

The other point made by Assmann, that writing is a medium of memory and storage and not a medium of communication, must now be addressed. Assmann makes some shrewd observations about the processes of the recording and canonization of cultural memory, but says little about how such written and canonized memories are communicated to others, especially in the societies in which they come into being. This raises a question that will arise elsewhere in this book. It partly involves the vexed questions of the extent of literacy and the existence and type of reading practices in ancient Israel and Judah, questions which cannot be answered with any confidence except, perhaps, for the latest parts of the pre-Common Era.[23]

In their *Dialektik der Aufklärung* T. W. Adorno and Max Horkheimer wrote towards the end of the book: 'Wenn die Rede heute an einen sich wenden kann, so sind es weder die sogenannten Massen, noch der Einzelne, der ohnmächtig ist, sondern eher ein eingebildeter Zeuge, dem wir es hinterlassen, damit es doch nicht ganz mit uns untergeht.'[24] An image

---

[23] For a review of the whole subject see A. Millard, 'Authors, Books, and Readers in the Ancient World' in J. W. Rogerson and J. M. Lieu (eds), *The Oxford Handbook of Biblical Studies*, Oxford: Oxford University Press, 2006, pp. 544–64.

[24] T. W. Adorno and M. Horkheimer, *Dialektik der Aufklärung* in T. W. Adorno, *Gesammelte Schriften*, Darmstadt: Wissenschaftliche Buchgesellschaft, 1998, vol. 3, p. 294; ET *Dialectic of Enlightenment* (trans. J. Cumming), London and New York: Verso and NLB, 1979, p. 256: 'If there is anyone today to whom we can pass the responsibility for the message, we bequeath it not to the "masses" and not to the individual (who is powerless) but to an imaginary witness – lest it perish with us.'

that both were fond of using was that of a shipwrecked person putting a message in a bottle in the hope that someone might find it. Adorno, writing about uncompromising modern music, described it as 'die wahre Flaschenpost'.[25] Is this how we should think of the 'counter-present' historical narratives in the Old Testament? Does the story of the discovery of the book of the law in the temple in the reign of Josiah (622) have any bearing on the matter, assuming that the book was really discovered and not planted (2 Kings 22.8)? Might it have been concealed in the temple like a message in a bottle in the hope that one day it would be found? These questions cannot be answered; but the fact that they can be posed draws attention to the connected questions of whether the narratives were communicated to anyone, or intended to be communicated, and if so, how. Were they 'sealed up among disciples' (cf. Isaiah 8.16) for use when times were more propitious? Whatever the truth, these narratives have survived to this day, and call out to be interpreted. How is this to be done?

'Hot' and 'cold' histories

In his book *The Savage Mind* (La Pensée Sauvage) the French social anthropologist Claude Lévi-Strauss distinguished between 'hot' and 'cold' societies. By the 'savage mind', Lévi-Strauss understood 'neither the mind of savages nor that of primitive or archaic humanity, but rather mind in its untamed state as distinct from mind cultivated or domesticated for the purpose of yielding a return'.[26] Putting it another way, we might say that Lévi-Strauss was referring to the spontaneous, instinctive responses of mind to phenomena, rather than responses conditioned by explicit theories, or reflection, ignoring the problem of speaking about minds in the abstract.

In a chapter entitled 'Time Regained' Lévi-Strauss discussed societies whose image of themselves was an essential part of their reality, and he considered how such societies responded to historical circumstances that challenged this self-understanding. A modern example would be the way in which post-war Germany had to come to terms with what had happened from 1933 to 1945. 'Cold' societies were those in which mechanisms were developed for neutralizing the effects of economic or social upheavals. It was not that such societies had no history, but that they were able to transform their history into a 'form without content'.[27] 'Hot'

---

[25] T. W. Adorno, *Philosophie der neuen Musik* in *Gesammelte Schriften*, vol. 12, p. 126. 'It is the true message in a bottle.'

[26] C. Lévi-Strauss, *The Savage Mind*, London: Weidenfeld & Nicolson, 1966, p. 219.

[27] Lévi-Strauss, *The Savage Mind*, p. 235.

societies, on the other hand, were those that were able to internalize and deploy the historical process in order to make it 'the moving power of their development'.[28]

Lévi-Strauss based his findings upon the study of tribal and aboriginal peoples. Assmann has adapted them to his work on cultural memory.[29] He emphasizes something that is already allowed by Lévi-Strauss, that there is no society that is either entirely 'hot' or entirely 'cold'. The two key words (which are in any case metaphors) describe options which exist in various ways and proportions in most if not all societies.[30] Examples of 'cold' institutions in otherwise 'hot' societies are given as initiation rites, or the army and the church. Meaning is expressed in these areas by recurrent and regular observances, and continuity is preferred to innovation or radical breaks with the past. Two sections on political power argue that it can be used to neutralize the effects of historical change, that is, serve the interests of a 'cold' society. One way is to use the past to legitimize the present political state of affairs, which can be described as the deliverance from a former state of disorder and anarchy which would certainly return if the now established political order were to be overthrown. The other way is by sternly repressing any movement for social change that arises from lower classes in the society. There is also a discussion about myth and history. While, from the point of view of their content, there is a difference between stories set in a beginning time (that is, myths), and stories set in what is claimed to be historical time, both types of narrative can function in the same way. They can serve both 'hot' and 'cold' interests. If their aim is to legitimize and preserve a status quo they will have a 'cold' function. However, they will plant the desire for change, that is, be 'hot', if they describe an ideal state of affairs that contrasts strongly with a society's present experience, thus stimulating hopes for something better.[31] Assmann devotes a whole chapter to the Old Testament, in two parts: Israel and the invention of religion, and Religion as memory, in the second of which he discusses Deuteronomy.[32] In what follows, some of his suggestions will be developed somewhat differently.

It can be argued that a classical example of 'cold' history in the Old Testament is the books of Chronicles, concerning which Wilhelm Martin Leberecht de Wette first argued in 1806 that the books of Chronicles had

---

[28] Lévi-Strauss, *The Savage Mind*, p. 234.
[29] Assmann, *Das kulturelle Gedächtnis*, pp. 68–70.
[30] Assmann, *Das kulturelle Gedächtnis*, pp. 69–70.
[31] Assmann, *Das kulturelle Gedächtnis*, p. 79.
[32] Assmann, *Das kulturelle Gedächtnis*, pp. 196–228.

used the books of Samuel and Kings as a primary source.[33] One of de Wette's most illuminating arguments will be referred to shortly. The books of Chronicles were probably written some time between 400 and 350 BCE to serve the needs of the small community in the Persian province of Yehud that was centred upon Jerusalem and its rebuilt temple.[34] They begin with nine chapters of genealogies from the time of Adam, that is, they integrate the mythical 'beginning time' into genealogies that extend to the time of David. 1 Chronicles 9 concentrates upon the families of the priests and Levites, as well as others who are described as servants of the temple including gatekeepers and singers. The history-like narrative proper begins with the reign of David, on whose work the Spirit of God rests. This is indicated by God's Spirit coming upon Amasai, the chief of David's band of thirty warriors, who says:

> We are on your side, David,
>> and with you, son of Jesse!
> Peace, peace be with you,
>> and with your helpers!
> Your God is your helper.
> (1 Chronicles 12.18 [Hebrew 12.19])

Chapters 13 to 16 of 1 Chronicles describe the bringing of the ark of God from Kiriath-Jearim to Jerusalem. The eight verses in 2 Samuel 6.12–19 that recount the ark's final movement from the house of Obed-edom to Jerusalem are expanded in 1 Chronicles to two chapters, 1 Chronicles 15 and 16, of which chapter 16 is largely devoted to extracts from Psalms 96, 105 and 106, which are described as having been sung when the ark was placed in its tent. David had already appointed the Levites and musicians who should serve the ark and its tent-shrine. The final eight chapters of 1 Chronicles are devoted to the preparations that David makes for building the temple; his organization of the duties of the priests, Levites, gatekeepers, musicians and other administrators, his giving to Solomon the plans for the temple-building and its furnishings and his organizing of the collection of gold, silver and precious stones for the work. 1 Chronicles ends with the prayer of David which includes words that have found their

---

[33] W. M. L. de Wette, *Beiträge zur Einleitung in das Alte Testament*, vol. 1: *Kritischer Versuch über die Glaubwürdigkeit der Bücher der Chronik mit Hinsicht auf die Geschichte der Mosaischen Bücher und Gesetzgebung*, Halle: Schimmelpfennig & Compagnie, 1806; reprint Darmstadt: Wissenschaftliche Buchgesellschaft, 1971.

[34] For literature and a review of the dating of Chronicles see L. L. Grabbe, *A History of the Jews and Judaism in the Second Temple Period*, vol. 1: *A History of the Persian Province of Judah*, London: T. & T. Clark International, 2004, pp. 97–9.

way into Christian worship at the time of the offertory: 'All things come from you, and we have given you what is yours' (1 Chronicles 29.14).

2 Chronicles continues the story from Solomon to the decree of Cyrus that the temple destroyed by the Babylonians should be rebuilt. Yet the narrative does not relate the history of a nation but the story of a religious people. This can be seen in many ways when the narratives of Chronicles are compared with those of Samuel and Kings. A good example, and one to which de Wette drew attention, is the incident of the coup d'état against Queen Athaliah in 2 Kings 11 and 2 Chronicles 23.[35] In the account in Kings, Athaliah's overthrow is a secret plot engineered by the priest Jehoiada and the captains of the guard who are responsible for the royal palace and the temple. The priest shows to the captains the legitimate king, the seven-year-old Jehoash who has been concealed from Queen Athaliah following her attempt to destroy the royal family after the death of King Ahaziah. The priest Jehoiada arranges for the guards who come off duty on the sabbath to remain on duty and to protect the boy king at a coronation ceremony in the temple. Athaliah is arrested and executed. In the account in Chronicles the plot is nation-wide involving the Levites from all the cities of Judah and the heads of all the fathers' houses in Israel. They are summoned to a great assembly, to which the legitimate king is shown. The plot is then carried out not, as in Kings, by the captains of the guard in secret but by the Levites and all Judah, with Athaliah apparently being the only person who is not in on the secret! The account in Kings ends with the people rejoicing at the death of Athaliah. In Chronicles the priest Jehoiada makes a covenant that the people should be Yhwh's people. This leads to a national religious revival in which images and altars to Baal are destroyed and the temple worship in Jerusalem is reformed.

Other instances of the transformation of Israel from a nation to a religious people in Chronicles include the conduct of warfare and the minimizing of the destruction of the temple in 587 BCE. Warfare in Chronicles is a religious affair in which God defeats Israel's enemies provided the people respond to the urgings of the inspired men who are raised up by God at the time of battle. Thus in 2 Chronicles 20, when Jehoshaphat is faced by great armies from the Moabites and Ammonites, a Levite named Jahaziel is inspired to reassure the people that victory will be theirs. 'You will not need to fight in this battle,' he proclaims. 'Take up your position, stand still, and see Yhwh's victory on your behalf' (2 Chronicles 20.17). In response, the singers go before the army singing the refrain from Psalm

---

[35] De Wette, *Beiträge*, vol. 1, pp. 91–8.

136, 'Give thanks to Yʜwʜ, for his steadfast love endures for ever.' Regarding the destruction of the temple by the Babylonians, only five verses are devoted to this disaster in 2 Chronicles 36.17–21 as the narrative moves to describe how God stirred up Cyrus king of Persia to issue a decree for the rebuilding of the temple.

In what sense is Chronicles 'cold' history? The answer is that the purpose of the books is to stress continuity with the past. Even if the temple has been destroyed and rebuilt, the worship that takes place in it was instituted by David, who is connected to the beginning of time by genealogies that go back to Adam. Anything in Samuel and Kings that has to do with successful rebellions is omitted or passed over in a few verses. Chronicles says nothing of David's desertion to the Philistines and although the departure of the northern tribes under Jeroboam is recorded, there is no mention of the coups d'état that led to the reigns of Omri and Ahab, nor of the prophetic revolution led by Elijah and Elisha that brought the downfall of the house of Omri. A brief mention that Jehu destroyed the house of Ahab and killed Ahaziah of Judah is the prelude to the story of Athaliah's attempt to usurp the kingship, which then leads to the story of the later restoration of the true king, the boy Joash. The picture that is paramount is one of stability reaching back to the beginning of time. Chronicles legitimates the community centred upon Jerusalem in the fourth century BCE as a community whose rationale is the temple and its worship, founded and established by David and continued faithfully at the time of the compilation of Chronicles.

According to Lévi-Strauss[36] a 'hot' society is one that internalizes the historical process in order to make it the moving power of its development. On this analogy a 'hot' history is a way of describing events in such a way that readers/hearers (if there are any!) are challenged to look critically at their situation with a view to changing and improving it. It will now be argued that the so-called Deuteronomistic History, which extends from Joshua to 2 Kings is an example of a 'hot' history.

There is a growing consensus that the origins of the Deuteronomistic History are to be sought in the situation that faced Judah in the immediate aftermath of the final destruction of the northern kingdom, Israel, in 722/1. This brought a wave of refugees from the north to the south, necessitating the enlargement of Jerusalem to help accommodate them. Indeed, it can be argued that this changed Judah into a 'hot' society, in the sense that the loss of the northern kingdom gave Judah a new identity and a

---

[36] Lévi-Strauss, *The Savage Mind*, p. 234.

new purpose. Under the leadership of King Hezekiah (*c.* 727–698) Judah took over the role of Israel – not in the sense of claiming to be the northern kingdom (this would have been manifestly absurd as well as untrue) but in the sense of claiming to be the true heir of a united kingdom that had been called Israel, and which had once embraced the northern kingdom, Israel, and the southern kingdom, Judah, and which was ruled from Jerusalem. This new identity expressed itself in two ways. First, Hezekiah tried, where possible, to expand his territory and/or influence to the north. Second, a 'hot' historical narrative began to be put together which emphasized the priority of Judah over its former northern neighbour. Abraham, the ancestor of Judah, was depicted as the grandfather of Jacob, the ancestor of the northern kingdom, while the latter was depicted as a rebellious nation that had broken away from a united kingdom ruled from Jerusalem by David and Solomon. This view of things enabled Judah to be 'hot' in the sense that there was a mis-match between representation and reality. Judah was claiming to be the true heir and representative of a nation that had once extended from Dan in the north to Beer-sheba in the south. This mis-match gave justification to Hezekiah for any move to expand his territory. I am assuming that we are dealing in the first instance with an unwritten cultural memory that both justified Hezekiah's action and provided the basis for the written version of the cultural memory.

By the time that this cultural memory had assumed something like its final form the situation had changed out of all recognition. Hezekiah's ambitions had been thwarted by Sennacherib's invasion of Judah in 701 BCE. A long period of Assyrian domination had been broken by a bid for independence under King Josiah (640–609), only for Judah to come eventually under the domination of the Babylonians, who exiled the king and nobles in 597, and destroyed Jerusalem and its temple in 587. The Deuteronomistic History received something like its final form probably in the territory of Benjamin in the early fifth century BCE, the Babylonians having transferred the administration of Judah to that area following the destruction of Jerusalem.[37]

Looked at as a whole, the Deuteronomistic History is characterized by change. This is in stark contrast to the stability represented in the books of Chronicles. The change, or rather changes, are ascribed to moral and religious factors. Although the latter predominate in that much is made of the disasters that result from rulers and the people turning to gods other than the God of Israel, this is not purely or mainly a cultic issue. Disloyalty to the God of Israel has profound *moral* and *social* implications. This is made

---

[37] P. R. Davies, *The Origins of Biblical Israel*, London: T. & T. Clark International, 2007.

clear by the fact that the Deuteronomistic History is prefaced by the book of Deuteronomy, a book that contains some of the most important legislation in the Old Testament in support of social justice for the poor and for women.[38] It is also true that in both Deuteronomy and the 'history' that it prefaces, there is a good deal of intolerance towards other nations. (On the other hand, stories such as those about Abimelech and Abraham in Genesis 20 certainly present the *non-Israelite* in a much better light than the Hebrew ancestor!) But this intolerance may spring from the bitter experience of how non-Israelite rulers exercised their power in relation to the poor and marginalized (cf. the story of Naboth's vineyard referred to above, pp. 21–2).

The Deuteronomistic History begins with the book of Joshua, the greater part of whose narrative section (chapters 12 to 21 are devoted largely to information about the territories, towns and villages allotted to the Israelite tribes) in chapters 2 and 6—8 deals with the conquest of Jericho and the subsequent defeat at Ai. A theme that emerges, and that will be repeated a number of times in the Deuteronomistic History, is that God's favour, and the material success that goes with it, cannot be taken for granted. The great fortress of Jericho falls when the priests carry the ark of the covenant around its walls for seven days. The insignificant town of Ai, whose name means 'ruin' in Hebrew, is the scene of a defeat because a certain Achan has kept spoil from defeated Jericho that should have been 'devoted' to God by being destroyed. It is worth noting at this point how wide of the mark all the attempts have been to defend the historicity of these narratives especially in the light of the fact that neither Jericho nor Ai were probably inhabited at the time of the presumed 'invasion' of Canaan by the Israelites in the late thirteenth century BCE. This is an object lesson in how the quest for confirmation of the historical accuracy of biblical narratives can divert attention from what they are actually about![39]

Chapter 9 is the story of how the Gibeonites deceived Joshua and the Israelites by coming to the camp at Gilgal dressed as though they had undertaken a very long journey. Joshua makes a covenant with them, one that he abides by when, three days later, his army arrives at the Gibeonite cities, which are in the land of Canaan. He does not destroy the cities, but makes their inhabitants hewers of wood and drawers of water. From

---

[38] See E. Otto, *Theologische Ethik des Alten Testaments*, Stuttgart: Kohlhammer, 1994, pp. 175–211.

[39] Bright, *History*, pp. 118–19 maintains that the evidence for the occupation of Jericho in the thirteenth century is inconclusive and requires an open mind to be kept. On Ai, he argues that Joshua 8 is probably an accurate historical memory of the Israelite conquest of Bethel, with later tradition wrongly associating the campaign with Ai. The 3rd edn (1980), pp. 130–1 repeats these points.

the point of view of what is being argued in this chapter, the incident shows that the Israelites have learned the lessons of Jericho and Ai. Even though they were lied to by the men of Gibeon, they feel bound to uphold an oath sworn in God's name (Joshua 9.18–21). This obedience to God has the outcome that Joshua is able to defeat a coalition of five kings in the area of Judah, and later to capture and destroy Hazor in the far north. However, lest the Israelites should conclude that God is now unconditionally on their side, two speeches of Joshua, in chapters 23 and 24, sound a warning note. The Israelite success in capturing the land will quickly turn to failure if the people forsake God.

The failure warned of by Joshua in the book of his name takes a rather special form in the book of Judges which follows it. An artificial framework which accommodates popular stories about local rulers and judges becomes the means of making 'hot' the narrative of the period between the 'occupation' and the rise of the monarchy. There is a recurring cycle of events in which the people turn to other gods, are then subjugated by a neighbouring (in one case, Canaanite) ruler, before God raises up a deliverer who frees the people and enables them to enjoy a period of peace, before the whole cycle is repeated. Yet this potentially monotonous account is enlivened not only by the vividness of the individual stories (of which that concerning Samson and Delilah is the best known, and that of Jephthah and his daughter has generated plays and musical dramas); the book is affected by a shadow that is cast back upon it from 1 Samuel, which follows it. This shadow is not only cast by verses such as that with which the book ends ('there was no king in Israel in those days; every man did what was right in his own eyes', Judges 21.25). It is also cast by the fact that none of the rulers who feature in the book is able to establish a dynasty.

Ehud (Judges 3) is left-handed – a factor which enables him to deceive and kill the Moabite oppressor of the Israelites, Eglon, but which was popularly viewed with disfavour. The Hebrew word for left-handed (*'itter*) takes the form of words that describe a physical defect.[40] Deborah, the judge at the time of the oppression by the Canaanite ruler Sisera (Judges 4—5), is a woman, and her commander, Barak, is not conspicuously brave (cf. Judges 4.8). Gideon, who delivers the Israelites from the Midianites, expressly refuses to rule over the people (Judges 8.22–3) while his son Abimelech, who has no such inhibitions, makes a disastrous attempt to become king (Judges 9). Jephthah has only one child, a daughter, who is

---

[40] The evidence is summarized by M. H. Segal, *A Grammar of Mishnaic Hebrew*, Oxford: Clarendon Press, 1927, pp. 108–9.

tragically the first person to meet him on his return from victory, he having vowed to God to offer as a sacrifice the first person who greeted him if he returned victorious (Judges 11). Later interpreters found this conclusion so distressing that they fastened upon a slight ambiguity in the Hebrew and understood the maiden's fate to be that she remained a virgin for the rest of her life.[41] Either way, Jephthah, without offspring, could not found a dynasty. The same is true of Samson (Judges 13—16), whose behaviour in any case might be considered to be inappropriate for one who might found a royal dynasty.

The inability to found a dynasty continues into 1 Samuel, where first, Samuel has sons who are said to turn aside after gain, take bribes and pervert justice (1 Samuel 8.1–3) and second, Saul has a son Jonathan, who acknowledges that David will succeed Saul as king (1 Samuel 20.14–16). When the first book of Samuel is reached, it becomes obvious who is casting the shadow back over the book of Judges: it is David, who establishes not only a dynasty, but one approved by God (2 Samuel 7). Yet even then there are surprises to come. David, the man after God's own heart (1 Samuel 13.14), is spared nothing as the story of his adultery with Bathsheba and his cynical treatment of her husband, Uriah, so that he is killed in battle, is unfolded in 2 Samuel 11—20, together with the disasters that beset his family and his kingship.[42] The man after God's own heart has feet of clay, as does his son, Solomon, who in spite of his magnificence is accused of being unfaithful to God (1 Kings 11.9–13). The result is that the kingdom is divided after his death. The story of the two kingdoms follows, with kings being judged according to the criterion of whether or not they abolished the high places. It ends with the loss of both kingdoms, yet with a possible gleam of hope in the favourable treatment accorded to Jehoiachin, the last of the Davidic kings, who has been in exile in Babylon for 37 years (2 Kings 25.27–30).

What makes the Deuteronomistic History 'hot' is the fact that it seems to anticipate a time when, under God's rule, the people of 'Israel' (Israel understood as a religious community yet one embodied in the tribal society of the pre-monarchic period, the united monarch and the kingdoms of Israel and Judah) will enjoy permanent peace and prosperity. Yet this hoped-for state never materializes. The occupation of their 'own' land by

[41] R. Bartelmus, *Theologische Klangrede: Studien zur musikalischen Gestaltung und Vertiefung theologischer Gedanken durch J. S. Bach, G. F. Händel, F. Mendelssohn, J. Brahms und E. Pepping*, Zurich: Pano, 1998, pp. 65–86.

[42] See also A. de Pury and T. Römer (eds), *Die sogenannte Thronfolgegeschichte Davids: Neue Einsichten und Anfragen* (OBO 176), Freiburg Schweiz: Universitätsverlag; Göttingen: Vandenhoeck & Ruprecht, 2000.

the Israelites does not fulfil that hope; it only exposes them to new dangers within and outside the land. The periods of 'rest' for the people in the book of Judges are short-lived. Even the establishment of the Davidic dynasty and the building of the temple do not bring a permanent 'golden age'. The two Israelite nations war with each other, and are eventually destroyed by more powerful nations.

At one level, the narrative is saying that the hoped-for enjoyment of peace and prosperity under God's rule can never be attained because human nature is incapable of doing what needs to be done in order to achieve it. Even the ideal king himself, David, falls short in this respect. The narrative thus looks beyond itself, and while it does not speak of the possibility of a new covenant (a notion which must not be simplistically identified with the New Testament), it is not forcing the issue to refer to Ezekiel 36.16–32 here. The prophet looks forward to a future restoration of the people in the promised land, a restoration that will involve the transformation of the people: 'I will take away the heart of stone from your body and give you a heart of flesh. I will put my spirit within you, and bring it about that you walk in my statutes' (Ezekiel 36.26–7). The paradox here is that a people made to obey God in spite of themselves would offer a service that was worthless in moral terms. The verses from Ezekiel, and the whole of the Deuteronomistic History, expose a fundamental flaw at the heart of reality, if one is going to take seriously the existence of the God of the Bible.

The same paradox is explored in a different way in another, arguably 'hot', history in the Old Testament, the narrative of the wilderness wanderings in the books of Exodus and Numbers. For the sake of convenience the narrative will be assumed to begin with Exodus 16, the chapter immediately following the accounts, and celebration, of the crossing of the Red Sea.

The first verse of Exodus 16 is simply a geographical notice of the route taken by the Israelites following their departure from Elim. It is followed by the first of the many complaints by the people about the harshness of conditions in the wilderness compared with what is claimed to be the plenty that they enjoyed in Egypt. Death in Egypt, they say, would have been preferable to life in the wilderness (Exodus 16.2). In order to meet these complaints God provides the people with the manna (which has been identified as a gum excreted from various flowering trees, especially the tamarisk) and quails (birds that migrate from Africa and Arabia to southern Europe). The next complaint (in Exodus 17) concerns the lack of drinking water. The life of Moses is threatened, and disaster is averted only when Moses performs a miracle by striking a rock with his rod, which produces water. An astonishing saying is attributed to the people: 'Is Yʜᴡʜ in our midst or not?' (Exodus 17.7). This is astonishing because, according to the narrative, the people concerned have been freed from slavery, have been miraculously delivered from a pursuing Egyptian army at the Red Sea, and have been fed with quails and manna. Something profound about human nature is being said here, whether consciously or not.

It was observed above that Ezekiel 36.27 appears to contain the paradox that if God makes people obey him, this service will be morally worthless. The same problem arises here in a different form. What does God have to do to convince people that he is 'in their midst'? Clearly, miracles are not the answer. They can satisfy people for a brief period but do not possess the power to bring a conviction that will not only last, but enable the recipients to surmount new crises. It is noteworthy that in the cultural memory of the Israelites this incident (if it can be called that, because it is not being maintained here that we are dealing with 'real' historical events) left its mark as the Massah and Meribah incident, two place names (if that is what they are) meaning respectively 'proof' and 'contention'. They are alluded to in Psalm 95.8: 'Do not become stubborn as you were at Meribah and at the time of Massah in the wilderness; there your fathers challenged me and put me to the test, even though they had seen what I had done.' The importance of this for present purposes is that we are dealing with a foundation narrative,[43] a narrative about those who experienced the deliverance without which Israel would not exist as a people with a religious vocation. Indeed, the narrative is a continuation of what Assmann calls 'willed remembering' in the story of the Exodus, with its reinforcement in the observance of the Passover.[44] The narrative is 'hot' in the sense that it raises questions that cannot be answered, and this confers on the account an 'openness' that will not allow it to be accommodated into an explanation that conveniently makes sense of everything. In some ways, it is irrational. Why do people who have been delivered from slavery feel resentful rather than grateful? How can people who have seen miracles performed on their behalf still doubt that divine power is on their side? Why is it that God persists in identifying himself with a people that is so obviously unfit for such attention?

These unanswered and unanswerable questions continue in the book of Numbers, especially from chapter 11, although reference also needs to be made to the incident of the Golden Calf in Exodus 32. Whatever may be the origins of this story, it not only fits in well with the previously

---

[43] Cf. Assmann, *Religion und kulturelles Gedächtnis*, p. 86.
[44] Assmann, *Religion und kulturelles Gedächtnis*, p. 18.

raised question (why should a people turn from the God who has delivered them from slavery to gods that they have manufactured themselves?); it enhances something that is hinted at in Exodus 16 and that becomes more prominent in the book of Numbers. That something is the suffering role of Moses, who is the man rejected by those whom he had delivered. Indeed, this theme may also be discerned in the narrative of the plagues in Exodus. Pharaoh orders the taskmasters to make the Israelite slaves provide their own straw for the making of bricks, the taskmasters having previously provided the necessary straw. The foremen of the Israelites meet and accuse Moses and Aaron of having worsened the conditions of the slaves by demanding that Pharaoh should let the people go to the wilderness to worship Yhwh (Exodus 5.20–1, cf. 5.1–2).

In Numbers, Moses has to endure not only the usual complaints about harsh conditions in the wilderness, including the boring menu of manna as opposed to the fish, cucumbers, melon, leeks, onions and garlic that they allegedly enjoyed in Egypt during their enslavement (Numbers 11.4–6). Moses has to face opposition to his leadership. The most painful comes from his own family, from his brother and sister Aaron and Miriam. They claim that Moses does not have exclusive rights to be God's spokesman. 'Has Yhwh really only spoken through Moses? Has he not spoken through us as well?' (Numbers 12.2). Aaron and Miriam are punished by God, Miriam by temporarily showing the signs of leprosy. The next crisis comes from the report of the spies sent out to reconnoitre the land of Canaan. The bad report of ten of them, that opines that it will be impossible for the Israelites to enter the land with any hope of success, makes the people murmur against Moses and Aaron (Numbers 14.1–3). It is proposed that a new leader should be chosen, who will take the people back to Egypt (Numbers 14.5). Another rebellion, led by Korah, Dathan and Abiram, appears to be an attempt to widen the circle of those who have access to priestly service. 'Every single member of the congregation is holy' they claim (Numbers 16.3), 'and Yhwh is among them; why then do you set yourselves up above the assembly of Yhwh?' The punishment meted out to these rebels (they are swallowed by an earthquake) causes the people to be indignant against Moses and Aaron (Numbers 16.41). They, in turn, are punished when a plague is sent upon them.

These chapters make grim reading; but for all their grimness they are exploring the theme of human ingratitude in the face of divine mercy, and how this is to be coped with. Although both Judaism (to a lesser extent) and Christianity have shared an aversion to the idea that God can suffer, this is what is going on in these chapters, with the suffering also falling particularly strongly upon Moses. This is emphasized in Numbers 20, which is a repetition of Exodus 17, in that the people cry out because of lack of water, Moses produces water from a rock by striking it with his staff, and the place is named Meribah, meaning 'contention'. Numbers 20, however, adds that God now passes sentence upon Moses and Aaron because of this incident. Although the narrative itself contains no hint of this, Moses and Aaron are accused of not believing in God (Numbers 20.12). Their sentence is that they will not live to lead the people into the promised land. Aaron dies at Mount Horeb at the end of Numbers 20. Moses is allowed to view the promised land from afar before he dies (Deuteronomy 34.1–4).

There is no resolution of anything in these narratives. One crisis follows another; displays of divine power do not convince the people that God is with them. The punishment of those who rebel against God teaches the people no lessons but, on occasion, provokes their indignation. Even the stories of Moses (and Aaron) have no 'happy' ending. In the case of Moses, whose reluctance to get involved in the divine project of freeing a people from slavery is well described in Exodus 3—4, the trials that he endures, at the hands of those he has helped to deliver from slavery, earn him no favours. He is not allowed to enter the promised land and successfully complete the task that he had begun.

At one level, the narratives not only present the people in a bad light, the very people, it must be remembered, who had been brought from slavery to freedom. They also present God in a bad light. What is the point of being able to inflict plagues upon the great civilization of Egypt, to be able to control the waters of the Red Sea, to be able to produce water from rocks in the wilderness and to bring plagues upon people if none of these things bring about the willing obedience of the people whose lives it was intended to transform? Yet in the narrative God does not abandon the project as hopeless, and neither does Moses, in spite of what he endures at the hand of the people as well as from God! The narrative expresses hope without describing the realization of any hope, except, perhaps, that in spite of everything the people do manage to complete the journey from Egypt to the threshold of the promised land. Also, the wishes of those who thought that it would be preferable to return to slavery are not realized. The journey is completed in spite of the obduracy of the people and the apparent inability of God to win their allegiance. The sufferings of Moses play a part in this.

The determination that this narrative displays, not to give up hope, is a remarkable feature of the Old Testament, and one that will be commented upon elsewhere in this book. It is a remarkable feature because in the ambiguous world in which humans live out their lives it is easier to give up hope than to go on hoping; just as it is easier to give up faith in God when confronted by the fact of evil than it is to go on believing. To this extent, the problem of good (that is, why people persist in believing when so much seems to count against it) is more perplexing than the problem of evil. The 'hot' narratives of the Old Testament raise the question why some, among the people of Israel and Judah, went on hoping, when so much seemed to count against such an attitude. This matter will now be explored further.

In the exodus and wilderness wanderings narratives it is the figure of Moses that is used to explore the issue of hope. In the Deuteronomistic History there is no comparable figure. While the tradition there *likens* Hezekiah and Josiah to Moses (2 Kings 18.6; 23.25) with Josiah getting the lion's share of the praise, they do not play the same role as Moses. That role is played by a succession of named and unnamed prophets, and perhaps it is no accident that the tradition also regards Moses as a prophet (Deuteronomy 18.15). Returning to Moses, it must be remembered that he is not an historical figure in the sense that a modern biography could be written about his birth, upbringing, career and death (although all these features are present in the narrative!). It may be that Martin Noth correctly described some of the features of the growth of the tradition about him in his *Überlieferungsgeschichte des Pentateuch*.[45] In terms of what is being argued in the present work, Moses is the creation of a cultural memory, a corporate or social phenomenon that embodies and articulates the experience and associations of a group within the complexes that we call Judah and Israel. It is here that it is important to see Moses not as an individual but as a symbol, or, if one will, a supreme example (in the literary sense) of what happens to people and groups who become involved in the project that pertains to the God of Israel.

The suffering that Moses endures is mainly recorded in Exodus and Numbers; but this suffering is not unique, even if it is rather more thinly scattered throughout the Deuteronomistic History. Thus, Joshua finds himself in a position similar to that of Moses, following the defeat of the people at Ai (Joshua 7.6–9). He questions the wisdom of God in bringing the people across the river Jordan if the result is to be the kind of debacle experienced at Ai. Gideon finds his life threatened after he has destroyed the altar of Baal and its Asherah (Judges 6.28–32). Jephthah suffers the tragedy that his vow to God commits him to sacrificing his only child, a daughter (Judges 11.29–40). The priest Eli experiences the loss of the

---

[45] M. Noth, *Überlieferungsgeschichte des Pentateuch*, Stuttgart: Kohlhammer, 1948; ET *A History of Pentateuchal Traditions*, Englewood Cliffs: Prentice Hall, 1972.

ark of the covenant and the death of his two sons in battle against the Philistines (1 Samuel 4.10–18). Samuel is rejected by the people when they request a king to rule them (1 Samuel 8.4–22). David experiences mayhem in his own family, with his son Amnon raping his half-sister Tamar, Absalom (Tamar's full brother) killing Amnon, and Absalom leading a revolt against David (2 Samuel 13—18). Elijah's life is threatened by Jezebel following his successful contest with the prophets of Baal on Mount Carmel (1 Kings 19). All of these set-backs or incidences of suffering can be seen as components of a cultural memory or memories that are themselves based upon actual experiences of people or groups within the circle or circles that produced the cultural memory. As in the more obvious case of Moses, so in the pages of the Deuteronomistic History the point is being hammered home that the project bound up with the God of Israel will bring frustration, despair and danger to those most closely involved in it; to those who believe most firmly in it. How is the persistence of these people, and the hope that sustains them, to be explained?

In his *Das Prinzip Hoffnung* Ernst Bloch accounted for hope by drawing attention to what he called the *Noch-Nicht-Bewußtes* (not-yet-consciousness).[46] This was a human capacity for sensing that which exceeded the limitations of understanding or possibilities, in given circumstances. In line with his Marxist convictions, Bloch argued that in given economic and social conditions, their *Noch-Nicht Bewußtes* capacity could enable individuals or groups to formulate revolutionary or utopian ideals which could become the driving force for social, moral, intellectual and artistic change. There would be opposition to such visions and to attempts to realize their practical implication. Ultimately, they could not be resisted as they were an essential part of the process whereby humanity became what it was.

It is not difficult to see the similarity between Bloch's account of hope and the notion of 'hot' societies (Lévi-Strauss was also strongly influenced by Marxism!). Assmann's application of the idea of 'hot' societies to 'hot' histories adds a neat twist in that 'hot' narratives can be seen as part of a cultural process that gives narrative and literary form to utopian ideals. In relation to the Old Testament it can be argued that it contains a very real and concrete phenomenon – a narrative witness to utopian ideals generated by the *Noch-Nicht Bewußtes* of particular individuals and groups. Attempts to put the ideals into practice were constantly frustrated but the visions were never destroyed. The remarkable thing about the Old Testament is the persistence of its visions of a better humanity and a better world.

---

[46] E. Bloch, *Das Prinzip Hoffnung*, Frankfurt a.M.: Suhrkamp, 1973, pp. 129–203.

This is a humanistic explanation of the persistent presence in the Old Testament of narratives that express hope. Can one go further? Should one go further? At one level this attempt at a 'communicative theology' can 'succeed' if it encourages readers who have no particular faith commitment to see the Old Testament from a different perspective – one that makes sense from the standpoint of writers such as Bloch, and which becomes a more effective part of the religious 'archive' which, as Jürgen Habermas has pointed out, can with certain reservations provide insights for modern philosophy and society.[47] Others, understandably, will not be satisfied, expecting a 'theology' to say things or make claims about God. An obvious rejoinder is to say that to describe what appear to be the human processes that bring things about is not to exclude God, if one has grounds for believing in divine involvement in the world of human affairs. Another approach to the same question would be to ask whether the religious forms in which the Old Testament narratives express hope – religious forms in the shape of stories about God communicating with humans, performing miracles, inflicting punishments – were an incidental or an indispensable part of the vision which sustained the groups responsible for these cultural memories.

This is a very important question because any responsible modern approach to the narratives is likely to be repelled by some of their content. What sort of God is the God of Israel when he helps Joshua to 'mow down' the Amalekites (Exodus 17.13), approves of the killing of three thousand men following the making of the Golden Calf (Exodus 32.28) and sends a plague of poisonous serpents upon the complaining people in the wilderness (Numbers 21.4–6)? If a modern reply is that these and similar narratives exhibit a naïve understanding of God and give no clue as to his real nature, the sceptic can claim with some justification that the case has been conceded; that it has been admitted that the religious form taken by the narratives is incidental, not essential to the hope that they are expressing. If the moral sentiments that they contain are problematic for modern

---

[47] J. Habermas, 'Religion in der Öffentlichkeit' in *Zwischen Naturalismus und Religion: Philosophische Aufsätze*, Frankfurt a.M.: Suhrkamp, 2005, pp. 119–54. See p. 149: 'Religiöse Überlieferungen scheinen, auch wenn sie sich einstweilen als das intransparente Andere der Vernunft präsentieren, sogar auf eine intensivere Weise gegenwärtig geblieben zu sein als die Metaphysik . . . Jedenfalls ist nicht auszuschließen, dass sie semantische Potentiale mit sich führen, die eine inspirierende Kraft für die *ganze* Gesellschaft entfalten, sobald sie ihre profanen Wahrhaltsgehalte preisgeben.' [Religious traditions seem, even when for the moment they present themselves as an opaque other in relation to reason, to have remained a present factor in a more intensive way than metaphysics . . . At any rate, the view must not be rejected that they contain the semantic potential to develop inspiring power for the whole of society if they give up their claims to articulate profane truth.]

readers, why keep on insisting that they nevertheless have some religious value?

The force of this argument is considerable and, perhaps, unanswerable in a satisfactory way to anyone who stands outside of Christian or any other faith. An attempt to deal with it may be possible with the help of a quotation from Dostoyevsky's *The Brothers Karamazov*. Ivan is debating the question of whether God created the human race, or whether the human race created God. Although he inclines to the second view he nonetheless qualifies it in this way:

> To be sure man has invented God. And what is so strange, and what would be so marvellous, is not that God actually exists, but that such an idea – the idea of the necessity of God – should have entered the head of such a savage and vicious animal as man – so holy it is, so moving and so wise and so much does it redound to man's honour.[48]

I would want to say of this quotation that it draws attention to the paradox that the human race, which is capable of so much barbaric destructiveness, as witnessed by the Holocaust and other atrocities in the twentieth century, is also capable of ideas of purity, forgiveness, self-sacrifice and respect for others especially the weak and disadvantaged, and capable of action to match these ideas. How is this possible? Is there no source for these virtues outside of humanity? If one is inclined to answer 'yes', then there will be a possible key to interpreting the 'hot' histories of the Old Testament theologically. Without denying any of the humanistic aspects of hope so movingly analysed by Bloch, it will be possible to see the 'hot' histories as the outcome of a divine–human encounter that sustained the human participants in a way that would otherwise have been beyond their capacity. Within this encounter their understanding of the divine was imperfect and corrupted by too ready an attempt to create God in their own image, and to attribute to him ingratitude and obtuseness. If, indeed, the 'greatness' of God is exhibited in these narratives it is not by way of miraculous demonstrations of power. These, as has been pointed out, did little to secure the loyalty or compliance of the people. The divine 'greatness' consists of the fact that it was able to absorb and outlast the ingratitude and obtuseness of the people freed from slavery; that the journey to the promised land was completed; that the destruction of Jerusalem and its temple was not the end of the story. The 'hot' histories have an 'openness' because the last word rests with God and not the human race.

---

[48] F. Dostoyevsky, *The Brothers Karamazov* (trans. David Magarshak), London: Penguin, 1982, p. 287.

2

Creation accounts as critiques of the world of human experience and human actions

In Chapter 1 ideas were combined from Jan Assmann and Claude Lévi-Strauss to suggest that histories in the Old Testament could be categorized as either 'hot' or 'cold', and that 'hot' histories contained an inner dynamic that enabled ancient Israel to survive and to overcome the great crises that threatened its very existence. Chapter 2 will pursue similar ideas concerning what will broadly be called creation accounts. Assmann argues that in a similar way to histories, what he calls 'founding memories' can have the function either of seeking to preserve the status quo that exists in the present, or of seeking to undermine it.[1] One of the ways that 'founding memories' can seek to undermine the present is by describing the beginnings of human culture in ideal or idyllic terms which are at variance with the state of affairs at the time when the beginnings are being described. This is the familiar idea of the lost Golden Age which may or may not return at the end of time. Another way in which the status quo can be challenged, of course, is by conceiving a future set of conditions which radically challenge those in the present. P. Bourdieu, in a discussion of Sartre's *Being and Nothingness*, writes of 'the power to create the meaning of the present by creating the revolutionary future which negates it'.[2] As will be argued, instances of this can also be found in the Old Testament; but for the moment, the focus will be on accounts of origins.

Narratives about the beginnings of creation in the Old Testament, or about the creation itself, are critical of the world in which readers or hearers of the stories had to live out their daily lives. To that extent these stories were 'hot'. They did not allow readers or hearers to be content with the world as they knew it, and they injected into their world-view an expectation of a restored world that provided both hope *and* critique. In this respect their function was different from how the stories have

---

[1] Assmann, *Das kulturelle Gedächtnis*, pp. 78–9.
[2] P. Bourdieu, *Outline of a Theory of Practice*, Cambridge: Cambridge University Press, 1977, p. 74.

been understood in the history of theology. For example, Genesis 1 has been used traditionally as the basis for a Christian doctrine of the creation of the world *ex nihilo*.[3] It is still a battleground today, as advocates of 'creationism' or 'intelligent design' try to defend its 'truth' against physical or biological scientific accounts of how the universe and the human race came into being.[4] Even theologians who do not follow that particular line, and accept the story as theology rather than history or science, still insist that it teaches that the universe is 'good' even though Old Testament specialists have pointed out that 'good' in the phrase 'God saw that it was good' does not mean morally good, but something like 'fit for the purpose for which it was intended'. Erich Zenger expands the sense of 'good' in Genesis 1 under the headings of 'beautiful' (God delights in what he has done) and conducive to life (*lebensfördernd*).[5] What interpreters often overlook, however, is the simple, but fundamentally important point, that Genesis 1 does *not* describe the world of human experience. While Genesis 1 indeed affirms that the God known to ancient Israel is the creator of the universe, the creation of that part of the universe inhabited by the human race is *not* what is described in Genesis 1! How can this be so?

Genesis 1.29–30 decrees that men and animals are to eat only plants and fruit. The passage reads:

> God said, 'Look, I am giving you every plant that produces seed everywhere in the earth, and every tree whose fruit produces seed; they shall be your food. As for the wild beasts, the birds of the heavens and the reptiles, all living creatures, their food will be every green plant.'

What does this imply? The mediaeval Jewish commentator Abraham Ibn Ezra (1089–1164) was clear that the human race and other living creatures were not permitted to eat meat until after the Flood,[6] and among modern commentators who take the same view is C. Westermann.[7] An interesting

---

[3] See, for example, Augustine, *City of God*, Book XI, chs 4–6.

[4] A useful history of 'creationism' and its variants is given in A. McCalla, *The Creationist Debate: The Encounter between the Bible and the Historical Mind*, London: T. & T. Clark International, 2006.

[5] E. Zenger, *Gottes Bogen in den Wolken: Untersuchungen zu Komposition und Theologie der priesterlichen Urgeschichte* (SBS 112), Stuttgart: Verlag Katholisches Bibelwerk, 1983, pp. 59–60.

[6] Abraham Ibn Ezra, *'Al HaTorah*, Jerusalem: Mossad Harav Kook, 1976, p. 19.

[7] C. Westermann, *Genesis* (BKAT 1), Neukirchen-Vluyn: Neukirchener Verlag, 1968, pp. 223–8. Westermann discusses various interpretations, but concludes that the biblical writer wanted to convey that things were different in the Urzeit, the primal age, from what they were later. See also S. R. Driver, *The Book of Genesis* (Westminster Commentaries), London: Methuen, 1904, pp. 16–17, who argues that the biblical writer portrays an *ideal*. '[H]e represents both men and animals as subsisting at first only on vegetable food.'

aspect of discussions about the verses has been the ignoring of the fact that *animals* as well as humans are forbidden to eat meat. Calvin, for example, who sets out the arguments for and against the verses being a ban on the eating of meat before the Flood, entirely confines the discussion to the way in which the verses affect *humans*.[8] But this is not what the text says. The implication of the inclusion of animals with humans in the ban on eating meat is that Genesis 1 describes the creation of a *vegetarian* world. It is only in the past thirty years or so that the full implications of this have been explored.[9]

P. Beauchamp, in his article published in 1989, draws a sharp contrast between Genesis 1.26–30 and 9.1–7. In the former passage the relationship between humans and animals is one of harmony, in spite of the fact that attempts have been made to interpret the Hebrew verbs translated as 'subdue' and 'have dominion' in an aggressive sense.[10] In Genesis 9.2 that harmony is no longer present:

> 'Fear of you and terror shall come upon every wild beast, every bird of the heavens, all reptiles and all the fish of the sea; they are delivered into your power.'

There is no harmony here. The verb translated as 'delivered' is used elsewhere in the Old Testament where Israel has victory over its enemies. Moreover, there is not only the dread of the human race on the part of other creatures; Genesis 9.6 envisages that humans will kill each other. What is portrayed is a world of violence, the world familiar to human beings. That violence is absent from Genesis 1.26–30, and the difference between the two worlds is that one is vegetarian and the other is not. The vegetarianism of Genesis 1.26–30 is not advocating that humans should be vegetarians (although the writer of these words is one). Vegetarianism is a way of describing a world at peace with itself. As Beauchamp says, the Bible does not think of peace between human beings without there being peace between humans and animals.[11] Genesis 1

---

[8] J. Calvin, *Commentary on the Book of Genesis*, Edinburgh: Banner of Truth Trust, 1965, pp. 99–100.

[9] See P. Beauchamp, 'Création et fondation de la loi en Gn 1,1–2,4' in F. Blanquart (ed.), *La Création dans l'orient ancien* (Lectio Divina 127), Paris: Les Éditions du Cerf, 1987, pp. 139–82; J. W. Rogerson, *Genesis 1—11* (Old Testament Guides), Sheffield: JSOT Press, 1991, pp. 44–6. The matter is also dealt with fully in U. Neumann-Gorsolke, *Herrschen in den Grenzen der Schöpfung: Ein Beitrag zur alttestamentlichen Anthropologie am Beispiel von Psalm 8, Genesis 1 und verwandten Texten* (WMANT 101), Neukirchen-Vluyn: Neukirchener Verlag, 2004, where a different conclusion in reached from that argued here.

[10] See Rogerson, *Genesis 1—11*, p. 43.

[11] Beauchamp, 'Création et fondation de la loi', p. 180.

is able to believe that a mastery over the earth is possible without exercising a mastery over the other beings, who are intermediate beings between the master and the earth. Genesis 1 teaches us that there is only true mastery over the earth if mankind does not enslave itself by enslaving its fellows.[12]

What is described in Genesis 1, therefore, is not the world of our experience. That world comes into being only after the Flood, a world in which human beings contribute significantly to the destructiveness, oppression and alienation which are so characteristic of it. The vegetarian world re-appears in visions of a new heaven and new earth in passages such as Isaiah 65.17–25, as in the following excerpts:

> Look, I am about to create new heavens and a new earth;
> the former things shall no longer be remembered or come to mind.
> Jerusalem will be my delight and my people will be my joy.
> No more shall be heard in her
> a sound of weeping or a cry of distress.
> There will not be found there
> an infant that dies before its time,
> nor an old man who does not complete his allotted span.
> The youth shall die a hundred years old,
> and whoever fails to reach a hundred years shall be considered accursed.
> They shall build houses and live in them;
> they shall plant vineyards and eat their produce.
> They shall not build for others to dwell there;
> they shall not plant for others to eat;
> The days of my people's lives shall be like those of a tree,
> and my chosen shall enjoy to the full the work of their hands.
> Before they call I will answer them,
> while they are still speaking I will hear.
> The wolf and the lamb shall feed together,
> the lion shall eat straw like the ox.[13]
> They shall not hurt or destroy on all my holy mountain, says YHWH.[14]

The narrative of the creation of the world of our experience is the story of the Flood in Genesis 6—9. Before this is discussed, however, it is necessary

---

[12] Beauchamp, 'Création et fondation de la loi', p. 170: 'elle a pu faire croire qu'une maîtrise de la terre était possible sans que fût exercée une maîtrise sur d'autres êtres, intermédiaires entre le maître et la terre. Gn 1 nous enseigne qu'il n'y a vraie maîtrise de la terre que si l'homme ne s'asservit pas lui-même en asservissant son frère.'

[13] Omitting 'dust shall be the food of the snake' as a gloss. See BHK.

[14] Isaiah 65.17, 19–22, 24–5. In the complete passage there is a tension between the promise of a new (i.e. renewed rather than recreated) heaven and earth, and a restored Jerusalem and Judah, which has given rise to the suggestion that a promise of renewal for Jerusalem has been expanded into a promise of the renewal of the heaven and earth. See C. Westermann, *Das Buch Jesaja: Kap. 40–66* (ATD 19), Göttingen: Vandenhoeck & Ruprecht, 1966, pp. 322–4.

to consider Genesis 4, a chapter of which it can be rightly said that it describes the violent world of our experience. In it, Abel is murdered by his brother Cain (Genesis 4.1–16), and Lamech boasts that he has killed a man who wounded him (Genesis 4.23). Further, the cursing of the ground in both Genesis 3.17–19 and 4.11–12 envisages conditions familiar from the world of human experience rather than the conditions of an ideal primal world. The easiest way round this difficulty is to invoke source criticism and to say that it is in the Priestly tradition that Genesis 1 describes an ideal world, and that the Priestly story of the Flood is the story of the creation of the world of our experience. Genesis 4 belongs to the non-Priestly tradition, and has a different outlook, albeit one that sees the corruption of an originally benign world by a breakdown in divine–human and human–human relationships. The opening chapters of Genesis have been subjected to various processes of addition and expansion, and this explains the literary tensions that can be discerned within them.[15]

For present purposes, Genesis 1 and Genesis 6—9, will deal with the Priestly tradition within these chapters, that is, Genesis 6.9–22; 7.6, 11, 13–16, 18–21, 24; 8.1–2, 3b–5, 13–19; 9.1–17. The narrative structure of the text makes it clear that it is in Genesis 6—9 that we find the account of the creation of the world of our experience. That the flood story in Genesis is linked to the account of creation in Genesis 1 has long been recognized. Creation in the Old Testament is understood as order, including the moral order, violation of which can undermine the created natural order. In Genesis 1 to 9 (and elsewhere, e.g. Job 38) the establishment of order involves setting limits to the potentially destructive forces that are part of nature. In Genesis 1 the waters are allocated to two spheres, which control their destructive potential. They are either above the firmament in a kind of metal dome in Hebrew cosmology – or gathered together under the firmament to provide a platform upon which dry land stands. The provision of water in the form of rain entails releasing water from above the firmament. The provision of water in the form of springs entails releasing water that is below the dry land. In Genesis 7 a flood is brought upon the earth when the forces that restrain the destructive potential of the waters are removed:

> on this day [the 17th day of the 2nd month of Noah's 600th year] all the fountains of the great deep burst through, and the windows of the heavens were opened. (Genesis 7.11)

---

[15] See especially M. Witte, *Die biblische Urgeschichte: Redaktions- und theologiegeschichtliche Beobachtungen zu Genesis 1.1–11.26* (BZAW 265), Berlin: W. de Gruyter, 1998.

After the earth has been covered by the flood, a passage similar in one important respect to the opening of Genesis 1 occurs:

> God caused a wind to blow over the earth, and the waters abated; the fountains of the deep and the windows of the heavens were blocked.
>
> (Genesis 8.1–2)

Commentators on this passage have been so concerned with identifying this wind or discussing its physical function that they have overlooked its close connection with those words in Genesis 1.2 that state that the spirit or wind of God was hovering on the face of the primal waters.[16] Thus the wind in Genesis 8.1–2 has been compared with the 'strong east wind' that drove back the waters of the Red Sea and created dry land for the Israelites to pass over (Exodus 14.21).[17] This, in turn, has raised the question whether the function of the wind in Genesis 8.1 was to dry the waters, and whether, in fact, this was physically possible. Gunkel comments that 'die Flut nimmt ab, indem die *stehenden* Wasser durch Wind vertrieben werden [the Flood abates as the *standing* waters are driven back by wind]'.[18] A similar observation is made by Westermann.[19] If, however, Genesis 8.1–2 is compared with Genesis 1, the similarities are striking. In each case there is a watery chaos – *tehom* in Genesis 1 and the flooded earth in Genesis 8. In each case a wind or spirit of God is moving or blowing across these waters. In each case, order is created out of the chaos by the imposition or reimposition of boundaries and limits. In the case of Genesis 1 this is the original ordering of the world, in which waters are assigned to their appointed places. In the case of Genesis 8 it is the blocking of the fountains of the deep and the windows of the heavens. Genesis 8.1–2, as it describes the creation of the world of our experience, thus parallels the account of the creation of the world in Genesis 1, and the wind of Genesis 8.1 links back to the wind in Genesis 1.2. The parallel between Genesis 1 and Genesis 8 is made clear in Genesis 9.1–3, where the mandate given in Genesis 1 to all mankind is renewed to Noah and his family.

---

[16] Witte, *Biblische Urgeschichte*, p. 139, observes, 'Mit dem Motiv des von Gott über die Erde gesandten Windes, der über die Erde zieht und die Wasser zurücktreibt (8,1b), knüpft der Verfasser an die Vorstellung in 1,2a an' ['with the motif of the wind sent by God over the earth, which sweeps over the earth and drives the waters back, the writer makes a connection with the idea in Genesis 1.2a'].

[17] So the Puritan commentator M. Poole, *A Commentary on the Holy Bible* (1685), Edinburgh: Banner of Truth Trust, 1962, p. 21.

[18] H. Gunkel, *Genesis*, 7th edn (GHAT), Göttingen: Vandenhoeck & Ruprecht, 1966, p. 145.

[19] Westermann, *Genesis*, p. 593.

> Be fruitful and increase, and fill the earth. Fear of you and terror shall come upon every wild beast, every bird of the heavens, all reptiles and all the fish of the sea; they are delivered into your power. Every creature that moves and lives shall be your food; as I once gave you the green plants, I now give you everything.
>
> (Genesis 9.1–3)

This is no longer a vegetarian world at peace with itself. It is a world in which the human race may kill and eat animals provided that they avoid eating their blood (Genesis 9.4). It is a world in which the non-human species live in fear and dread of the human race and in which, as verse 6 makes clear, humans will kill each other regardless of the fact that they are made in God's image. If Genesis 1 and Genesis 6—9 are compared, it will be seen that Genesis 1 is a critique of the world described in 6—9. The former world results from the creative word of God. The world of our experience is a compromise world, born of human wickedness and necessarily adapted to the destructive creature that humanity is, or has become. It is possible to describe the Old Testament as the story of a divine project to form a type of humanity that would be capable of living in the kind of world described in Genesis 1 – a topic which will be dealt with in a later chapter. In terms of the 'hot' and 'cold' distinction, Genesis 1 and Genesis 6—9 taken together are 'hot' accounts. Paradoxically, they ascribe the origin of the world to the God revealed to Israel, but also affirm that the world of human experience is not the world that God intended. This means that God cannot, and humanity should not, be content with the world and humanity as they are, and this dissatisfaction should become a driving force that inspires humanity to press towards the ideals expressed in Genesis 1 and the prophetic visions of the future, such as in Isaiah 65.

The account of creation in Job 38—41 has in common with Genesis 1 the view that creation is about order. In Genesis 1 the establishment of that order is described; in Job it is presumed. The waters, for example, have their prescribed limits:

> who enclosed[20] the sea with doors,
> when it burst from the womb in flood;
> when I fashioned its garment from clouds,
> and made deep darkness its swaddling band?
> I prescribed bounds for it,[21] and set a bar and doors.
> I said, 'This far may you come, and no more,
> here shall your mighty waves be halted.'[22]
>
> (Job 38.8–11)

---

[20] Reading mî sāk, cf. BHK.
[21] Reading huqqō, cf. BHK.
[22] Reading yišbot gᵉōn, cf. BHK.

But the description of order also has some charming touches:

> Have you been in the storehouses of the snow,
> or seen where the hail is kept,
> which I have preserved ready for times of trouble,
> for days of battle and war?
> By which way is light distributed,
> or the east wind made to scour the earth?
>
> (Job 38.22–24)

We have a picture of a set of storehouses containing items such as snow, hail, light and wind. We are tempted to ask whether God is the warehouse keeper, or whether each storehouse has its own janitor!

But if Job 38—41 has in common with Genesis 1 the idea of creation as order, it disagrees fundamentally about the purpose of creation. According to Genesis 1 (and this is still the case in the compromise world of Genesis 6—9) the human race is the climax of the creation, and is given authority to act as God's steward in relation to it. In Job this is far from being the case. The very form of Job 38—41, in which Job is asked a series of unanswerable questions, serves to stress that humankind is in no position to assume that the creation exists primarily for its benefit. Here are just some of the questions designed to put Job and humanity in their place:

> Where were you when I laid down earth's foundations?
> Have you ever issued a command to the morning,
> or told the dawn where it should be?
> Have you been to the sources of the sea,
> or wandered in the depths of the deep?
> Where is the way to where light dwells,
> and where does darkness reside?
>
> (Job 38.4, 12, 16, 19)

And alongside these unanswerable questions are other questions that imply that things happen in the created order that have no connection with or relevance to the human race:

> Who carved out a channel for the torrents of rain,
> and made a path for the thunderbolt,
> to bring rain on land without inhabitants,
> on desert where no one lives;
> to refresh land waste and desolate,
> and clothe dry places[23] with grass?
>
> (Job 38.25–27)

---

[23] Reading tsāmē. Cf. S. R. Driver and G. B. Gray, *The Book of Job together with a New Translation* (ICC), Edinburgh: T. & T. Clark, 1921, part II, p. 305.

And such thoughts lead into chapters 39—41 in which members of the created order are described, such as the wild ass, the ostrich and the hawk. These are spoken of as being of concern to God, and then comes a section on the creature that is the first of the works of God, that is, the climax of creation. Whether Behemoth is taken to be the hippopotamus[24] or, more likely, the crocodile,[25] makes no difference to the argument here. It is to be doubted whether anyone, asked to suggest what might be the climax of God's creation, would choose either the hippo or the crocodile! What is important is that it is not the human race, at any rate, not according to Job 40—1.

One of the important things that has to be accepted if the Old Testament is to be understood fully, is that it does not speak with one voice. Various types of Reformed theology may well have claimed that there are no contradictions in the Bible and that no one Church 'may . . . so expound one place of Scripture, that it be repugnant to another' as Article XX of the 39 Articles of Religion of the Church of England puts it. But such ideas must be put to one side. Reality is far too complex to be summed up adequately in human categories of thought (which is one of the messages of Job 38—41!) and in the Old Testament it is the diversity of voices and their discordances that enable profound insights about reality to be articulated. Job 38—41 contradicts the idea that the human race is the climax and most important feature of the created order. In the context of the book of Job as a whole, this view is meant to counteract the idea that Job's undeserved sufferings demand from God an explanation satisfactory to human understanding. From the perspective of the latent meanings embodied in Job 38—41, the passage is a warning against an anthropocentric view of the world; one in which any action can be justified if it furthers what the ruling and controlling powers among humanity decide to be in the interests of and benefit for humanity. To this extent, Job 38—41 is 'hot'. It challenges a thought-paradigm and invites alternative ways of thinking about the place of humans in the world, and how they should act in it.

The third creation account to be considered in this chapter is the opening of the book of Ecclesiastes (or Qoheleth, to give it its Hebrew name). On the face of it, it is a very 'cold' account, with its stress on repetitiveness and the impossibility of there being anything new in the world. Here, it will be argued that its stress upon the inscrutability of the created order gives the text considerable 'heat'. The main part of the passage is as follows:

---

[24] Thus in the footnote to the RSV of Job 40.15, and in the text of the *EU* (Nilpferd).
[25] Thus in the text of the NEB and REB of Job 40.15.

A generation passes away, a generation is born,
but the earth remains unchanged.
The sun rises and the sun sets,
and returns to the place where it rises.[26]
The moon[27] goes to the south,
and circles to the north;
the moon[28] goes round,
and returns to its circuit.
All streams flow into the sea,
but the sea is not filled;
the streams never cease to flow
to the place to which they go.
All things are wearisome;
no man can find words for it;
no eye is satisfied with seeing,
no ear filled with hearing.
What has been is what will be,
what has been done is what will be done;
there is absolutely nothing new under the sun.
Is there something of which it is said
'Look, this is new'?
It has already existed
in the times before we were born.
Former things are not remembered,
neither will those who live after us remember the later things that
    come to pass.

I, Qoheleth,[29] was king over Israel in Jerusalem. I applied my mind to enquire and to search out by wisdom all that is done under heaven. It is a grim business that God has given to occupy the human race. I have seen everything that is done under the sun and indeed, all is nothingness;[30] an attempt to herd[31] the wind.   (Ecclesiastes 1.4–14)

The perception in recent years that Qoheleth is a 'modern' book, one that resonates with the pessimism that is engendered by the atrocities and injustices of today's world, has led to an explosion of scholarly literature

---

[26] Reading *šāʾaf* and adding *hōlēk*.
[27] Reading *yarēach* for *rūach*. This was proposed privately by G. R. Driver and I have not seen it suggested elsewhere, although it seems to me to be highly plausible.
[28] Reading *yarēach* for *rūach*.
[29] The Hebrew, which is variously translated as preacher, teacher, philosopher, spokesman, is left untranslated.
[30] The Hebrew suggests that which is insubstantial and has no lasting substance or profit.
[31] The enigmatic Hebrew *rᵉʿūt* is connected with the verb to pasture flocks.

on this text.[32] It has also generated a variety of differing interpretations. At one extreme Aarre Lauha claims that Qoheleth's faith in God is not that of the faith of Israel.[33] He argues that for the writer of the book, God is distant. He is not the God who could be addressed in prayer. That whereas in wisdom teaching and the psalms the incomprehensibility of God leads to worship, in Qoheleth it leads to bitterness. This, of course, begs the question about what constituted 'the faith of Israel' and arguably uses a modern view of the essence of religion to show the alleged inferiority of Qoheleth's faith in comparison with that of 'Israel'. It is tempting to ask why, if Qoheleth felt so bitter about God, he bothered to write the book that bears his name, and why it was received into the Jewish canon as Scripture. A different approach is found in an article by Norman Whybray, which maintains that the opening chapter of Qoheleth is not about the futility of life, but is an invitation to readers to observe the processes of nature with awe and wonder.[34]

Before proceeding further, the matter must be addressed whether it is possible to speak of Qoheleth as the author of his book, or at any rate, the opening chapters. Theories that the book has been subjected to various sets of interpolations by different editors have long been maintained.[35] Recently, Martin Rose has suggested that the book owes its final form to several rereadings of the original work of Qoheleth the wise, respectively by a disciple and a theologian redactor.[36] The view taken here will be that of A. A. Fischer, who takes Ecclesiastes 1.3—3.9 to represent substantially what he calls 'der Traktat des Kohelet'.[37] For the moment only the first chapter will be considered. The poem in 3.1–9 will be dealt with in a later chapter. The passage will be commented on in the light of some observations made in Charles Taylor's book *Sources of the Self: The Making of the Modern Identity*.[38]

In these observations Taylor refers to nineteenth-century European writers and painters of the 'realist' school (Zola, Flaubert, Courbet and Manet)

---

[32] See the invaluable surveys by O. Kaiser, 'Die Botschaft des Buches Kohelet'; 'Beiträge zur Kohelet-Forschung' in Kaiser, *Gottes und der Menschen Weisheit* (BZAW 261), Berlin: de Gruyter, 1998, pp. 126–200.

[33] A. Lauha, *Kohelet* (BKAT 19), Neukirchen-Vluyn: Neukirchener Verlag, 1978, p. 17.

[34] R. N. Whybray, 'Ecclesiastes 1.5–7 and the Wonders of Nature', *JSOT* 41 (1988), pp. 105–12.

[35] See the brief surveys by Lauha, *Kohelet*, pp. 4–7; Kaiser, 'Beiträge', pp. 152–7.

[36] M. Rose, *Rien de nouveau: Nouvelles approches du livre de Qohéleth. Avec une bibliographie (1988–1998) élaborée par Béatrice Perregaux Allisson* (OBO 168), Fribourg: Editions Universitaires Suisses; Göttingen: Vandenhoeck & Ruprecht, 1999.

[37] A. A. Fischer, *Skepsis oder Furcht Gottes?* (BZAW 247), Berlin: de Gruyter, 1997.

[38] C. Taylor, *Sources of the Self: The Making of the Modern Identity*, Cambridge: Cambridge University Press, 1989.

and obviously, there is a danger in comparing these artists with a writer some two thousand years earlier in the ancient Near East. Neither can one know whether Qoheleth had in mind what Taylor says about the 'realists'. However, the connection, if there is one, is suggestive.

Taylor argues that the 'realists' were determined 'to show things in their crude, lowly reality and to dispel any illusion of a deeper meaning inhabiting them'.[39] He goes on to say that 'the premiss of realism then and now is that we somehow in the normal course of things fail to see things aright, that we grasp them only through a veil of illusion which lends them a false enhancement of significance, woven by our fears and self-indulgence. It takes courage and vision to see them as they are.'[40]

Two things are particularly striking about this. The first is that it is commonly held that Ecclesiastes is an attack upon the optimistic world-view of the so-called wisdom literature as found, for example, in the book of Proverbs.[41]

That world-view envisages the kind of universe in which thrift and moral uprightness are rewarded and sloth and wrongdoing are punished. Job's friends entertain similar opinions. If Qoheleth is deliberately seeking to undermine this view, then, to paraphrase Taylor's words, he is trying to tear away a veil of illusion which lends to reality a false enhancement of significance. The second striking thing is that he uses the device of having been a king as part of his attack upon the wisdom outlook. Wisdom was, of course, associated with the royal court, whose scribes learned to write by copying the proverbs that expressed the wisdom outlook. More importantly, the claim of the writer of Ecclesiastes to have been a king and to have enjoyed wealth and pleasure put him in an impregnable position from which to attack the wisdom teaching. According to that teaching he must have been thrifty and upright in order to be blessed by having wealth and pleasure to enjoy. According to his own viewpoint his advantages had enabled him to see through the illusions which distorted the perception of reality of some, at least, of those among whom he lived. Taylor suggests that such portrayals of reality bring about what he calls a kind of transfiguration. The ability to confront and acknowledge harsh reality sets people free from any power these conditions may have over them. What is revealed is not so much any truths about these realities, but rather truths about the people themselves, truths that may leave them unwilling

---

[39] Taylor, *Sources*, p. 431.
[40] Taylor, *Sources*, p. 431.
[41] Lauha, *Kohelet*, p. 14. A slightly different view is found in Rose, *Rien de nouveau*, pp. 94–5, who notes Qoheleth's criticism of 'wisdom' teaching but locates him within its broad ambit.

to accept things as they are. How much of this can be taken back to Ecclesiastes is no doubt a matter of opinion, but it may not be going too far to say that the book would presumably not have been written unless the author had wished to communicate his 'realistic' view of the world. His 'realism' had resulted not in a passive acquiescence and acceptance of a monotonous, repetitive and apparently meaningless world. It had moved him to communicate something, presumably in the hope that it would persuade others to see the world 'realistically' and to act accordingly as they were able.

Taylor's illuminating observations address the matter subjectively; they indicate how people subjectively may face reality by stripping it of any illusions that mask its harshness. A similar thought can be found in Adorno's *Minima Moralia,* in the passage about seeing past the beauty of a blossoming tree to the dark shadow of the reality of which it is part.[42] Must the matter rest here, or can and should anything be said about the relation of the world to God that is implied by Qoheleth?

The negative remarks about Qoheleth's faith in God found, for example, in Lauha, imply that there is only one genuine type of experience or knowledge of God and that Qoheleth lacks this. It is a way of reading the Old Testament from the perspective of a type of orthodoxy that privileges certain strands of religious experience. This brings with it the danger that the theological witness of the Old Testament becomes restricted and diminished, because those who approach it in this way know in advance what it says, or ought to say, about God. The view taken in the present work is that the Old Testament speaks with many voices and that readers will do well to listen to them rather than decide in advance which are the most congenial. Starting from this position it can be suggested that Qoheleth's desire to present reality in all its harshness derives not only from his humanistic outlook, but also from his religious faith. This faith, in so far as it can be deduced from the book of Ecclesiastes, may indeed have involved a relationship with God that was formal and distant rather than personal and intimate, but this does not mean that it was unreal or invalid. It had the effect of giving him the courage to be critical of the world as he saw it – a world that he believed to have been created by God – and critical of the lot of humanity within it. If this is correct it

---

[42] T. W. Adorno, *Minima Moralia* in *Gesammelte Schriften,* Darmstadt: Wissenschaftliche Buchgesellschaft, 1998, vol. 4, p. 26, 'Noch der Baum, der blüht, lügt in dem Augenblick, in welchem man sein Blühen ohne den Schatten des Entsetzens wahrnimmt . . .'; ET *Minima Moralia, Reflections from Damaged Life* (trans. E. F. N. Jephcott), London: Verso, 1978, p. 25, 'Even the blossoming tree lies the moment its bloom is seen without the shadow of terror . . .'

raises the question, not wholly irrelevant in today's world, whether it is better to be pious while being indifferent to, or the cause of, human suffering, as opposed to being sensitive to human suffering and active in seeking to alleviate it, while not passing all the religious tests that would be administered by 'committed' believers.

The most explicit statement in the book concerning religious observance occurs in 5.1–2 [Hebrew 4.17—5.1] which reads

> Watch your step when you go to the house of God.
> To approach in order to listen,
> is better than sacrifices offered by fools.
> It is their ignorance that makes them do wrong.
> Do not be rash with your mouth,
> or hasty with your heart,
> to bring a matter before God.
> God is in heaven and you are upon earth.
> Let your words, therefore, be few.

The opening statement is remarkable given that the main function of temples, including that in Jerusalem, was to enable sacrifices to be offered. They were not centres of preaching, unless the suggestion of Rex Mason is taken up, that there was a tradition of preaching in Jerusalem's Second Temple.[43] The function of sacrifices was to enlist divine support to maintain the status quo; but if, for Qoheleth, the status quo was riddled with injustice, it is easy to see why he regarded the offering of sacrifices as the work of fools performed in ignorance. The prophetic critique of sacrifice comes to mind here, with the difference that the prophets (probably) objected mainly to the hypocritical offering of sacrifices, whereas the objection of Qoheleth (on the view being advanced here) would be that they enlisted the support of God for the maintenance of an unjust world.[44] Again, the counsel against bringing matters rashly before God can be seen as a warning against regarding God as a means whereby humans can achieve their own goals. God is not that kind of commodity.

God, as conceived by Qoheleth, may therefore be remote, and certainly not an object to be manipulated to meet specific human requirements. But there is an admirable integrity about Qoheleth's faith. It requires him to be honest and realistic about the world in which he lives, and about the God whom he believes to be responsible for it. Modern readers might well ask

---

[43] R. Mason, *Preaching the Tradition: Homily and Hermeneutics after the Exile*, Cambridge: Cambridge University Press, 1990.

[44] Rose, *Rien de nouveau*, pp. 342–4, surveys scholarly opinions about Qoheleth's attitude to the sacrificial cult.

why, given his view of the world, Qoheleth wanted a God at all. But this would have made the world more intolerable than it already was. Even the mere notion of an inscrutable God can be the source of feelings of transcendence that make humans aware of their limitations and creatureliness, and which engender hopes for better possibilities. To sum up, Ecclesiastes 1.3–18 is 'hot'. It describes a created order that implies a world that evokes not so much awe and wonder as resignation and indignation. It strips away the fantasies that mask its harsh realities. To refer back to Taylor, it can set people free from the power that harsh realities may have over them. If they believe in God, it may purge their conception of the divine from all that trivializes it.

The next creation account to be discussed is the book of Jonah. Jonah is not usually regarded as a creation narrative, and traditionally, discussion has centred on whether the work was historically true, or whether it was a parable or an allegory; whether Jonah was a real person or a symbol for Israel, the people for God.[45] The suggestion that the book was concerned with creation was made by Ludwig Schmidt in his book *De Deo*, published in 1976.[46] Schmidt's argument depended upon the isolation in Jonah of an original *Grundschrift* or basic story, which consisted of Jonah 1.2; 3.3–10; 4.1, 5a, 6–11. This told of Jonah's preaching against Nineveh without any mention of his reluctance to do this, and of Nineveh's repentance. God's act of mercy was grounded in the fact that he was the creator. This basic story was added to by subsequent editors in such a way as to turn the book into a prophetic 'legend'. However, it is not necessary to follow Schmidt's literary analysis in order to appreciate the value of his basic suggestion and to develop it by reading the book in its 'final form'.

The central passage of Jonah occurs at 1.9 when the sailors in the vessel that is in danger of sinking ask Jonah who he his, and where he comes from. He replies,

> I am a Hebrew; and it is Yʜwʜ, the God of heaven, whom I fear, who made the sea and the dry land.

The passage unequivocally links the God of the Hebrews with the creator of the world.[47] Yʜwʜ is not just another god; he is the one who made the sea and the dry land. Earlier in the chapter (1.6) the sleeping Jonah is aroused by the sailors with the words

---

[45] See the discussion in J. A. Bewer, *Jonah* (ICC), Edinburgh: T. & T. Clark, 1912, pp. 3–11.

[46] L. Schmidt, *'De Deo': Studien zur Literarkritik und Theologie des Buches Jona, des Gesprächs zwischen Abraham und Jahwe in Gen 18.22ff. und von Hi 1* (BZAW 143), Berlin: de Gruyter, 1976.

[47] H. W. Wolff, *Jona* (BKAT 14.3), Neukirchen-Vluyn: Neukirchener Verlag, 1977, p. 92.

Get up and call upon your god! Perhaps the god will spare us a thought, so that we do not perish.

The world of the sailors is one in which there are many gods, whose relationship to the human race is probably one of indifference, an indifference that might be overcome by especially desperate or fervent petition. With this implication, the narrative is deeply into irony, because the cause of the storm that threatens the survival of the ship is not the indifference of a god, but the active intervention of Jonah's God, Yhwh, who is punishing the prophet for deliberately refusing to go to Nineveh, as God has commanded him. Readers are left to muse on the fact that Jonah both confesses that Yhwh is the maker of the sea and the dry land, and also presumes that he can escape from the prophetic task entrusted to him by the creator by embarking on a ship that is going in the opposite direction from Nineveh![48]

Jonah's belief in God is sufficiently adult to realize that the tempest that threatens the ship has come about because of his disobedience. He tells the sailors to throw him overboard for the sake of saving the ship. The sailors, in doing this, assume that they are sending Jonah to his death. They pray that Yhwh(!) will not hold them responsible for Jonah's life, and offer sacrifice to him and vow vows (1.16).[49] Presumably, Jonah himself expects to die. The fact that he does not drown, but is swallowed by a great fish, is a further demonstration of the power of God, who made the sea and the dry land.

When Jonah finally carries out his mission, and his warning of Nineveh's imminent destruction brings about the repentance of the king and the people, Jonah's annoyance at being deprived of the spectacle of Nineveh's destruction leads him to set up an observation post outside the city, in case he is not disappointed, and the city is destroyed after all. He is protected from the sun by a plant, probably a castor bean, which reaches a height of 4 metres and has many large leaves that can provide shade.[50] When the plant withers and no longer affords protection, Jonah is angry, and asks God to take his life. God's answer is as follows:

> *You* have pity on the plant that cost you no toil, and which you did not make grow, which grew up in a night, and withered in a night. Should not *I* have pity for Nineveh, a great city in which there are more than a hundred and twenty thousand persons who do not know their right hand from their left, as well as much cattle?
>
> (Jonah 4.10–11)

---

[48] D. Gunn, 'Jonah' in J. D. G. Dunn and J. W. Rogerson (eds), *Eerdmans Commentary on the Bible*, Grand Rapids: Eerdmans, 2003, p. 699.

[49] Gunn, 'Jonah', p. 699, suggests that the sailors have been 'converted' to Yhwh by Jonah's willingness to be thrown overboard.

[50] M. Zohary, *Plants of the Bible*, Cambridge: Cambridge University Press, 1982, p. 93.

There is quite a complicated argument here. Jonah had entertained some affection for the castor bean, but this was not based upon the creator–created relationship. Jonah did not create the castor bean, and did not make it grow. His affection for it was purely selfish – it afforded him shelter from the heat of the sun. God, it is implied, did create it and make it grow. If Jonah felt some affection for a plant simply because it was useful to him, how much more should God feel affection for it because he made it; and affection not just for the castor bean, but also for the 120,000 inhabitants of Nineveh together with their cattle. God's mercy in sparing the people and their cattle comes from his relationship with them as their creator.

But we need to probe more deeply than this. We can say that Jonah stands for a part of the human race, a human part that believes in a creator God, but refuses to draw any practical conclusions from this belief. It thinks that God's commands can be ignored and that the creator will have no power to see that they are carried out. It can attach itself to a created item that is of use to it, while being indifferent (if that is an appropriate word in the context) to the fate of thousands of fellow human beings and the non-human creatures on which they rely. This behaviour is contrasted in Jonah with other parts of the human race which do take seriously a belief in a creator God. The sailors, having cast Jonah into the sea, fear YHWH greatly, offer a sacrifice to him and make vows. The inhabitants of Nineveh take the message of Jonah so seriously that their public demonstration of repentance could hardly be more thorough. The book of Jonah is, of course, not just about creation and attitudes to it. But it can arguably be read as a 'hot' account of creation, one that poses the question about the nature of belief in creation. Is such belief primarily a matter of intellectual assent, or does it have implications for the way in which people should live in a created world, and how they should regard their fellow creatures, both human and non-human?

I want to conclude by mentioning a well-known disagreement among Old Testament scholars on the subject of creation, and by linking it to something in Charles Taylor's *Sources of the Self*. The discussion was begun in 1936 by Gerhard von Rad in an essay entitled 'The Theological Problem of the Old Testament Doctrine of Creation'.[51] Von Rad's basic point was

---

[51] G. von Rad, 'The Theological Problem of the Old Testament Doctrine of Creation' in B. W. Anderson (ed.), *Creation in the Old Testament*, London: SPCK, 1984, pp. 53–64; German original (1936) reprinted in 'Das theologische Problem des alttestamentlichen Schöpfungsglaubens' in *Gesammelte Studien zum Alten Testament* (ThB 8), Munich: Chr. Kaiser, 1961, pp. 136–47.

that belief in God in the Old Testament resulted from the conviction that Israel had been chosen and redeemed by God. There were no independent speculations about the origins of the universe, speculations that attributed these origins to a creating deity. Rather, belief in Yhwh as redeemer was the starting-point of Israelite belief, and as the faith of Israel developed it increasingly saw its redeemer as also the lord and creator of the universe. As von Rad put it:

> in genuinely Yahwistic belief the doctrine of creation never attained to the stature of a relevant, independent doctrine. We found it invariably related, and indeed subordinated, to soteriological considerations.[52]

Von Rad's thesis was challenged in 1973 by Hans Heinrich Schmid in an article entitled 'Creation, Righteousness and Salvation: "Creation Theology" as the Broad Horizon of Biblical Theology'.[53] Schmid outlined the views of creation in the ancient world, and especially their emphasis on the link between cosmic order and moral order. This entailed what has been called 'the connection of act and consequence' (Tat–Ergehen–Zusammenhang), and Schmid traced this throughout the Old Testament, reaching the following conclusion:

> the belief that God has created and is sustaining the order of the world in all its complexities, is not a peripheral theme of biblical theology but is plainly the fundamental theme . . . it seems to me to be of the highest significance that the description of the order of creation in the Bible and the description of creation found in the surrounding countries are largely in agreement.[54]

I do not intend to enter into the details of the discussion as it subsequently developed, except to say that in my view, subsequent research has tended to support von Rad's view rather than that of Schmid.[55] What the discussion raises is the question of where we get our ideas about the origin and nature of the universe from. Do we get them from general observation of the world around us (which is, roughly, Schmid's view) or do we bring other resources to bear on how we view the world, such as the

---

[52] Von Rad, 'The Theological Problem', p. 62; German, p. 146.

[53] H. H. Schmid, 'Creation, Righteousness and Salvation: "Creation Theology" as the Broad Horizon of Biblical Theology' in Anderson, *Creation in the Old Testament*, pp. 102–17; German original, 'Schöpfung, Gerechtigkeit und Heil: "Schöpfungstheologie" als Gesamthorizont biblischer Theologie', *ZThK* 70 (1973), pp. 1–19.

[54] Schmid, 'Creation, Righteousness and Salvation', p. 11; German, p. 15.

[55] See J. Halbe, '"Altorientalisches Weltordnungsdenken" und alttestamentliche Theologie: Zur Kritik eines Ideologems am Beispiel des israelitischen Rechts', *ZThK* 76 (1979), pp. 382–418.

belief in our redemption (which is, roughly, von Rad's view). I want to link this second alternative with some remarks of Taylor, bearing in mind that Taylor has wrongly taken the statements about God seeing the universe as 'good' in a moral sense. However, this does not invalidate the general point. Taylor writes as follows:

> The goodness of the world is not something quite independent from God's seeing it as good. His seeing it as good, loving it, can be conceived not simply as a *response* to what it is, but as what *makes* it such.

Taylor goes on to speak of the importance of 'a transformation of our stance towards the world whereby our vision of it is changed' (p. 449), something that he says has traditionally been connected with the notion of grace and which can also be connected with 'the creative imagination'. In the course of a discussion of Dostoyevsky, Taylor summarizes that writer's thoughts as follows:

> what will transform us is an ability to love the world and ourselves, to see it as good in spite of the wrong . . . But this will only come to us if we can accept being part of it, and that means accepting responsibility . . . Loving the world and ourselves is in a sense a miracle, in face of all the evil and degradation that it and we contain. But the miracle comes on us if we accept being part of it. Involved in this is our acceptance of love from others. We become capable of love through being loved.   (p. 452)

This may seem to be a long way from the theme of creation accounts as critiques of views of creation but arguably, the distance is not great. I would maintain that what gave the Old Testament writers the courage to compose critical accounts of the created order was their conviction of being loved and sustained by a God who had in view a better future for both them and the created order. This conviction of being loved sustained them also in cases where communication became distorted, as I shall try to show in Chapters 4 and 5.

Additional Note on Proverbs 8.22–32

Proverbs 8.22–32, if not a creation narrative, is indisputably about creation. It reads as follows:

> It was YHWH who created me at the beginning[56] of his works,
> before his deeds long ago.

---

[56] Taking r'ēšît as an adverb of time. See the discussion in A. Müller, *Proverbien 1—9: Der Weisheit neue Kleider* (BZAW 291), Berlin: de Gruyter, 2000, p. 232, note 4.

From eternity was I woven,[57]
from the very first, before the beginning of the earth.
When there were yet no deeps, was I born,
no springs of gushing water.
Before the mountains were sunk,
before the hills, was I born.
When he had not yet made land or fields,
nor the first of the soils of the world,
when he established the heavens, I was there;
when he determined a horizon on the face of the deep,
when he fastened the clouds overhead,
and fixed firm the springs of the deep;
[when he gave the sea its limit,
so that the waters should not transgress his command],[58]
when he set fast the foundations of the earth,
then was I with him, the master workman,[59]
I was his delight[60] each day,
playing before him always,
playing in his inhabited world,
delighting in the human race.

The relationship of Proverbs 8.22–32 to Genesis 1 is not easy to determine. The word *tehōm* meaning 'primaeval deep' occurs at Genesis 1.2 and Proverbs 8.24 (in the plural) and also at verses 27 and 28. The idea of creation as order, so fundamental to Genesis 1, is also found in Proverbs 8.22–32. Verse 27 reads 'when he determined a horizon on the face of the deep' and verse 29 (assuming it to be original and not a later gloss) has 'when he gave the sea its limit'. There are, however, fundamental differences between the two accounts. Proverbs 8 presupposes the existence of humanity, and does not describe its creation, neither is there any mention of the non-human inhabitants of the earth. Indeed, with the repetition of the words 'when there was yet no . . .' the passage arguably has more in common with the creation narratives of Israel's neighbours than with Genesis 1.[61] The main aim of the passage, in any case, is not to describe the creation of the world but to explain the position of wisdom in it. She is the speaker in these verses, and she is able to demonstrate her superior

---

[57] Reading nᵉsakkōtî. Cf. BHK and Müller, *Proverbien*, p. 233, note 3, and the use of skk at Psalm 139.13.

[58] The words in brackets are omitted by Codex Vaticanus of the LXX. Cf. BHK and Müller, *Proverbien*, p. 235, note 7.

[59] For this rendering see Müller, *Proverbien*, p. 236, note 2.

[60] Reading šaʿašuʿāv, cf. BHK.

[61] See the section 'when there was yet no . . .' in Westermann, *Genesis*, pp. 59–64.

relationship to the rest of creation by claiming that she was brought into being by YHWH before anything else existed.

The passage has generated an enormous amount of discussion about its relationship to ancient Near Eastern accounts of creation, about the place of personified wisdom in relation to YHWH, and about whether wisdom is in any way a participant with YHWH in the creative process. The passage has been particularly important for feminist interpreters of the Old Testament.[62] Some of the interpretative issues have hinged upon the translation of the Hebrew, especially the word *ʾamōn* in verse 30. The translation given above makes clear that the view taken in the present work is that there is no question of wisdom having any part in the creative process.

The main matter of concern here is whether Proverbs 8.22–32 is 'hot' or 'cold' – whether it sets up a dialectic between an ideal created order over against the world as we experience it. It will be argued here that the passage is 'cold', and that this has, and has had, implications for the use of the Old Testament in ethics. The passage is 'cold' in the sense that it assumes that the kind of world described in Genesis 1 is the world of our experience. This slightly contradicts the point made above, that the Proverbs passage seems to have a greater affinity with some ancient Near Eastern creation accounts than with Genesis 1, but this point is essentially a scholarly rather than a readerly one. It is only because scholars can collect together creation narratives from various cultures in the ancient world that the comparisons with Proverbs 8 can be made. This would have been impossible for the biblical writers, and does not occur to 'ordinary' readers of the Bible. From their perspective, Proverbs 8 has a connection with Genesis 1 because they share common subject matter.

Proverbs 8 supplies something that is partly missing in Genesis 1, taken alone. Genesis 1 does indeed indicate the purpose of the creation, which is that humankind created in the divine image should have dominion over the non-human creatures in the world. But how is this to be done? Proverbs 8, in the context of Proverbs 1—9, supplies the answer in terms of wisdom. The wisdom that was the first of God's created things has an intimate knowledge of the divine purpose. This knowledge can be available to human beings who desire it. By seeking, and obeying, wisdom, humans can live in harmony with the created order and its maker. This

---

[62] See G. Baumann, '"Zukunft feministischer Spiritualität" oder "Werbefigur des Patriarchats"? Die Bedeutung der Weisheitsgestalt in Prov 1—9 für die feministisch-theologische Diskussion' in L. Schottroff and M.-T. Wacker (eds), *Von der Wurzel getragen: Christlich-feministische Exegese in Auseinandersetzung mit Antijudaismus*, Leiden: E. J. Brill, 1996, pp. 135–52.

point of view sets in train something that has wide implications, and which finds expression in so-called apocryphal books such as the Wisdom of Solomon and Ben Sirah (Ecclesiasticus).[63]

The issue that concerns the present work can be seen most clearly when Proverbs 8.22–32 is compared with Ecclesiastes 1. Is the world of our experience one from which it is possible to deduce principles for living (roughly, what Proverbs 8.22–32 is claiming with the help of the concept of wisdom) or does it present itself as something that invites us to strip away the fantasies with which we surround ourselves (which is what Ecclesiastes 1 is saying, according to the interpretation above, pp. 53–4)? Is the world of our experience something that we must learn to live in harmony with, or is it something that needs to be challenged and changed? Much Christian ethical thinking has, of course, preferred the first alternative, whether that has been in terms of 'natural law' – principles deduced from the nature of things – or in terms of 'creation ethics' – the view that the Bible contains or reveals the 'maker's instructions' for how we should live.[64] The view taken in the present work is that the paradox expressed in the contrast between the ideal world of Genesis 1 and the compromise world of our experience in Genesis 9 must be maintained at all costs. This does not mean that nothing of value for ethics and living can be deduced from the world of our experience. It does mean that constant vigilance is needed, lest the attempt to deduce principles from our world becomes, whether deliberately or not, a way of accepting and affirming it. Proverbs 8 must be read with this point in mind. As Marx famously observed, 'the philosophers have only *interpreted* the world, in various ways; the point is to *change* it'.[65]

---

[63] See further E. Otto, *Theologische Ethik des Alten Testaments* (TW), Stuttgart: Kohlhammer, 1994, pp. 256–63.

[64] For 'natural law' see N. H. G. Robinson, *The Groundwork of Christian Ethics*, London: Collins, 1971, pp. 124–6; for 'creation ethics' see O. Barclay, 'The Nature of Christian Morality' in B. N. Kaye and G. J. Wenham (eds), *Law, Morality and the Bible*, Leicester: Inter-Varsity Press, 1978, pp. 125–50.

[65] K. Marx, 'Theses on Feuerbach XI' in K. Marx and F. Engels, *The German Ideology*, London: Lawrence & Wishart, 1970, p. 123.

3

Aspects of communication: interpersonal relationships

The first two chapters have indicated that human behaviour is seen in the Old Testament as problematic. The narratives of the exodus and the wilderness wanderings wrestle with the fact that the liberated people regret that they have been liberated, and that no amount of miraculous interventions on the part of God can persuade them otherwise. The narratives about the creation suggest that the created order needs to differ from that which God would ideally have it be, because otherwise it would be quickly destroyed by the human race. It is a disturbing thought that in today's world, the human race has actually acquired the power to destroy the earth, and that it is not neglecting to use this power to that end.

The present chapter will explore what the Old Testament contains on the subject of the nature of humanity. In this respect it will resemble those standard Old Testament theologies that have sections on anthropology, in the sense of the nature of humanity. It will also differ from them in a number of ways. First, no attempt will be made to describe some independent entity such as 'man' (or 'woman'). No doubt it can be argued, for example, by psychologists, that human beings share characteristics that can be classified with various personality types or traits;[1] and Old Testament scholars have similarly tried to elucidate the *Grundstrukturen* implied by the Old Testament narratives about human being and beings.[2] No such assumptions will be made here. Second, no attempt will be made to impose upon the texts to be discussed a theological doctrine, such as that of the 'fall' of the human race, or 'original sin'. This is not to deny that such doctrines may contain valuable insights into the nature of humanity; it is to affirm that the method adopted here is to try to allow the texts to speak for themselves in so far as modern awareness of 'reader response' criticism

---

[1] See, for example, E. Fromm, *Man for Himself: An Inquiry into the Psychology of Ethics*, London: Routledge, 2003.

[2] See the section 'Gemeine Grundstrukturen?' in H. D. Preuss, *Theologie des Alten Testaments*, vol. 2: *Israels Weg mit JHWH*, Stuttgart: Kohlhammer, 1992, pp. 140–2 and the literature there cited.

allows this to be possible. Another type of approach that will be avoided is set out in words quoted by Preuss from H. Seebass,

> Die im Alten Testament überlieferten Texte wollen Menschen überhaupt nicht anders erkennen als vor dem 'Angesicht' ihres Gottes.[3]

This is an assertion that cannot be proved or disproved, and which in any case does not contribute to the interpretation of the texts in question. A third point to be made in regard to what follows is that it will concentrate upon texts that deal with human interaction. The implication will be that what humans are is closely bound up with how they act towards each other. The Old Testament contains a good deal of material on this subject, only some of which will be able to be discussed. The first narrative to be considered, the story of Cain and Abel in Genesis 4.1–16, reads as follows in my translation:

> Adam knew his wife, Eve, carnally. She became pregnant and gave birth to Cain. She said 'I have gained[4] a man, just as YHWH did.'[5] She gave birth again, to his brother, to Abel. Abel became a shepherd, Cain a worker of the land. In due course Cain brought some of the produce of the land as an offering to YHWH and Abel also brought an offering, the fat portions of the firstlings of his flock.[6] YHWH looked favourably on Abel and his offering, but unfavourably on Cain and his offering. Cain was very angry and his face fell. YHWH said to Cain 'Why are you angry, and why has your face fallen? Surely, if you do well there is recognition. If you do not do well, sin crouches, ready to entice you.'[7] Cain said to his brother Abel 'Let us go into the open field.'[8] When they reached the open field Cain rose up against his brother Abel, and killed him. YHWH said to Cain 'Where is your brother Abel?' Cain answered 'I do not know. Am I my brother's guardian?' YHWH said 'What have you done? Your brother's blood is crying out to me from the ground. From now on you are cursed from the ground which opened its mouth to receive your brother's blood shed by your hand. When you work the land it will no longer yield its strength to you. You will be a wanderer and fugitive

---

[3] Preuss, *Theologie des AT*, p. 140, quoting H. Seebass, 'Über den Beitrag des A. T. zu einer theologischen Anthropologie', *KuD* 22 (1976), pp. 41–63; the quotation is on p. 43. 'The Old Testament texts that have been handed down deal with the human race only insofar as it is seen before the "face" of its God.'

[4] This rendering tries to bring out the connection in Hebrew between the name, Cain, and the verb, *kanah*.

[5] For a full discussion of this well-known crux see Westermann, *Genesis*, pp. 396–7. The view taken here is that Eve exclaims that she has brought a man into existence, just as God brought Adam into existence.

[6] Taking the *vav* before 'of their fat portions' as a *vav explicativum*.

[7] Reading leᶜphattoteka with BHK and omitting verse 7c as a gloss from 3.16.

[8] Following the Samaritan, Greek and Syriac versions.

in the land.' Cain replied to YHWH, 'my guilt is too heavy to bear. You have driven me out this day from the face of the earth, and I shall be hidden from your presence. I shall be a wanderer and fugitive in the land and any one who finds me will kill me.' God said 'It will not be so.[9] Anyone who kills Cain will be punished sevenfold.' So YHWH put a mark upon Cain so that anyone who found him would not kill him.

This narrative has provided much ammunition for scholarly speculation about the origins of its basic elements. Stories about brothers in conflict are well-known motifs in folk literature[10] and appear elsewhere in the Old Testament (cf. 2 Samuel 13.28–29). Conflicts between groups subsisting by using different food-producing strategies (e.g. agriculture versus animal husbandry) have been noted in the Sumerian text of *Dumuzi and Enkimdu*[11] and also posited in Genesis 4 (note that Cain is a farmer and Abel a shepherd). Another line of interpretation has suggested a connection between Cain and the Kenites, a group of itinerant metalworkers whose genealogy is found later in Genesis 4 (verses 17–22) and who appear, for example, in Judges 4.17–21 in the form of Jael the wife of Heber the Kenite. Dietrich has suggested that one of the purposes of the narrative is to explain why the Kenites have no permanent possession of land.[12]

What follows in the present work is indebted to Horkheimer and Adorno in the *Dialektik der Aufklärung*, in that their Excursus on the story of Odysseus uses an ancient narrative in order to draw conclusions about the main dilemma and its underlying rationality. The recent publication of Adorno's original version of the Excursus gives added interest to this treatment.[13] The Odysseus story is described as an *Urgeschichte*: not an ancient story but one that articulates deep and fundamental insights about the nature of humanity. It describes Enlightenment which, for Horkheimer and Adorno, is not an intellectual movement in the Europe of the seventeenth and eighteenth centuries, but a permanent feature of the growth

---

[9] Reading with the versions l'ō kēn.
[10] S. Thompson, *Motif-Index of Folk Literature*, Bloomington: Indiana University Press, 1966, vol. 6, pp. 101–2; H. Gunkel, *Das Märchen im Alten Testament*, Tübingen: J. C. B. Mohr (Paul Siebeck), 1921, p. 130, ET *The Folktale in the Old Testament*, Sheffield: Almond Press, 1987, p. 143.
[11] *ANET*, pp. 41–2.
[12] '"Wo ist dein Bruder?" Zu Tradition und Intention von Genesis 4' in W. Dietrich, *'Theopolitik': Studien zur Theologie und Ethik des Alten Testaments*, Neukirchen-Vluyn: Neukirchener Verlag, 2002, pp. 159–72. Westermann, *Genesis*, pp. 385–8 gives an overview of the different approaches to the interpretation of the narrative.
[13] T. W. Adorno, *Gesammelte Schriften*, vol. 3, and 'Geschichtsphilosophischer Exkurs zur Odyssee' in R. Tiedemann (ed.), *Frankfurter Adorno Blätter*, Munich: Edition Text and Kritik, (V) 1998, pp. 37–88.

and development of the human race. Part of the dialectic is what they believe to be the endemic fact that human progress comes about only as one part of the human race dominates other parts and uses them for their own advancement. This is illustrated in the Odysseus story by the incident of the navigation of the ship of Odysseus past the Sirens. Odysseus fills the ears of the sailors with wax so that they cannot hear the alluring calls of the Sirens or any orders of Odysseus. Odysseus himself is bound to the mast so that he can take no action. The narrative thus indicates that the human race can avoid disaster only by depriving some of its members of their freedom, while its leaders have to put restrictions on their freedom to action. Naturally, Horkheimer and Adorno do not regard this as an ideal situation, and the purpose of their writing is to analyse the human situation with a view to it being changed, if this is possible. How they proceed is not the concern of this chapter. Their treatment of the Odysseus story has been outlined as an introduction to a discussion of the narrative of Cain and Abel, which will be treated as an *Urgeschichte* in the sense of Horkheimer and Adorno – a narrative that articulates fundamental insights about the nature of humanity.

Cain is the first human being to be begotten by humans, which puts him in pole position to embody and articulate the nature of the human kind that is produced by humankind. It has long been noted, of course, that if Cain and Abel were the first humans after Adam and Eve, Cain could not properly be concerned about other people meeting and killing him. This difficulty was dealt with by older commentators on the assumption that the Genesis narrative was selective in its history of the human race, and that Adam and Eve must have had other offspring not mentioned in the account.[14] This kind of difficulty is of no relevance here. The bringing by Cain and Abel of their offerings to God, and the acceptance of that of Abel but the rejection of that of Cain, has occasioned much theological reflection on the reason for God's attitude. The view taken here is that this is a narrative device which sets up the potential between the brothers either for mutual acceptance and cooperation, or for antagonism and violence. Cain opts for the latter. In the spirit of Horkheimer and Adorno it can be said that according to the narrative, violence is endemic in the human race when it is threatened either from without (God represents a force outside of humanity that can be benevolent or hostile) or from within (the success of one human party and the failure of another). There is, however, an element in the narrative that takes us beyond Horkheimer and Adorno.

---

[14] See, for example, Poole, *A Commentary on the Holy Bible*, p. 13.

In verse 7 Cain is warned that sin is crouching, ready to entice him. This phrase has caused enormous difficulty to commentators. Westermann concludes that it belongs to a later stage in the transmission of the story and that it should be used only with caution, or not at all, in interpreting the Cain and Abel narrative.[15] Von Rad entertains the same suspicion about the phrase's relationship to the original story, but acknowledges that in its present form, the meaning of the words is that sin is an objective power that stands outside of humanity and which desires to make humanity its possession.[16] It is tempting to ask whether von Rad's interpretation was in any way affected by his having lived through the bombing of Leipzig and Jena in the Second World War, and by his experience in a prisoner of war camp which reminded him of paintings of hell, and which made tangible the situation of Godforsakenness.[17] The view taken here is that the words constitute a profound insight into the nature of evil in relation to human relationships.

It is not necessary to postulate the existence of a devil, or fallen angels, or to speculate about the possible origins of evil in order to take seriously the fact that it exists – that the evil that occurs in the world is not simply the sum of individual acts of wrongdoing, but that it seems to have a power and existence of its own.[18] Part of this is structural and can assume quite innocent forms, such as the inability of social services to deal with individual cases of illness or hardship because regulations produce situations that can be described as Kafkaesque. In other cases, structures can be overtly oppressive, as in regimes in which individuals have no right to think differently from the ruling ideology. Economic systems also embody evil when their structures allow parts of the world to enjoy excessive wealth while other parts are denied clean drinking water and basic medical provision. All this, of course, goes beyond what is implicit in Genesis 4, but it is necessary to reflect upon it if justice is to be done to Genesis 4. In the passage, the proto-human Cain, the first offspring of human parents, is being warned that if certain choices are made, this will enable a power of evil to enter into human affairs and to begin to subvert them in directions unintended and unforeseen by the one making the choice. While this

---

[15] Westermann, *Genesis*, p. 410.

[16] G. von Rad, *Genesis* (ATD), Göttingen: Vandenhoeck & Ruprecht, 1972, p. 77.

[17] R. Smend, 'Gerhard von Rad' in *Deutsche Alttestamentler in drei Jahrhunderten*, Göttingen: Vandenhoeck & Ruprecht, 1989, p. 241. Witte, *Biblische Urgeschichte*, p. 249, links Genesis 4.7 with 1.26–28, and sees it as the work of a redactor who asserts that the task of the human race is to have dominion over sin as well as over the animals, etc.

[18] See H. Häring, *Das Böse in der Welt: Gottes Macht oder Ohnmacht*, Darmstadt: Wissenschaftliche Buchgesellschaft, 1999.

power of evil has a kind of independent existence, it depends upon human choices and actions in order to gain strength and to assume forms that then shape and control human destinies. This fact is only too painfully obvious in today's world, where, for example, decisions to go to war, even for the most justifiable reasons, open the door to escalations of violence and destruction that were never envisaged or intended by those opting for war, and which can often amount to a greater disaster than the one the warlike action was intended to remedy.

In Genesis 4 Cain has not yet taken the decision to murder Abel; but the warning about not giving opportunity to evil is ignored, and the murder takes place. The immediate outcome is deception on the part of Cain, deception which includes an element of self-justification: 'Am I my brother's guardian?' Another outcome is the cursing of the ground that has been polluted by Abel's blood. No doubt this is an expression of the Old Testament view that creation is a matter of order, including the moral order, and that violations of the moral order adversely affect the natural order. At the level of personal relationships the point is that competition for resources leads to their exploitation and to their uneven distribution in the world. The narrative keeps using the word 'brother' in verses 8, 9, 10 and 11. The human race is meant to act in solidarity and cooperation. This is what the term 'brother' implies. Cain has violated this obligation of solidarity and to this extent has become less human than he would be if he acted in consort with Abel.

Sentence is passed upon Cain. This is done by God, a point to which I shall return. But it can also be said that the sentence is passed by the human race. There is a paradox here. Cain represents the human race, as the first-born of human parents, and in this role his first recorded action is one of fratricide. Yet the human race has come to regard such behaviour not as constitutive of human nature (for all that there have been many instances of it in the history of the world and especially in the twentieth century), but as a denial of it. This view has been partly influenced by the Judaeo-Christian tradition and its rootedness in the Bible.[19] But it has also been brought about by a sense of shame and responsibility within human nature. The narrative speaks of Cain being driven out from where he is so that he becomes a wanderer and fugitive; and parallels have been noted between this motif and the story of Adam and Eve being driven from the Garden of Eden.[20] It is also possible to see this as a self-imposed exile, in which Cain

---

[19] R. Kather, *Person: Die Begründung menschlicher Identität*, Darmstadt: Wissenschaftliche Buchgesellschaft, 2007.

[20] Dietrich, '"Wo ist dein Bruder?"', pp. 162–3.

is driven by the need to distance himself from the consequences of what he has done, as the enormity of the deed becomes clear to him.

So far the narrative has been read as an *Urgeschichte* in the sense of the Excursus on Odysseus in *Dialectic of the Enlightenment*. The proto-human Cain represents the human race in paradoxical terms. It ought to function in the solidarity presupposed by the term 'brother', and does not. At the same time it is conscious of this failing and seeks to justify and excuse it, and to flee from its consequences. Further, it is not just human actions that are involved. There is an outside force of evil that depends upon human failure in order to gain strength and to assume forms that affect human lives. Breakdown in communication in personal relationships has implications that reach out beyond those immediately involved.

So far, nothing has been said about the role of God in the narrative. This will be remedied, again with reference to the Odysseus narrative in *Dialectic of the Enlightenment*. In the Odysseus story the humans are confronted by supernatural powers that they mostly need to overcome in order to survive. They do this by a mixture of resourcefulness and cunning, which is designed to enable them to achieve their aims in spite of opposition from supernatural powers. These powers are inferior to human beings. Their behaviour can be judged by humans, who need to learn that they are better than the gods, and to behave accordingly.

In the Cain and Abel story, God is not a malevolent power inferior to the human actors. He is the guarantor of justice who upholds the rights of the oppressed. The murder of Abel does not go unnoticed or unpunished. Yet there is also an unexpected side to God's behaviour. Cain is indeed punished by God, but he also receives God's undeserved mercy. In reply to Cain's anguished cry that in his wanderings he will be at the mercy of anyone who wishes to kill him, God answers 'Not so!' Even if one does not want to go as far as Eberhard Jüngel and declare that this is the first instance in the Bible of the justification by God of the godless,[21] it has to be admitted that this is a remarkable response on the part of God. It can be read as an expression of hope – that the inhumanity of the human race towards itself does not have to be the last word, and that through the mercy of God good can come out of evil. Indeed, it is necessary that this should be so, as a reaction to the fact that evil takes advantage of human wickedness in order to strengthen and fashion itself. God's mercy engages with this aspect of evil, otherwise there would ultimately be no hope for humanity. This point emerges strongly as the chapter proceeds. One of the

---

[21] E. Jüngel, *Das Evangelium von der Rechtfertigung des Gottlosen als Zentrum des christlichen Glaubens*, Tübingen: Mohr Siebeck, 1998, pp. 7–10.

descendants of Cain, Lamech, boasts in a fragment of poetry, that he had killed a man because the latter wounded him – hardly a proportionate response (Genesis 4.23–24). The human race's propensity to violence is thus confirmed. Yet the chapter ends on a note of hope. Eve gives birth to a son whose name, Seth, is taken to mean that he is a replacement for the murdered Abel. This replacement is attributed to God (Genesis 4.25), who is therefore presented as the one who restores what humankind has destroyed. The final verse of the chapter records that 'at that time, people began to worship YHWH by name'.[22] Seemingly against the odds, the human race is capable of seeking after God as well as practising violence against itself.

The next narrative to be considered is the Jacob–Esau–Laban cycle of stories, found in Genesis 25.19–34; 27.1—33.20. In their present form the stories are post-exilic. The change of the name Jacob to Israel (Genesis 32.28) is an exilic phenomenon, as indicated by the occurrence of the connection of the two names, Jacob and Israel, in Isaiah 40—48.[23] The possible reason for this is that following the destruction of Jerusalem in 597–587, the community was governed from the Benjaminite town of Mizpah, with Bethel taking the place of Jerusalem as the main cult centre.[24] The heartland of the groups associated with traditions about Jacob now became the Benjaminite part of the former northern kingdom of Israel, as the location of the people of God. The renaming of Jacob as Israel (see also the Priestly account in Genesis 35.10) was an assurance to the community situated in territory associated with Jacob, that God's promises to his people Israel were still in force.

The complex history of the growth of these traditions to their present form is not the subject of the present discussion.[25] The stress will be on their present form, and on the fact that in this form they are a kind of founding story, in the sense that the main character, Jacob, is the one whom the tradition regards as the progenitor of the nation and its constituent parts. Before this point is reached, however, it can be noted that the cycle is made up of various elements and themes, including motifs

---

[22] The text and translation are not completely certain. The LXX attributes this act (the worship of YHWH) to Seth's son Enosh.

[23] See J. W. Rogerson, 'Die Neubesinnung auf die Identität Israels in der exilischen Epoche' in H. Irsigler (ed.), *Die Identität Israels: Entwicklungen und Kontroversen in alttestamentlicher Zeit* (Herders Biblische Studien 56), Freiburg: Herder, 2009, pp. 101–9.

[24] Davies, *Origins of Biblical Israel*, pp. 159–71.

[25] See E. Blum, *Die Komposition der Vätergeschichte* (WMANT 57), Neukirchen-Vluyn: Neukirchener Verlag, 1984, pp. 66–203; R. G. Kratz, *Die Komposition der erzählenden Bücher des Alten Testaments*, Göttingen: Vandenhoeck & Ruprecht, 2000, pp. 270–5, 278–80.

found in folk-literature about brothers in conflict. The mysterious narrative about the wrestling of Jacob at the river Jabbok has been a rich source of speculation about folklore and other possible sources.[26]

The first episode to be considered is the well-known story of Jacob cheating Esau out of his birthright (Genesis 25.27–34). In the narrative Esau is the hunter, presumably on whose prowess in that art the whole family depends for the luxuries that they are able to eat from time to time. Jacob's profession is not mentioned, but it can be presumed that he is a transhumant shepherd, which is implied by the information that he dwelt in tents (Genesis 25.27). Whether or not the narrative reflects a clash of ways of life (as in the case of Cain and Abel: in the present story a clash between the hunter-gatherer type and the transhumant shepherd type),[27] the story in its present form describes behaviour that violates human decency, not to mention obligations that ought to obtain in families. Jacob takes advantage of his brother's feeling of total exhaustion in order to get him to forswear his birthright, that is, his privileges as the first-born to succeed his father as head of the family, as well as, possibly, the right to inherit two-thirds of the family possessions (cf. Deuteronomy 21.15–17). The fact that the character of Esau in the story is criticized by some commentators as being that of a rather simple person who puts the satisfying of bodily needs above matters of principle[28] only makes matters worse. It is no doubt easy in life for the competent and intelligent to outwit the inefficient and dull members of the human race, but this is no way to act, especially in a family. On the contrary, in a properly functioning family the more gifted and advantaged have an obligation to support its less fortunate members.

The narrative in Genesis 27.1–45 in which Jacob cheats Isaac out of his father's blessing repeats the basic theme of this birthright story, but in darker colours. Isaac asks Esau to catch and prepare some savoury food, perhaps deer (whose availability is indicated by its mention in the list of permitted animals for food in Deuteronomy 14.4–5) as a preliminary to granting him his blessing. Rebekah overhears this request, and urges Jacob to upstage his brother by bringing two young goats from the flock, so that she can prepare savoury food from them for Isaac. This move needs further reflection. Israelite shepherds rarely ate meat from their flocks, because by doing so they diminished the size of the flock on which they depended. Palestinian sheep, for example, apparently produced only one

---

[26] See W. Dietrich, 'Jakobs Kampf am Jabbok, (Gen. 32.23–33)' in '*Theopolitik*', pp. 173–83.

[27] Westermann, *Genesis*, p. 509.

[28] J. Skinner, *Genesis* (ICC), Edinburgh: T. & T. Clark, 1910, p. 362.

offspring each year.[29] A passage in the book of Proverbs (Proverbs 27.23–27) exhorts readers to know well the condition of their flocks, and warns against their dissipation:

> riches do not last for ever;
> and does a crown endure to all generations?

The Proverbs passage describes the value of the flocks: goats provide milk when the grass has gone; the lambs provide wool for clothing. There is no mention of the animals being eaten for food. It is likely that readers/ hearers of Genesis 27.9 would have been surprised if not amazed at the profligacy of Rebekah's suggestion. They would most likely have understood the social conventions implied by the passage to be that Isaac's family only ate meat that was hunted and killed; certainly not meat from the family's flocks. Rebekah's proposal and Jacob's acquiescence implied a squandering of resources that were not solely theirs.

The next episode involves Jacob in not only deception, but dishonesty in the name of God. Isaac, surprised at the speed at which a meat dish had been brought before him, seeks to reassure himself that all is well. In answer to the question how his son found the game so quickly, Jacob replies 'Yhwh your God granted me success' (Genesis 27.20). This dishonest invocation of the name of God is followed by an outright lie. 'Are you really my son Esau?' asks Isaac, to which Jacob replies 'I am' (Genesis 27.24). The whole exercise has been one of distorted communication designed to mislead Isaac and to manipulate the situation to Jacob's advantage. The fact that Jacob now has to flee because of Esau's threats to kill him is, perhaps, no less than he deserves. His disregard for the obligations of responsibilities within family groups has not only led to the family's break-up, but also to his exclusion from it. Like Cain, he has become an exile.

The next part of the narrative contains an element of irony. Rebekah, having been party to the breakdown in relationships in her inner family, now counsels Jacob to flee for help to her wider family (Genesis 27.43)! The welcome that Jacob receives there (Genesis 29.1–14) contrasts signally with his own disregard for family solidarity. Yet even in his new-found family, solidarity is valued less than exploitation.

Jacob enters into an agreement with his maternal uncle, Laban, that he will serve him for seven years in return for the marriage of Laban's younger daughter, Rachel. This is a well-known arrangement in social anthropology[30]

---

[29] See the article by Y. Amitov, 'Ts'on' in *Enziklopedia Ha Miqrait* (Hebrew), vol. 6, Jerusalem: Bialik Institute, 1971, pp. 645–9.

[30] *Notes and Queries in Anthropology*, 6th edn, London: Routledge & Kegan Paul, 1951, p. 116.

and it is strange that Westermann[31] insists that Jacob offers his service as a free man (which he does), but not in return for the marriage. In this, Westermann probably misunderstands what social anthropology calls bride-wealth.[32] Laban's deception of his nephew whereby Jacob discovers that he has been given not Rachel, but her elder sister Leah, is a common motif in folk-literature,[33] but it also has a grounding in social reality. An unmarried woman in a patriarchal society is in a vulnerable position, and Laban's deception in arranging her marriage is understandable. It is ironic, from the narrative viewpoint, that Jacob the younger brother who tricked his elder brother by deceit, now finds himself married to the elder, not the younger daughter, by being himself deceived. He is obliged to serve for a further seven years in order to gain the hand of Rachel.

Jacob is now married to two sisters, a sororal arrangement according to the social anthropologists[34] and one incidentally forbidden in Leviticus 18.18. Whether Jacob's marriages are of the type that make him a member of his wives' kin is a matter of dispute.[35] At any rate, when he intimates to Laban that he wishes to return to his own kin, Laban is reluctant to let him go. The implied social background is understandable. Laban has acquired a son-in-law and eleven great nephews/grandsons (Genesis 30.1–24), a body of manpower to be much desired. Its loss would be a blow to any farming group. Jacob only gets his way, first, by arranging with Laban to be considered the owner only of the sheep and goats that have unusual colouring or markings (Genesis 30.31–43), and, second, by using Laban's absence at sheep-shearing to take the opportunity to escape. In between, he ensures the increase of his unusual coloured flocks by setting up variegated white peeled rods in front of the breeding females. The narrative is far from clear here. Jacob has claimed ownership only of black sheep and speckled goats, and it is hard to see how anyone could have believed that rods with variegated white streaks would produce black sheep. The commentators suspect that a straightforward narrative has been added to by later editors.[36] Whether or not the colours of animals can be scientifically influenced in this way, it was apparently accepted in the ancient world that they could be.[37]

---

[31] Westermann, *Genesis*, pp. 568–9.
[32] See the note by Skinner, *Genesis*, p. 384 and W. R. Smith, *Kinship and Marriage in Early Arabia*, 2nd edn, London: A. & C. Black, 1907, pp. 207–8.
[33] Thompson, *Motif Index*, vol. 5, p. 356, number T. 131.2.
[34] *Notes and Queries*, p. 118.
[35] See Skinner, *Genesis*, p. 384.
[36] Westermann, *Genesis*, p. 585.
[37] Skinner, *Genesis*, p. 393.

On discovering the flight of Jacob, Laban is not only distressed by the loss of his daughters and their offspring, and of his flocks, but also by the loss of what in Hebrew are called *teraphim* (Genesis 31.19) which are stolen by Rachel. These are usually understood to be household gods, images of varying sizes, which were believed to afford protection to a household, and which may also have enabled the household that possessed them to feel a link with the deceased ancestors of the family.[38] Their loss would therefore be keenly felt, and their theft becomes significant in the dialogue between Jacob and Laban in Genesis 31.25–54, when Laban catches up with the fleeing Jacob.

Laban regrets that Jacob's flight by stealth deprived him of the chance to bid farewell to his daughters and grandchildren. Although Jacob is now in his power, Laban is ready to respect the word that came in a dream from God, that he should do no harm to Jacob. However, the theft of the teraphim puts this in a different light. Jacob agrees that if the teraphim are found, the thief shall be put to death. He does not know of Rachel's treachery, who is also able to frustrate Laban's search by sitting on the teraphim and refusing to stand up on the ground that 'the way of women' is upon her. Laban's failure to find the teraphim moves Jacob to a bitter outburst in which he accuses Laban of exploiting him during the twenty years that he has lived with him. The fact that he arrived on Laban's doorstep as a fugitive seems to be forgotten. Laban now seeks a reconciliation, and it is difficult not to feel sympathy for him. He is losing his daughters, their children and his flocks, not to mention the household gods that protect his family and link it with the past. His behaviour is more humane than that of Jacob, and he proposes a covenant between them, part of which is that Jacob will not ill-treat Laban's daughters, nor take wives in addition to them, which would amount to ill-treatment, for it would mean that they were now being less favoured than the new wives.

On reflection, Jacob does not come out of this narrative particularly well. Having caused the disruption of the family in which he grew up, he has now caused the disruption of the wider family that gave him refuge. His outburst of righteous indignation against Laban has only been made possible by the deception of his wife, Rachel. She, it must be noted, is the mother of Joseph (Genesis 30.23–24) and later of Benjamin (Genesis 35.16–19 – she dies giving birth to him), the eponymous ancestors of the group that made up the heartland of Israel during its historical existence, and the heartland of the community in exile in the sixth and fifth centuries before the reassertion of the primacy of Jerusalem.

---

[38] S. Schroer, 'Terafim' in *NBL*, vol. 3, pp. 816–17.

The last part of the narrative of Jacob proper (in the story of Joseph in Genesis 37—50 he is an incidental figure) is his reconciliation with Esau in Genesis 33. Jacob does everything he can to prepare for this potentially difficult reunion by sending gifts to his brother ahead of their meeting (Genesis 32.13–21). In the event, his reception by Esau is remarkable. Whereas Jacob describes himself as Esau's servant (Genesis 33.5) and calls Esau 'lord' (Genesis 33.13), Esau calls Jacob 'my brother' (Genesis 33.9). The one who has more than enough reason to want revenge for how he had been treated is the one who demonstrates by his welcome of Jacob, what the word 'brother' ought to mean in practice.

While the Jacob–Esau–Laban cycle is characterized by deception and mistrust at the level of human relationships within the wider kin group, the two narratives that centre upon God's interventions confront human fickleness with divine grace. The first account, Jacob's dream at Bethel, is probably meant to legitimate Bethel as the sanctuary that is to be used following the destruction of Jerusalem (Genesis 28.10–57).[39] Within the Jacob cycle it records an initiative taken by God when Jacob is on the way from his father's house to that of Laban. Its imagery of the ladder occupied by angels ascending and descending may draw upon the fact that, where possible, temples in the ancient world were situated on the tops of hills, and were reached by broad flights of steps. Whatever the origin of its promise of the land of Israel to Jacob's descendants at a time when Jerusalem had been destroyed and its elite citizens had been taken into exile, within the narrative as a whole it is a declaration that God's design to use the Hebrew nation to bless the families of the earth (Genesis 28.14) cannot be frustrated by human inability to behave as befits those who are brothers.

Adverse comment has often been made on the self-centred nature of the vow that Jacob vows to God following this encounter (Genesis 28.20–22). God is definitely seen as an object of use to Jacob, whose loyalty will depend on God's continuing usefulness. Yet the importance of this vow is its difference from the prayer of Jacob that precedes the mysterious struggle with God in Genesis 32.22–32. That incident has evoked many reactions[40] but the most convincing interpretation, in my view, is that of

---

[39] Davies, *Origins of Biblical Israel*, p. 171.

[40] In addition to Dietrich, '*Theopolitik*', pp. 173–83, see H. Utzschneider, 'Das hermeneutische Problem der Uneindeutigkeit biblischer Texte – dargestellt an Text und Rezeption der Erzählung von Jakob am Jabbok (Gen. 32.23–33)' in *Gottes Vorstellung: Untersuchungen zur literarischen Ästhetik und ästhetischen Theologie des Alten Testaments* (BWANT 175), Stuttgart: Kohlhammer, 2007, pp. 17–32.

Karl Elliger.[41] Elliger does not concentrate upon the elements in the story that have, unsurprisingly, fascinated many interpreters: the fact that Jacob's assailant must depart before dawn; that although apparently defeated by Jacob he nonetheless disables him; the reluctance of the assailant to disclose his name coupled with his progressive development in the story from a man to some kind of manifestation of God. Elliger regards those as incidental to the main point, which is that Jacob's struggle is the answer to the prayer that he prays in Genesis 32.9–12. Here for the first time in the characterization of Jacob in the narratives we meet a Jacob whose fear of what might happen leads him to pray in a way which, while not entirely free from self-interest, at least contains a glimmer of honesty:

> I am too insignificant for all the steadfast love and all the true dealings which you have shown to your servant, for only with my staff did I cross this Jordan: and now I have become two companies. Save me, I pray, from the power of my brother, Esau, for I fear that he may come and kill me, the mothers with the children.　　　(Genesis 32.10–11 [Hebrew 32.11–12])

We can note, in passing, the irony of the fact that Jacob calls Esau his brother. If violence is what is to be expected from a brother, this is only because Jacob has made this a convention by his own actions.

According to Elliger, Jacob's mysterious encounter in Genesis 32.22–32 is God's answer to Jacob's prayer. The struggle gives Jacob the reassurance for the future that he seeks – his name is changed to Israel, with the implication that he will be the ancestor of that nation; but the reassurance comes with a price. As Elliger remarks, the attack of God upon Jacob must be taken seriously.[42] If God is to be gracious to Jacob, that gracious act must involve judgement. That is indicated in the narrative by the permanent injury that Jacob sustains (Genesis 32.25, 31). Jacob's new name, Israel, is partly explained in the narrative by the words 'you have striven with God and with men, and have prevailed' (Genesis 32.28). But it is not Jacob who has ultimately prevailed, but God. God has somehow fashioned out of a lying trickster an ancestor through whose descendants he purposes to bless the nations of the world.

---

[41] K. Elliger, 'Der Jakobskampf am Jabbok: Gen. 32,23ff als hermeneutisches Problem', *ZThK* 48 (1951), pp. 1–31. See J. Rogerson, 'Wrestling with the Angel: A Study in Historical and Literary Interpretation' in A. L. Loades and M. McLain (eds), *Hermeneutics, the Bible and Literary Criticism*, London: Macmillan, 1992, pp. 131–44.

[42] Elliger, 'Der Jakobkampf', p. 27, 'Wir haben kein Recht, den Angriff Gottes zu verharmlosen, als sei er nur ein Spiel und nicht bitterernst gemeint' [We have no right to minimize the attack of God as though it were a game and not meant in the most deadly earnest].

I propose next to consider the continuation of the story of Jacob – that of his eleventh son, Joseph, which covers Genesis 37—48, 50. Chapter 38, the story of Judah and Tamar, has been regarded as an intrusion into the Joseph narrative,[43] and although Robert Alter has pointed to the chapter's many literary links with its larger context[44] it will not be discussed here. Any reader of the Joseph story will immediately recognize how greatly its narrative coherence differs from what has preceded it in Genesis. Although smaller, complete, units of narrative are not lacking in the earlier chapters, they are interspersed with genealogies and short summaries that prevent these earlier chapters from presenting a long, continuous and coherent narrative. Genesis 37, 39—48, 50 is different. The chapters have a coherence that is matched in the Old Testament only by the so-called Court Chronicle in 2 Samuel 9—20. Whether this coherence came about because one writer was responsible for the whole, or because two stories have been woven skilfully together, or because there have been minor interpolations into a single narrative, is a topic that has occupied the attention of experts, but which will be disregarded here.[45] The cycle is evidently a late composition, seeking to give an answer, among other things, to the question how and why the Israelites found themselves in Egypt prior to their enslavement and the Exodus. Kratz[46] makes the interesting suggestion that it presupposes the flight to Egypt of a number of Israelites following the assassination of Gedaliah, the Babylonian-appointed governor of Judah (Jeremiah 43—44). This happened around 582 BCE.

For the purposes of the present chapter, attention will be paid to the personal relationships that are found in the story. They are centred upon eleven brothers, and their aged father, Jacob. The claims of Joseph, on the basis of a dream, that he will rule over his brothers, naturally arouses their hostility and leads to a plot to dispose of him. His unpopularity is increased by the fact that Joseph is his father's favourite son. The plot is able to be carried out when Joseph is sent by his father from somewhere in the south of Canaan, to where his brothers are pasturing the flocks, at Dothan near the southern edge of the Valley of Jezreel (Genesis 37.12–17). Some of the brothers wish to kill Joseph. Reuben, the first-born and therefore their leader, dissuades them from doing this. Instead, they put Joseph

---

[43] So H. Gunkel, *Genesis*, 3rd edn (GHAT), Göttingen: Vandenhoeck & Ruprecht, 1910, p. 410, 'Die Erzählung gehört nicht zum Hauptfaden des J., der die Josephgeschichte behandelt, sondern ist erst nachträglich hier eingesetzt worden' [The narrative does not belong to the main thread of J, which handles the story of Joseph, but has been added here subsequently].

[44] R. Alter, *The Art of Biblical Narration*, London: George Allen & Unwin, 1981, pp. 3–13.

[45] See Blum, *Komposition*, pp. 230–44; Kratz, *Komposition*, pp. 281–6.

[46] Kratz, *Komposition*, pp. 285–6.

into a pit, from which Reuben later hopes to rescue him. From the narrative point of view he might have two motives: that of brotherly regard for Joseph, or fear of his father's wrath, given Reuben's position of responsibility as the eldest brother. In fact, the narrative is not coherent at this point (Genesis 37.22–36), which is why many commentators have suspected that two sources, or versions, of the story have been combined together. In one, Judah takes the lead and persuades his brothers not to kill Joseph but to sell him to some passing Ishmaelites. In the other, Reuben takes the lead and persuades the brothers to put Joseph in the pit, meaning, as already noted, to rescue him later. However, while the brothers are elsewhere, a group of passing Midianites finds Joseph in the pit, pulls him out, and takes him to Egypt. Reuben returns to find the pit empty. The brothers have to decide how to break to Jacob the news of Joseph's disappearance. Conveniently, the special robe given by Jacob to his son is in their possession. They dip it in the blood of a slain goat, bring it to Jacob, and leave it to him to conclude that Joseph has been killed by a wild animal. Perhaps it is accidental that Jacob deceived his father Isaac by killing animals from the flock, and is now himself deceived because an animal from the flock has been killed and its blood used to stain Joseph's coat. At any rate, Jacob, the deceiver of his father, is now deceived by his sons. In both cases, this is because brotherly rivalry has prevailed over brotherly solidarity.

There is no need at this point to elaborate on Joseph's prowess in Egypt, his wrongful imprisonment because of the false accusations of his master's wife, and his advancement to power in Egypt because of his ability to interpret dreams. Neither is it necessary to dwell on the tricks that he plays on his brothers when they are forced to come from Canaan to Egypt to buy grain. The climax of the narrative is reached, as has often been pointed out, in Joseph's words at Genesis 45.5–8, when he reveals to his brothers that he is, in fact, Joseph:

> Do not be grieved or angered because you sold me here. It was in order to preserve life that God sent me ahead of you. For these past two years the famine has been in the land, and there will be neither ploughing nor harvesting for another five years; so God sent me ahead of you.[47] It was not you who sent me here, but God.

These words have been taken to mean that the author of the Joseph narrative embraced a view of providence that was 'modern' rather than

---

[47] Omitting the remainder of verse 7 as a later insertion, with Westermann, *Genesis*, I, 21, pp. 153–4.

'ancient'. This is most strongly expressed by Gunkel, who argues that the author sees God's involvement not in extraordinary, miraculous-type happenings, but as an unseen hand directing everything to fulfil his purposes.[48] I doubt whether Gunkel and those who follow him are correct here. The whole notion of divine providence is problematic, especially for a world that has experienced world wars and genocides.[49] It also raises the question of free will and moral responsibility. There is no suggestion in the narrative that Joseph's brothers were acting other than out of spite and jealousy, for which they were morally responsible, and for which the tricks played on them by Joseph are something of a punishment. From the narrative perspective it can be said that Joseph's words were no more than a way of helping him to be reconciled to his brothers by finding a way of excusing them for what they had done, and thereby breaking down any barrier of guilt that divided them from him. It is one thing to look back over a series of events and to discern a pattern in them, and quite another thing to assert that our perceived pattern must have been intended and brought about by God. That approach carries with it the danger that we begin to create God in our own image, and to see him serving our purposes. All that faith requires is the hope that God somehow ultimately has the last word. What happens before this is not to be encompassed by our inadequate understanding. In the case of the Joseph story, God certainly has the last word up to a point, but it is unwise to draw any conclusions about how the author thought that this became possible. If he was supplying an answer to the question of how the Israelites got to Egypt prior to their oppression and the Exodus, did he think that the forced labour to which the narrative says the Hebrews were subjected was also intended by God? This is the kind of dilemma that presents itself if the approach suggested by Gunkel is logically pursued. If the narrative is read in a more

---

[48] Gunkel, *Genesis*, p. 459, 'Man beachte diesen tiefen Gedanken von göttlicher "Vorsehung": hier sucht das religiöse Empfinden Gott nicht mehr in einer einzelnen Begebenheit, die aus dem Kreise der sonstigen, regelmäßigen Dinge ihrer Art nach herausfällt, . . . sondern man findet Gottes Hand in einem an sich ganz natürlichen Geschehen; man sieht betroffen und erschüttert eine solche Zweckmäßigkeit des Geschehens und erkennt darin Gottes Hand, der im verborgenen die Dinge so ordnet, daß sie seinen Zwecken dienen müssen' [One notes these deep thoughts about divine 'providence'; here, religious sensitivity does not seek God in a particular event which falls outside the regular course of happenings . . . rather, God's hand is found in a quite natural occurrence. Amazed and astonished, one sees a purposefulness in the course of events and God's hand in them is recognized, who so orders things in secret that they must serve his purposes].

[49] For an outline of the theological difficulties involved in providence see G. Ebeling, *Dogmatik des christlichen Glaubens*, Tübingen: J. C. B. Mohr (Paul Siebeck), 1979, vol. 1, pp. 328–30.

mundane way it can be seen to express a different point, which is that circumstances favour the brave and the determined, in spite of hindrances within a tightly knit family. Joseph's brothers did him a favour by abandoning him or selling him to slavery, depending on which strand of the storyline is followed. Had he remained with his brothers in Canaan as a shepherd, it is difficult to see how he could have realized his ambitions unless by resorting to the kind of trickery that his father had excelled in. Dreamers, whatever the source of their visions, have to break the mould into which their background and upbringing threatens to press them. Breaking free can often be helped unwittingly by the antagonisms that dreamers provoke within family circles. What they contribute to the benefit of mankind is nicely illustrated by the story of Joseph.

The three stories considered so far have had in common the fact that they concerned rivalries among members of families, in fact between brothers and, in the case of Jacob and Laban, between an uncle and a nephew. They could be supplemented by other narratives that concern male rivalries within families such as that between Amnon and Absalom (2 Samuel 13) and Adonijah and Solomon (1 Kings 1). A particularly gruesome instance is the case of Abimelech, who kills seventy brothers who have been born by various wives to his father Gideon (Judges 8.31; 9.1–6). Readers will best understand these stories if they have grown up in large families in which parents had pronounced favourites among their children. What of other relationships?

The three accounts in Genesis 12.10–20; 20.1–18 and 26.6–11 of what has been called 'the ancestress in danger' indicate the callousness that husbands can display towards their wives if their own safety is threatened. Whether or not the stories are oral duplicates of an original motif or are literary compositions dependent in some way on each other is beside the point here. In each case an ancestor (Abr(ah)am twice and Isaac once) pretends that his wife is his sister to avoid the danger that the foreign ruler in whose jurisdiction he is temporarily residing will take the wife into his harem, and kill the husband. In each case the supposed sister is indeed taken into the ruler's harem and it is left to God to protect her in various ways. The context of the first occurrence is striking. God has just promised to Abram that he will make of him a great nation (Genesis 12.1–3) but as soon as Abram finds himself in danger he betrays his wife in order to secure his own safety. The second occurrence of the story is noteworthy because it puts the foreign ruler, Abimelech, in a much better light than Abraham. Abimelech is able to make the point to God that he has acted honestly on the basis of Abraham's assertion that Sarah was his sister, not his wife (Genesis 20.5).

The examples given so far have been of men behaving badly towards each other, or towards their wives. What of relationships between women? These are obviously less prominent in a text that concerns itself with the world as ruled by and in the interests of men; but examples are not lacking. The most obvious story is that of the treatment of her servant-girl Hagar by Abraham's wife, Sarah. It comes twice, in Genesis 16 and 21.8–21. Again, it is not important for present purposes whether or not these are duplicate accounts of a piece of tradition. In the first version Sarai (as she is then called) persuades Abram to have a child by means of her Egyptian servant, Hagar. This kind of surrogate marriage appears to have been common in the ancient world, and also occurs in the Jacob story, where his two wives, Leah and Rachel, give their servants Zilpah and Bilhah to Jacob in order to bear surrogate children.[50] Success in Hagar becoming pregnant leads to a change in the relationship between Sarai and Hagar. Exactly how the Hebrew *vateqal* in Genesis 16.5 should be rendered is disputed. Strictly speaking it means that Sarai was lightly esteemed in her servant's eyes. This may have more to do with the increase in her status as the mother of Abram's son than simply a feeling of contempt or disdain, or even superiority towards a barren woman.[51] At any rate, the change in relationship is intolerable for Sarai, and she complains to her husband, who reminds her that Hagar is completely in her power. Sarai 'deals harshly' with her. Presumably she treats Hagar in such a way as to make it clear that Hagar is still subordinate to her. Hagar flees. It cannot be said that either Abram or Sarai come well out of the incident as narrated. It is Sarai who takes the initiative in using Hagar as a surrogate mother, and Abram who takes no steps to protect the woman he has made pregnant. The incident also draws attention to another aspect of human behaviour that is hardly commendable, the fact that there is such a thing as slavery; that some people lose their freedom and have to live their lives subject to the whims and interests of those who have gained power over them. How Sarai had come to have an Egyptian woman as a servant is not indicated by the narrative. Hagar may have been treated as a chattel by her father, and sold for profit, or she may have been the victim of jealousy on the part of her siblings, as in the case of Joseph. Whatever the circumstances, Hagar is not allowed to be a person in her own right. The sequel to the story (Genesis 16.7–14)

---

[50] See Westermann, *Genesis*, I.14, pp. 284–7. Westermann also provides a sketch of the history of interpretation of the passage noting a shift of emphasis in twentieth-century scholarship from the view that it is primarily an explanation of the origin of the Ishmaelites to the view that it is a family story of women in conflict.

[51] Westermann, *Genesis*, I.14, p. 286.

contains various motifs: the naming of the child to be born, as Ishmael, a characterization of the nature of Ishmaelites, and the reason for the name of a holy site. What matters for present purposes is that the inhumanity practised upon Hagar by Sarai and Abram leads to divine intervention by means of an angel of Yʜwʜ who, like the more mysterious angel in the incident of Jacob's wrestling, is perceived to be none other than God (Genesis 16.13). The Hebrew of the end of the verse is notoriously difficult, but enough is certain to indicate that Hagar perceives Yʜwʜ to be one who sees and responds to her need. She, it must be remembered, is not an Israelite, nor is the child that will be born the child of promise. The divine concern for justice and compassion is universal in scope.

It is the 'child of promise' who is an important factor in the second account of disharmony between Sarah and Hagar, in Genesis 21. Sarah becomes pregnant, according to God's promise (in Genesis 17.15–21; 18.9–15) and gives birth to Isaac. When he has been weaned, Abraham celebrates with a great feast.

The age of Isaac when he was weaned would be around three, according to usual practice in ancient Israel. The age of Ishmael, his half-brother, is harder to determine because of conflicting information in the text. If the evidence of the Priestly tradition in Genesis 16.15–16 and 21.5 is followed, Ishmael must have been aged 14, because he was born in Abraham's eighty-sixth year while Isaac was born in his hundredth year. This does not tally with Genesis 21.14 and 18, which verses imply that Ishmael was young enough for his mother to pick him up and carry him. The matter of Ishmael's age is relevant to the translation of the Hebrew verb *mesaheq* in verse 9. A tradition that goes back to Tyndale's translation (also Luther's) takes the verb to mean 'mocking'. This is also reflected in the NEB's 'laughing at'. Would a child small enough to need to be carried by his mother be capable of mocking? Most modern translators and commentators take the verb to mean 'playing with', and that is the sense that is most likely. It also has the effect of making Sarah's reaction less defensible. Seeing the two children playing together reminds her that Isaac is not an only child, and that his elder half-brother, Ishmael, may have or consider that he has a claim on Abraham's wealth. This in turn affects the status of Sarah over against Ishmael's mother, Hagar. As Westermann points out,[52] Hagar appears in the narrative not so much as Sarah's slave but, rather, as Abraham's. The two women are rivals, the mothers of Abraham's sons. Sarah therefore fears that if Ishmael gains a secure place in Abraham's household this will be to the advantage of Hagar, and at her own expense.

---

[52] Westermann, *Genesis* I, 16, p. 415.

She therefore insists that Abraham should 'cast out' (NEB 'drive out') the slave woman and her son. Whether intentionally or not, the language ascribed to her illustrates how immoral actions are easier to justify to their initiators if other humans are described in less-than-human terms. Ishmael is described not as Abraham's son but the 'son of this slave woman'. The term 'slave woman' implies a less-than-human status for Hagar. It is noteworthy that the narrator comments that Sarah's request disquieted Abraham because it affected 'his son'. Whatever Abraham thought of Hagar's status, Ishmael was his son, not the son of a slave woman!

Why, then, did Abraham allow Sarah to have her way? One answer is that this was necessary for narrative reasons. The story is the explanation for the origin of the Ishmaelites, a people living in the Negev region (see Genesis 25.12–18), and therefore needing to have their ancestor growing up there. There are also theological reasons, although at first sight they are not particularly reassuring for modern readers. Abraham reluctantly evicts Hagar and Ishmael because God tells him to do so, on the ground that God will thereby give to both children abundant posterity. It would be helpful for anyone living in any age to have the advantage of long-term reliably accurate forecasts of the outcome of moral decisions, and modern readers can only count Abraham to have been most fortunate to have benefited in this way! The biblical writer is clearly trying to excuse Abraham for having acted inhumanely. Indeed, the divine speech to Abraham rather spoils the continuation of the story in verses 15 to 21, in which the assistance given by God to Hagar and Ishmael contrasts strikingly with the callousness shown by Sarah and Abraham. It is hard not to sympathize with the conclusion of Gunkel, that the divine speech to Abraham in verses 12–13 is a later insertion.[53]

What the story shows about human nature is that under certain conditions the need of humans to survive and to protect their own interests overrides any obligation that they might have towards others, on the ground of their common humanity. Sarah sees in Ishmael a threat both to her own future and to that of her son, Isaac. In requesting Abraham to evict Hagar and her small son, she seemingly has no regard to the threat to their future that her action will bring about. There is not even, apparently, any feeling of sympathy that one mother with a small child might have for another woman in a similar position. But Hagar is not a mother or a proper person in Sarah's eyes; she is 'this slave woman'. The position of the 'slave woman' is unenviable. As though it is not bad enough that she has somehow lost her freedom and is forced to live apart from her family

---

[53] Gunkel, *Genesis*, p. 229.

and people, she has also to suffer the fate of being cast out when it suits her master and mistress, and all because on the orders of the master and mistress she has been a surrogate mother. The second part of the story, in which God assists Hagar and her son and is 'with the lad' (verse 20) as he grows up, shows that from the divine point of view Hagar and Ishmael are not less than human. Sarah may not be moved to compassion by the thought of the plight of the evicted, defenceless, woman and her son, but God certainly is (verse 17). Inhumane human action once again does not have the last word.

I want to move now from narratives that are concerned with how human relationships are reflected in action, to one which is concerned with dialogue and with intellectual and moral relationships. I shall discuss the dialogues between Job and his so-called comforters in the book of Job. For these purposes the prologues and epilogue of the book, in which God first allows the Satan to afflict Job with a series of major disasters, and then restores him to his former prosperity (Job 1—2; 42.10–17), will be regarded as narrative devices to provide an intelligible framework for the dialogues. In these dialogues, Job's friends treat him with little regard. They are self-appointed representatives of a way of interpreting the world and God which allows of no contradiction. The truth has no existential claim upon them other than of reinforcing their own prejudices. The more frustrated they become with Job because of his refusal to compromise his integrity, the more they question his honesty, even to the point of making scurrilous allegations against him. This will be illustrated from extracts from the dialogues.

The position that the comforters maintain is that the universe is a moral universe, and that the misfortunes that Job has experienced must be justly deserved punishments for gross acts of wickedness.

In an opening speech, Eliphaz stresses the frailty of humans at the moral and intellectual level. This then enables Bildad to add that in these circumstances, it is the accumulated wisdom of the ages and their elders that discloses the truth about human affairs. The implication is that Job, a mere mortal individual, is wrong to pit himself against the accumulated wisdom whose champions the comforters are. Eliphaz asks:

> Can a mortal be more righteous than God?
> or a man be more pure that his creator?
> If God puts no trust in his heavenly servants,
> and finds fault with his angels,
> will he trust creatures of clay,
> who are fashioned from dust,
> and weaker than the moths?

Destroyed from morning to evening,
they perish with no lasting name.[54]

(Job 4.17–20)

Bildad adds:

> Enquire of former generations,
> and consider what out forebears learned.
> We belong only to yesterday and know nothing;
> we merely cast shadows on the earth.
> But the ancients will teach and inform you,
> and bring words from the depths of their hearts.

(Job 8.8–10)

What was it that the ancients taught? In the words of Zophar the received wisdom was as follows:

> Surely you know from the beginning,
> since man was first put on the earth,
> that the triumph of the wicked is short-lived,
> and the glee of the ungodly is momentary.
> If his pride ascends to the heavens,
> and his head even touches the clouds,
> yet will he perish completely like his faeces;
> those who saw him will ask 'where is he?'
> Like a dream he will fly away and be lost,
> chased away, like a vision of the night.

(Job 20.4–8)

But Job is not convinced that this ancient wisdom is either true or applicable to his plight, and his refusal to agree with it forces his interlocutors to deploy different tactics. If he maintains his denial of having committed any grievous offence, two dangers will follow. He will, in effect, accuse God of being unjust; and he will become a stumbling-block to the belief of others that God is just. This latter danger is spelled out by Eliphaz:

> You undermine the reverend fear of others,
> and hinder their access to God.

(Job 15.4)

It is the fourth comforter, Elihu, who charges Job with attributing injustice to God:

> Far be it from God to do evil,
> and the Almighty that he should do wrong!

---

[54] Reading shem for mesim with BHK.

86

> According to a man's works he rewards him,
> and according to his conduct gives what he deserves.
> In very truth, God does no evil,
> and the Almighty does not pervert justice.
> Did another give him charge over the earth,
> or make him responsible for the world?
> Is a hater of justice in charge of all things?
>
> (Job 34.10b–13, 17a)

If Job's comforters are not willing to listen to his arguments, part of his anguish is that he is prepared to listen to them and to acknowledge something of the force of what they say:

> Everything you say, I am familiar with;
> I am not inferior to you.
> I could say exactly what you are saying,
> if I were in the same position as you.
> I could bluster against you with words,
> and answer you with wags of my head!
>
> (Job 13.1–2; 16.4–5)

Job's openness, however, gets him nowhere with his opponents, and they try to browbeat him by trying to convince him that he has been concealing from himself what he is really like. Their spokesman is Eliphaz:

> Surely you have taken pledges from your brothers for no reason,
> and stripped the naked of their clothing.
> You refused a drink of water to the weary,
> and gave no food to the hungry.
> You helped the powerful to govern the land,
> and the favoured ones to live in it.
> You sent the widows away empty handed,
> and robbed the orphans of their power.
> No wonder snares surround you
> and you fear a sudden fate.
>
> (Job 22.6–10)

Elihu is even more forthright:

> Job says that he is innocent,
> and that it is God who denies him justice.
> 'In spite of my innocence I am considered a liar,' he claims,
> 'I am deeply wounded, yet without offence.'
> Has there ever been a man like Job,
> who drinks up scoffing like water,
> who loves the company of evil-doers,
> and likes to go about with the wicked?

He even says that one gains no benefit
from doing the will of God . . .
Intelligent people will tell me,
and discerning people agree,
that Job does not know what he is talking about,
and there is no sense in his words.
Would that Job were seriously examined,
on account of replies like those of the wicked!
He adds rebellion to his sins,
and multiplies words against God.[55]

(Job 34.5–9, 34—37)

In vain does Job try to defend himself. He is one, his comforters are four.
They know the truth; he is honest enough to have doubts about it.

Whoever heard what I had done praised me for it;
those who observed me agreed I did well.
For I rescued the poor when they cried to me,
and the orphan who had no protector.
I was blessed by those facing ruin,
and made the heart of the widow rejoice.
I dressed as it were, in goodness;
justice was my cloak and my turban.
I was eyes to those who were blind,
and feet to those who were lame.
To the needy, I acted as father,
and took on the cause of strangers.
I smashed the fangs of the wicked,
and rescued the prey from his teeth.

(Job 29.11–17)

At the end of the book, it is God who vindicates Job for saying what is right
(Job 42.7) while the friends are condemned. To this extent the book is an
encouragement for honesty, and a judgement upon those whose certainty
that they are in the right prevents them from treating as fully human those
who disagree with them. It is tempting to see this aspect of the book of Job
in the light of some of the observations of Kierkegaard, in his *Training in
Christianity*.[56] This was the beginning of Kierkegaard's assault upon the
state Lutheran Church of the Denmark of his day (1848), which he accused
of making Christianity so plausible and undemanding that it had ceased
to exist. Kierkegaard called this the deification of the established order, which

---

[55] Omitting bēnēnū yispoq as a scribal gloss.

[56] S. Kierkegaard, *Training in Christianity* (trans. W. Lowrie), London: Oxford University Press,
1941.

led, in his view, to the secularization of everything.[57] It is not difficult to see how this description – the deification of the established order – can be applied to Job's comforters, with the result that by secularizing everything they could find no space for Job's experience of God. Job, on the other hand, can be understood in terms of Kierkegaard's insistence that the suffering witness to truth passes judgement on the established order:

> it is . . . this God-relationship of the individual which must put every estab-
> lished order in suspense, so that God, at any instance He will, by pressure
> upon the individual has immediately in his God-relationship a witness, a
> reporter, a spy, or whatever you prefer to call it, one who in unconditional
> obedience, or by unconditional obedience, by persecution, suffering, and
> death, puts the established order in suspense.[58]

This is saying something very profound about the Old Testament conception of what it means to be human, if it is legitimate to read Job from the
perspective of Kierkegaard. It is saying that while reason is an important
characteristic of humanity, it has its limits; that there are experiences that
reason cannot understand or explain. When individuals find themselves
confronted by such experiences they have two alternatives: to deny the
implications of the experiences in the face of reason, or to insist on their
existential claim in opposition to reason. The second alternative, of course,
runs the danger of becoming a charter for fanaticism and fundamental-
ism, and its genuineness can only be tested by whether or not its outcomes
ultimately do good or evil. The suicide bomber whose convictions kill and
maim innocent people is very different from those whose convictions
move them to forsake marriage or a successful career in order to devote
themselves to dangerous charitable or medical work in uncongenial parts
of the world. Judged from this angle, the book of Job comes out on the
right side. Whatever may have been the circumstances that led to its composition, and it is difficult to suppose that *no* genuine experience of suffering and vilification underlies it, the book has been an inspiration to
many readers down the centuries as they have faced experiences for which
there was no rational explanation.

These observations will now become the link to the final part of this
chapter, which will deal with the seeming irrationality of human self-
sacrifice on behalf of others. I am reminded of the moving passage in Imre
Kertész's semi-autobiographical *Kaddish for a Child Not Born*.[59] Kertész, a

---

57 Kierkegaard, *Training*, p. 92.
58 Kierkegaard, *Training*, p. 92.
59 I. Kertész, *Kaddish for a Child Not Born* (trans. C. W. and K. A. Wilson), Evanston, Ill.:
   Northwestern University Press, 1997.

survivor of Auschwitz, relates how he owed his survival to the action of someone known as the 'Professor', who gave Kertész his food ration when sick prisoners were being transported on ox-drawn carriages. The action of the 'Professor' was one for which there was 'no explanation . . . because it [was] not rational'.[60] Earlier he writes,

> what is really irrational and what truly cannot be explained is not evil, but contrarily, the good. . . . Instead of the lives of the dictators, it is exclusively and for a long time now, the lives of the saints that interest me. This is what I find interesting and incomprehensible, this is what I cannot find a rational explanation for. And even Auschwitz . . . proved to be a more fruitful field of exploration in this respect.[61]

There is, in the Old Testament, an obvious instance of irrational, sacrificial behaviour, that of the Moabite young woman Ruth, in the book of her name. Whatever the origins and purpose of the book,[62] it presents a strikingly different picture of human behaviour compared with the examples discussed earlier in this chapter.

Ruth is a young widow, her deceased husband (either Mahlon or Chilion: the exact one is not specified in the text) having been the son of Naomi, who had taken refuge, together with her husband Elimelech, in Moab when their home village in Bethlehem was struck by famine. Naomi has also become a widow, as has another Moabite young woman, Orpah, who, like Ruth, had married one of Naomi's sons. Naomi determines to return to Bethlehem, and urges her daughters-in-law to return to their former homes in the hope that they may find new husbands. Orpah heeds this advice, but Ruth refuses to do so. She clings (Hebrew *davaq*) to Naomi and refuses to leave her. Her resolution to stay with Naomi come what may is expressed in one of the most noble passages in the whole of the Old Testament:

> Do not urge me to abandon you,
> or not go with you.
> Wherever you go, I shall go,
> Wherever you lodge, I shall lodge.
> Your people will be my people;
> Your God, my God.
> Where you die, I shall die.

---

[60] Kertész, *Kaddish*, p. 34.
[61] Kertész, *Kaddish*, p. 32.
[62] It is probably to be dated in the post-exilic period, perhaps the fifth century BCE. That it was composed as a criticism of the policies of Ezra and Nehemiah is possible, but not demonstrable. One of the best brief summaries is by B. I. Riesener, 'Rut', in *NBL*, vol. 3, pp. 384–6.

This is my oath before Yʜwʜ:
Only death will part me from you.
(Ruth 1.16–17)

The reader of the book of Ruth knows that things will work out well for
Ruth, and that she will find a husband, in Boaz. From the point of view
of the character in the story, Ruth does not know what lies ahead. She is
committing herself to a dangerous course of action by insisting on her
loyalty to Naomi. She is leaving her own country and the protection of
her Moabite relatives, to go to a country prone to famine, together with a
woman whose own prospects are uncertain. Although Naomi has relatives
in Bethlehem, as the sequel to the story shows, she will nonetheless be
economically and socially vulnerable as a widow with no immediate male
dependants. Ruth's action is irrational viewed from the perspective of her
enlightened self-interest. It stands in stark contrast to the survival tactic of
Sarah in bringing about the expulsion of Hagar and Ishmael from her
household, and in even starker contrast to the scheming ambition of Jacob.

If the narratives that have been discussed in this chapter are understood
as *Urgeschichte* in the sense of Adorno, that is, as stories that give expression to rationalities that underly the human need to survive and prosper
in a world distorted and fragmented by human encounter with the envi-
ronment and other humans and their power structures, the following conclusions can be drawn. The predominant rationality is one of self-interest.
At its best it protects not just particular individuals, but their immediate
dependants. Sarah is concerned for the future of her son Isaac, Rebekah for
the advancement of her son Jacob. Rachel is loyal to her husband Jacob
rather than her father Laban. At its worst, self-interest is contemptuous of
kin ties that ought to bind humans in solidarity. Cain murders his brother Abel, and Jacob tricks Esau, while Joseph's brothers plot Joseph's downfall. Examples of the rationality of self-interest can be multiplied in the
Bible, especially the so-called Court Chronicle of 2 Samuel 9—20, where
David commits adultery and (in effect) murder, Amnon rapes his half-
sister Tamar, Absalom murders Amnon, and Joab disposes of Absalom in
warfare, against David's explicit orders. Standing in sharp contrast to the
rationality of self-interest is the rationality of self-sacrifice. Its clearest
expression is in the story of Ruth; but it is also implicit in Moses' tragic
commitment to the leadership of his people, and Jeremiah's witness to a
truth that costs him dearly. God is cast in many human images in the Old
Testament. The one that comes closest to the truth is that which sees the
rationality of self-sacrifice as the clue to God's nature.

4

Disrupted communication:
social relationships

Society does not consist of people; it consists of communication between people. This is one of the fundamental positions of the late Niklas Luhmann for whom, as a consequence, social structure was a network of expectations governed by symbolically generalized media of communication.[1] By 'symbolically generalized media of communication' Luhmann meant, as an example, truthfulness in the sphere of academic research.[2] The expectation in the academic world is that researchers can be relied upon to present the results of their research honestly and accurately. Only so will the results of research command universal acceptance and create a sphere of communication that rises above personal or sectional interests. It will thus be a generalized medium of communication. 'It is not possible to say that something is true because I want it to be true or because I suggest that it is so.'[3] Luhmann's notion of communication was correspondingly broad, comprising not only speech and writing but also mediums of exchange (e.g. money), the owning of property and the exercise of power.[4] He also made the point that the systems underlying these mediums of communication were largely invisible, expanding the point made by F. de Saussure, that language system as opposed to language use was largely unknown to users of most languages.[5]

---

[1] N. Luhmann, *Die Moral der Gesellschaft*, Frankfurt a.M.: Suhrkamp, 2008, p. 212, 'Gesellschaft ist das umfassende Sozialsystem aller kommunikativ füreinander erreichbaren Handlungen' [Society is the comprehensive social system of all communicative actions that are available to each other]; 'Struktur ist für Luhmann nichts anderes als ein Netz verläßlicher Erwartungen und Erwartungserwartungen' [Structure for Luhmann is nothing other than a network of dependable expectations and expectations of expectations] (Detlev Horster in the Nachwort, pp. 375–92, 382). For the 'symbolisch generalisiertes Kommunikationsmedium' see Horster, at pp. 377–9.

[2] Luhmann, *Die Moral*, pp. 378–9.

[3] Luhmann, *Die Moral*, p. 379, my translation.

[4] N. Luhmann, *Einführung in die Theorie der Gesellschaft*, Darmstadt: Wissenschaftliche Buchgesellschaft, 2005, pp. 87–180.

[5] Luhmann, *Einführung*, pp. 92–7.

If human societies are to be thought of as systems of communication, as networks of expectations governed by symbolically generalized notions such as truthfulness, in what way can communication become distorted or disrupted? An obvious answer comes from the notion of truthfulness. If totalitarian regimes and their official media of communication constantly distort the truth, it will not be long before nobody believes them. A recent example in Britain of the undermining of trust has been the revelation that television programmes that asked viewers to vote to choose the winners of competitions were in fact taking no notice of the voting, and were choosing the winners in an arbitrary way. When it was discovered that a flagship children's programme called *Blue Peter* had been guilty of this breach of trust, there was much consternation.

Another notion similar to that of truthfulness is respect – respect for other people as well as their possessions. This notion, indeed, is embodied in the legal systems of modern Western nations, which protect people from harm to their persons and possessions. Yet there are ways in which the respect due to people can be abused in ways not covered by law, for example, by tolerating structural arrangements that condemn whole populations to poverty in a world of plenty, or, in wealthy nations, to unemployment, or to homelessness. Such things disappoint the expectations that notions such as respect engender.

For what follows in this chapter Luhmann's ideas will be taken up in the sense that texts will be examined that express outrage or condemnation in regard to social situations that disappoint expectations. This, it can be argued, is sounder methodologically than attempting to reconstruct the social structures in ancient Israel in order to subject them to moral critique. The obvious advantage is that the concentration is upon the texts rather than scholarly attempts to discover what lies behind the texts. Also, the difficulty is avoided that we probably know much less about the social structure of ancient Israelite society than is often supposed. Attractive as the view is that ancient Israel was once an egalitarian segmentary society, it has to be said not only that the evidence for this has never been compelling, but that the idea that we can know anything at all about ancient Israel in the period 1000 to 750 BCE, let alone 1250 to 1050, goes against all the trends of current research.[6] Given that the Old Testament traditions only reached their present form some time after the sixth century BCE, one cannot be confident that they can allow us to reconstruct social conditions

---

[6] See J. W. Rogerson, 'Was Early Israel a Segmentary Society?' *JSOT* 36 (1986), pp. 17–26; reprinted in D. J. Chalcraft (ed.), *Social-Scientific Old Testament Criticism: A Sheffield Reader*, Sheffield: Sheffield Academic Press, 1997, pp. 162–71; Davies, *In Search of 'Ancient Israel'*.

with any accuracy in earlier periods. In fact, there is no need to do this. The texts have a rhetorical power that is not dependent upon their time or milieu of production, although this should not prevent one from considering suggestions that have been made about these things in relation to passages discussed.

In order to justify this conclusion reference will be made to one of the most recent attempts to describe the social situation in Judah in the period from the eighth century BCE to the exile in the sixth century, that of R. Kessler.[7] The ground shared by Kessler with most of the scholars with whom he engages is that the criticism of social abuses by the eighth-century prophets (especially Isaiah and Micah) presupposes a radical change in the social situation in Judah in the eighth century. It is also claimed that the altered situation attracted criticism from later prophets, including Zephaniah, Jeremiah, Habakkuk and Ezekiel. What was this crisis, and what caused it? Kessler reviews the theses of Alt, who blamed 'Canaanizing' administrators; Loretz, who cited 'Rent Capitalism'; Kippenberg, who invoked the idea of an emerging class system; and Rüterswörden, who focused attention upon the *śarim*, a group or class of nobility.[8] The 'Rent Capitalism' theory gets short shrift with regard to the eighth century, because it assumes that the social conditions in Judah at that time were no different from those elsewhere in the ancient Near East, whereas Kessler advocated the view that there must have been a decisive change in social conditions in order to provoke the prophetic criticism. It has to be asked, however, whether the conclusion follows from this premise. Why did there need to be a decisive change in order to provoke prophetic criticism? The history of social reform provides many examples of social abuses that were tolerated for a long time before an individual or group felt moved to criticize them. The anti-slavery movements of the eighteenth and nineteenth centuries are a case in point. In fact, at the end of the examination of his chosen prophetic texts Kessler has to content himself with the conclusion, 'Was die Krise dann aber ausgelöst hat und warum das wahrscheinlich um die Mitte des 8. Jahrhunderts geschehen

---

[7] R. Kessler, *Staat und Gesellschaft im vorexilischen Juda vom 8. Jahrhundert bis zum Exil* (SVT 47), Leiden: E. J. Brill, 1992.

[8] A. Alt, 'Der Anteil des Königtums an der sozialen Entwicklung in den Reichen Israel und Juda' in idem, *Kleine Schriften zur Geschichte des Volkes Israel*, Munich: C. H. Beck, 1968, vol. 3, pp. 349–72; O. Loretz, 'Die prophetische Kritik des Rentenkapitalismus: Grundlagen-Probleme der Prophetenforschung', *UF* 7 (1975), pp. 271–8; H. G. Kippenberg, *Seminar: Die Entstehung der antiken Klassengesellschaft*, Frankfurt a.M.: Suhrkamp, 1977; U. Rüterswörden, *Die Beamten der israelitischen Königszeit: Eine Studie zu śr und vergleichbaren Begriffen* (BWANT 117), Stuttgart: Kohlhammer, 1985.

ist, läßt sich nach dem gegenwärtigen Stand der Forschung nicht sagen.'[9] Somewhat surprisingly Kessler rejects two possible solutions to the problem. The first, taking account of the traditions about Elijah and Elisha in the books of Kings, would be that prophetic critique of social abuses in the eighth century was not an innovation, and that Isaiah and Micah had their forerunners in Elijah and Elisha in the previous century. This, of course, would presuppose that the traditions in the books of Kings preserved genuine reminiscences of the activities of Elijah and Elisha in the ninth-century in the northern kingdom, Israel, something that Kessler accepted in a brief discussion of 2 Kings 4.1–7, the story of Elisha coming to the rescue of a woman who feared that a creditor would take her two sons into slavery in settlement of her debts. His argument, that the Elisha story concerned someone on the margins of society whereas the prophetic critiques of Isaiah and Micah presupposed the quite different situation of threats to free citizens and their families, is hardly convincing, and demonstrates the fragility of the view that there must have been a radical change in social arrangements in eighth-century Judah.[10] The second solution, barely considered by Kessler, is that the invasions of Judah by Assyrian armies in the latter part of the eighth century were responsible for a breakdown in normal social conventions. His treatment of military matters confines itself to a brief history of the militia in Judah from the time of David and Solomon, and the provisioning of garrisons such as Arad. Attention is drawn to extra-biblical materials such as the ostraca from Arad. But there is no investigation of the likely results of the wholesale invasion of the land by an enemy army such as that of the Assyrians.[11] Eckart Otto, in his book on war and peace in the Old Testament and the ancient Orient, provides a thorough account of the organization, ideology and aims of the Assyrian army, as well as a description of the course and results of the Assyrian invasions of Israel and Judah in the eighth century.[12] He rightly draws attention to Isaiah 1.7–9, a passage not discussed by Kessler, as a description of the results of the Assyrian invasion of Judah in 701 BCE:

> Your land is desolate,
> your cities burned with fire.
> Before your very eyes strangers

---

[9] Kessler, *Staat und Gesellschaft*, p. 125. 'What caused the crisis and why it happened probably around the middle of the eighth century cannot be determined in the present state of scholarship' (my translation).

[10] Kessler, *Staat und Gesellschaft*, p. 123.

[11] See Kessler, *Staat und Gesellschaft*, pp. 139–48 for his discussion of the militia and garrisons.

[12] E. Otto, *Krieg und Frieden in der Hebräischen Bibel und im Alten Orient: Aspekte für eine Friedensordnung in der Moderne*, Stuttgart: Kohlhammer, 1999, pp. 37–75.

devour the produce of your land . . .
Only Sion is left
like a booth in a vineyard,
a lodge in a cucumber field,
like a besieged city.[13]

This is a description of the aftermath of an invasion; but it is known that steps were taken to fortify Jerusalem, and possibly other strategic towns, in preparation for the invasion,[14] and it is not impossible that with the appearance of Tiglath-pileser III and his armies in Syria-Palestine from around 734 BCE Judah was put on what we today would call an emergency footing.

Bearing in mind what was said above about how little is known about the social situation and structure of Judah and Israel in the pre-exilic period, something that Kessler's investigation of Judah confirms, albeit unintentionally, it is perhaps perilous to draw conclusions. However, in what follows it will be assumed that if there was a crisis in eighth-century Judah, it was brought about not by internal developments, but by the need to respond to the external threat posed by Assyrian military ambitions.

I propose to begin with Micah 2.1–11:

1. Woe to those who plan wickedness
   and evil deeds[15] upon their beds.
   When daylight comes they
   carry out their plans,
   because they have the power to do so.
2. They covet fields and seize them,
   houses, and take them by force.
   They oppress a man and his household,
   a man and his inheritance.
3. Therefore thus says YHWH:
   Be warned: I am planning evil[16]
   from which you will not be
   able to free your necks!
   You will no longer walk about haughtily;
   it will be an evil time.
4. On that day a proverb will be
   told against you,

---

[13] Otto, *Krieg und Frieden*, p. 70; H. Wildberger, *Jesaja* (BKAT 10.1) Neukirchen-Vluyn: Neukirchener Verlag, 1972, pp. 20–1.

[14] Otto, *Krieg und Frieden*, p. 68.

[15] Reading po'ᵉlê for pō' ᵉlê.

[16] Omitting 'against this family'.

a lament will be wailed:
'We are utterly ruined.
The land of YHWH's people[17] is
measured out.[18]
No one can restore them to me;[19]
Our fields have been parcelled out.'[20]

5. Therefore there will be
no one to apportion to you
lands by lot
in the assembly of YHWH.[21]

6. 'Do not preach' they preach. 'Do
not preach about such things.
Such insults do not apply to us![22]

7. Is the house of Jacob accursed?[23]
Is the patience of YHWH exhausted?
Are these truly his doings?
Do not his words work what is good[24]
to those who walk uprightly?'

8. But you rise up as an enemy
against my people.[25]
You strip the garment from him
who desires peace,[26]
from those who live securely and
turn away from war.

9. You drive out the women of my people
from their pleasant homes,
and take away from their infants
my glory for ever.

---

[17] Reading ʿam YHWH for ʿammi.

[18] Reading yimmad with LXX.

[19] Reading vᵉʾēn mēšiv with BHS and omitting lᵉšôvēv.

[20] Reading yᵉḥullāq.

[21] R. Kessler, 'Arbeit, Eigentum und Freiheit: Die Frage des Grundeigentums in der Endgestalt der Profetenbücher' in R. Kessler and E. Loos (eds), *Eigentum, Freiheit und Fluch: Ökonomische und biblische Einwürfe*, Gütersloh: Kaiser, 2000, pp. 64–88, argues that Micah 2.4–5 is a later insertion into the passage dating from the end of the Babylonian exile when the land was re-divided. This is not the view taken here. J. Jeremias, *Die Propheten Joel, Obadja, Jona, Micha* (ATD 24.3), Göttingen: Vandenhoeck & Ruprecht, 2007, pp. 150–1, following H. W. Wolff, *Micha* (BKAT 14), Neukirchen-Vluyn: Neukirchener Verlag, 1980, pp. 37–8, 49–50, argues that these verses contain some exilic additions.

[22] Reading yassigēnu and presupossing sîn for sāmeq.

[23] Reading heʾarūr with BHS.

[24] Reading dᵉvārāv yētiv, cf. BHS.

[25] Reading veʾattem ʿal ʿammi.

[26] Reading mēʿal šᵉlēmîm cf. Wolff, *Micha*, p. 40.

10. Arise and go; this is no resting-place.
    For a trifle[27]
    you would commit[28]
    grievous mischief.
11. If a man went about in
    the spirit of falsehood and lies
    saying, 'I will preach to you
    about wine or strong drink,'
    this would be the ideal preacher
    for this people!

The fact that so much emendation is required in translating this passage must make any interpretation of it uncertain. Yet this much can be said: there is a prophetic condemnation of the forcible seizure of land and houses, and of the eviction of women and children from where they live. A coming judgement is spoken of in which the fate which the dispossessors inflicted upon their victims will be inflicted upon them. This message is unwelcome. 'Do not preach such things,' the prophet is told. 'They do not apply to us.' The prophet insists that they do, and adds that what his opponents really mean is that they want a prophet who speaks not about justice and wickedness, but about wine and strong drink.

In what circumstances could fields and houses be forcibly taken from the owners while those responsible denied that they had done anything wrong? Even Ahab, in the story of Naboth's vineyard, had to rely upon his wife's cunning to get him the vineyard, which she did by having Naboth falsely convicted of blasphemy, for which he was executed (1 Kings 21). Why did Ahab not forcibly seize the vineyard? Again, it does not seem as though the Micah passage is referring to the seizure of land as part of the settlement of outstanding debts. A possible answer is that the background to the passage is the fortifying of towns in the Shephelah along the route to Lachish, in anticipation of an Assyrian campaign. Micah, as an inhabitant of one of these towns, if Moresheth is to be identified with Tell-el-Judeideh, would have a particular interest in such a process. It may be that a situation of 'national emergency' not only provoked the need for military advisers to ride roughshod over the inhabitants of small towns in the building of defences; it may have provided the opportunity for unscrupulous officials to seize properties that were not strictly needed for the purposes of defence.

As a working hypothesis, this makes sense of parts of the passage. Verses 3–5, which predict that those who seize land will find themselves dispos-

---

[27] Reading meʾūmāh.
[28] Reading taḥbᶜlū.

sessed, possibly envisages the defeat of the Judahite military leaders and the seizure of their lands by the occupying force. In verse 8 the prophet declares in the name of God that the people who are being criticized have become the enemy of what God calls 'my people'. In other words, from this perspective the real enemy is not the foreign one that threatens the nation; it is the leaders of the nation, a nation which exists to serve their interests, and which they could not call 'our nation' in the way that God calls it 'my people'. There is also the admittedly difficult second part of verse 8:

> You strip the garment from him who desires peace,
> from those who live securely and turn away from war.

If this translation, with the alterations to the text that it requires, is sound, it implies the forceful coercion within the militia of those who oppose armed resistance in the coming emergency. The continuation of the passage in verse 9, although this is no more than a guess, may mean that the forcible recruitment of men into the militia has profound implications for the women and children who are their dependants.

If this interpretation of the passage is on the right lines it can be explained, in Luhmann's terms, with reference to different systems and their expectations. We hear today from many quarters the insistence that the first duty of a government is to protect its citizens, especially in the 'war on terror'. This duty, it is held, is so overriding, that governments are entitled to curtail certain civil liberties. Although it is only reluctantly admitted, if at all in official circles, even the British government has apparently connived at the use of the torture of suspects in order to gain information about terrorist activities. In ancient Israel and Judah national needs could also have overridden individual liberties. Those who have most to lose when a country is threatened by an invading army are those in charge of the nation. If they are to resist successfully, they need to mobilize all the resources available. Citizens who are usually of little importance to leaders suddenly become significant. Their unsolicited or forced involvement in the defence of what is controlled by the leaders, is a necessary price to pay.

From the point of view of the leaders of Judah, their expectations were that they should defend the land at all costs, and that they had the duty and right to requisition citizens and their property to this end. The view of Micah was different. The people could not be protected by actions which in effect made the leaders their enemy. The end did not justify the means. Perhaps Micah saw the duty of the leaders in terms of submission to the enemy, on terms that would protect the ordinary citizens even if it meant loss to the leaders. We do not know. What is clear is that there was disrupted communication in the sense that what Micah had to say was not welcome. The verb used to describe his preaching, *ntp*, means to drip. A good colloquial rendering would be 'spout'. The NEB renders it as 'rant' and we can presume that Micah's hearers deliberately used an insulting word in order to convey their contempt for what he was saying.

Modern readers may have some sympathy for this opposition to Micah. Was he saying that leaders of a country should leave its citizens defenceless against an advancing enemy? What would have been the outcome for European history if those in Britain who wanted to make peace with Hitler in 1940 had had their way? Micah's world, of course, had not perfected genocide in the way that today's world has done, although Israelite tradition would later represent its peaceful occupation of Canaan in terms of a successful war of annihilation of the land's previous inhabitants (cf. Joshua 10.40). Micah's generation had yet to experience what conquest by an aggressive empire such as the Neo-Assyrian empire would entail at the practical level. His words, and the reaction to them of those he spoke against, were an example of conflicting expectations. Those of the rulers were that they should defend the land, which meant their interests, and that they could legitimately ride rough shod over the ordinary citizens and force them to take part in war. Micah's expectations were that the primary duty of the leaders was to protect the citizens against being deprived of their land and their livelihood, and the break-up of their families. Put in modern terms, the loss of sovereignty was a lesser evil than the treatment of citizens by their leaders as objects for manipulation and coercion.

This interpretation has been based upon a difficult piece of Hebrew that requires sufficient emendation to make any approach tentative. The same cannot be said for Jeremiah 34.8–17. Here, there is the different problem that an original passage has been subjected to later editing which distorts its meaning. However, this is easily detected. In its present form the passage reads:

> The word that came to Jeremiah from YHWH after king Zedekiah made a covenant with all the people who were in Jerusalem to declare liberty to them, that everyone should set free his male and female Hebrew slaves, so that no one would enslave his Jewish brother. All the princes and all the people who entered into the covenant agreed that each should set free his male or female slaves and enslave them no more; and they obeyed and set them free. But later they changed their minds and forced back into slavery the men and women whom they had set free. The word of YHWH came to Jeremiah,[29] saying, 'thus says YHWH.[30] I made a covenant with your fathers

---

[29] Omitting 'from YHWH' with LXX and Pesh.
[30] Omitting 'the God of Israel' with LXX.

on the day I brought them out of Egypt, out of the house of slavery, saying, "at the end of seven years you must set free your Hebrew brother who has sold himself to you; when he has served you for six years you must set him free". But your fathers did not listen to me or take note of what I said. But today you have repented and done what is right in my eyes by proclaiming liberty each to his neighbour, and you made a covenant in my presence in the house which is called by my name. Then you changed your minds and profaned my name and took back the men and women you had set free[31] and forced them to become slaves once more. Therefore thus says YHWH: You have not obeyed me by proclaiming liberty each to his brother and his neighbour; therefore I am going to proclaim liberty for you: the liberty brought by the sword, and pestilence and famine. And I will make you an object of loathing to all the kingdoms of the earth.'

The passage goes on in verses 18–22 to condemn all those who have transgressed God's covenant, and threatens King Zedekiah and his princes with capture by the Babylonians, and the city of Jerusalem with destruction.

Anyone who has tried to translate this passage from the Hebrew will be aware of the awkwardness of its syntax at certain points, and even its contradiction in verse 14, where the Hebrew says that a slave must be released at the end of seven years after serving for six years. The Greek version has six on both occasions as well as a somewhat shorter text, especially in verses 10–11. These matters are dealt with exhaustively by McKane.[32] There is an obvious intrusion, in the form of verses 13–14, which remind the people of Judah that God gave to their forebears a law limiting slavery to six years. This obviously has little to do with the context, and McKane shrewdly disposes of the arguments of those who have defended the unity of the passage. As he remarks, 'the objections raised against their integrity [i.e. verses 13–14] are overwhelming. An exceptional proclamation which emancipated all slaves, male and female, and which was an extraordinary response to a situation of dire threat is a different matter from a law whereby slaves are set free after six years' service.'[33]

The verses preceding the passage indicate what the situation was that produced the temporary release of the slaves. It was that in around 588 BCE the Babylonian army had captured all the cities of Judah except for Jerusalem, Lachish and Azekah (Jeremiah 34.6–7). An assault against Jerusalem was either actual or imminent. The slaves were released,

---

[31] Omitting l^ĕnaphšām.

[32] W. McKane, *Jeremiah* (ICC), Edinburgh: T. & T. Clark, vol. 2, 1996, pp. 866–84.

[33] McKane, *Jeremiah*, vol. 2, p. 879.

presumably on the assumption that, as free citizens, they would be more willing to contribute effectively to the defence of the city than they would as slaves. Their freedom was revoked when the Babylonian threat seemed temporarily to recede (cf. Jeremiah 34.21).[34]

Both actions, the emancipation and its reversal, can only be viewed with the utmost cynicism. Before this is commented upon, however, it should be noted that I have no opinion on whether or not the passage was composed by or derived from the prophet Jeremiah, or whether it can be ascribed to any of the sources that have been proposed for the book. It seems to me to be highly probable that the verses derived from an actual event during the siege of Jerusalem, and that the injustice that it embodied was such that the incident was remembered and incorporated into the book of Jeremiah. In its present form it has been subjected to editing or reformulation by the post-exilic editors of the book.

From the communicative point of view the incident is horrendous. Masters and slaves in ancient Israel presumably did not communicate with each other except for the former to give orders to the latter. The story of Joseph in Genesis 39 in which the slave quickly became effectively in charge of the household is romance rather than reality. The sudden reversal of this situation, when the slaves were set free, presumably did little to alter the relationship between masters and slaves. In a besieged city, were the freed slaves (and their dependants?) suddenly expected to fend for themselves? The law in Deuteronomy 15.12–14, whether or not it was known about in 588 BCE, at least recognized that a freed slave needed material support on being released. The master is commanded to furnish the freed slave liberally out of his flock, his winepress and his threshing floor. What were the freed slaves in besieged Jerusalem to eat? Did they have any claim any longer on their former masters to provide them with food? Is the reason why it was possible for them later to be re-enslaved the fact that the alternative was starvation? Looked at in this way, the freedom given to the slaves was practically almost meaningless. So why was it done? It has already been suggested above that there was the hope that freed slaves would be more willing to fight for the defence of the city; but there is also another possibility. If the meaning of the complaint in Lamentations 5.8 'slaves rule over us' is that a victorious army might put slaves in charge of their former masters, this would be another reason for

---

[34] Cf. W. Dietrich, '"... den Armen das Evangelium zu verkünden". Vom befreienden Sinn biblischer Gesetze' in idem, '*Theopolitik*', p. 186.

emancipating the slaves before the city fell.[35] Again, the action would be governed by self-interest on the part of the slave owners and, incidentally, expose the freed slaves to greater personal risks, if a victorious army was disposed to treat slaves more generously than defeated citizens. The whole incident offends common decency; yet it may be that the Old Testament was in conflict with the customs and expectations of the time in condemning it. The institution of slavery was based upon its own logic and rationality, which must now be examined in detail.

In 2 Kings 4.1–7 the following narrative occurs:

> A certain woman of the sons[36] of the prophets cried out to Elisha, saying, 'Your servant, my husband is dead, and you know that your servant feared Yнwн; and the creditor has come to take my two sons to be slaves.' Elisha said to her, 'What can I do for you? Tell me, what do you have in the house?' She said, 'Your servant has nothing[37] except a jar of oil.' He said, 'Go and borrow vessels from your neighbours round about – empty vessels, as many as you can. Go and shut the door behind you and your sons and pour into those vessels. Whenever one is full, put it aside.' She went from him and shut the door behind herself and her sons. They brought the vessels to her and she poured. When the vessels were full she said to her sons,[38] 'Bring me another vessel.' They said[39] to her, 'There are no more vessels;' and the flow of oil ceased. She came and told the man of God. He said, 'Go, sell the oil and pay your debts, and keep your sons alive with the rest.'[40]

In spite of the legendary nature of the story, the social situation that it implies is clear. A widow has got into debt. Perhaps this happened while her husband was ill and unable to work to provide for the household. She had had to borrow in order to feed her family. The creditor needed to be repaid and her only way of meeting the debts was to sell her sons into slavery. If her reply, to the effect that all she had in the house was a vessel of oil, can be taken literally, she may already have sold everything else to meet her obligations. It is noteworthy that Elisha does not remonstrate with the creditor or criticize the system that has brought the widow to

---

[35] According to H.-J. Kraus, *Klagelieder*, 4th edn (BKAT 20), Neukirchen-Vluyn: Neukirchener Verlag, 1983, p. 89, the 'slaves' are auxiliary troops of the Babylonian army. O. Kaiser, *Klagelieder* (ATD 16.2), in H.-P. Müller, O. Kaiser and J. A. Loader, *Das Hohelied, Klagelieder, Das Buch Ester*, Göttingen: Vandenhoeck & Ruprecht, 1992, pp. 194–5, leaves open the possibility that the 'slaves' may be locally recruited.

[36] Omitting 'the wives of' with LXX.

[37] Omitting 'in the house' with LXX.

[38] Reading the plural with the LXX. Hebrew has 'her son'.

[39] Hebrew 'he said'.

[40] Reading vᵉ'et bānaiki tᵉhayyē, cf. BHK.

such a state of distress. His action is designed to help the widow survive within the system by providing the means with which she can repay her debts. There is no implication that the creditor was acting unfairly or unjustly.

The arrangements implied in the story were necessary if, in a subsistence economy, people were not to starve to death. The creditor was not providing loans for investment, nor lending money in order to make a vast profit.[41] In a subsistence economy the failure of a household to produce sufficient food to eat in a given year could come about in several ways. There could be a failure of the rains, or the crops could be smitten with blight or mildew, or devoured by a plague of locusts (cf. Amos 4.9). Injury, illness, or death affecting the main breadwinner would also have grave consequences for the provision of food for a household. In this situation, what could be done? Ideally, members of the extended family could come to the aid of those in need; but suppose that they, too, were affected by the failure of the rain or the loss of harvest through disease or predator insects? In such circumstances recourse would have to be made either to private individuals who had been able to store grain, or to a local town where there were public buildings for such purposes. The story of Joseph, in which grain stored in good years was made available for sale in the years of famine, illustrates this point (see Genesis 41—47). Genesis 47.13–25 describes how Joseph made slaves of the Egyptians in return for selling them grain, once they had nothing else left to sell. From a modern point of view this may seem totally unacceptable, although rich nations easily tolerate starvation in so-called underdeveloped regions. But in a subsistence economy the alternatives were either that people were allowed to starve to death, or that they survived by being loaned provisions. But these provisions had to be paid for. This was not simply a matter of justice. Those who were in a position to store grain and make it available in times of want would not do so if their debtors reneged upon their debts. As a last resort the creditor was able to enslave a debtor who had no other way of paying what was owed. In itself, the system was logical and not immoral; nonetheless it produced results that led to disrupted communication in the society. The forcible removal from a widow of her two sons in the Elisha story (their ages are not stated and the Hebrew word for 'son' gives

---

[41] A good summary of the economic arrangements implied in the story is given by M. Leutzsch, 'Das biblische Zinsverbot' in Kessler and Loos, *Eigentum*, pp. 108–10. See also in the same volume U. Duchrow, '"Eigentum verplichtet" – zur Verschuldung anderer: kritische Anmerkungen zur Eigentumstheorie von Gunner Heinsohn und Otto Steiger aus biblisch-theologischer Perspektive', p. 23, where attention is drawn to the observations of Heinsohn and Steiger about the amoral logic of economic systems.

no clue as to their ages, but presumably they were not old enough to match the productivity of their late father) would hardly benefit the family unit, nor the individual members of it. The way that the story is narrated is therefore a tacit criticism of the debt/slavery arrangements, and an instance of the way in which communication by way of narrative and writing can be a means of social critique and reform.

This position, that writing about the consequence of economic and social reforms is a way of communicative critique aimed at reform, will now be continued in this chapter with regard to property and trade. The approach will be based upon actual passages, together with a critical evaluation of attempts that have been made to conjecture the social situations that have produced them. While the outcome of these evaluations may be negative rather than positive, this will not affect the point that the texts are criticizing arrangements whose effects are socially disruptive, even if less is known about the arrangements than is often claimed. A locus classicus is Isaiah 5.8–10.

> Woe to you who attach house to house,
> who join field to field, till no room remains
> and you are left to dwell alone in the land.
> Yнwн of hosts has sworn in my hearing,[42]
> surely, many houses will become ruins,
> large, splendid ones will have no occupants.
> Ten plots of vineyard will yield only one measure of wine,
> And a quantity of seed produce
> only a tenth of what is sown.

The social background to this passage is not known. Premnath has tried to explain it in terms of a developing latifundialization (i.e. the development of large estates – from the Latin 'latifundium' – large estate), a process which he traces from the emergence of the monarchy in Israel.[43] However, his account is too dependent on a view of the Israelite state under David and Solomon which makes it far more powerful than can have been the case. Rightly much more cautious is the position of Kessler.[44] He doubts whether the text speaks of estate-building, which would result in the central control of agriculture within an estate with the divided workforce consisting of slaves and day labourers. Rather, he envisages the takeover by some property owners of the property of others who have fallen on hard times, so that they become day labourers on their former properties. This

---

[42] Adding nišbaʿ – cf. BHK.
[43] D. N. Premnath, 'Latifundialization and Isaiah 6.8–10', *JSOT* 40 (1988), pp. 47–60.
[44] Kessler, *Staat und Gesellschaft*, pp. 35–7.

happens by way of the mechanisms of loans and debts outlined above (p. 104). Kessler rightly remarks that the Hebrew verbs that describe the acquisition process, *ng*ʿ and *qrv* in the hiphʿil, do not imply violence, nor breach of the law. What in fact is being implicitly criticized is an economic mechanism that inevitably arises from the possession of property in the sense of land that can be bought and sold. It invariably results in the concentration of property in the hands of some, and the loss of property to others, not to mention those in no position to own any property in the first place.[45] Property, as a medium of social communication, is therefore highly disjunctive, and this was probably the case from the very beginning in ancient Israel and Judah.

How did people come to possess private property in ancient Israel and Judah? It is commonly supposed that land was originally owned communally and that innovations such as the rise of the monarchy led to the break-up of this old order and the emergence of the order that attracted prophetic criticism.[46] There may well have been good practical reasons why land, at least land attached to villages, was held in common. Such an arrangement would enable a social unit larger than the nuclear family to come to the aid of households that had become unable to sustain themselves with regard to the production of food.[47] It is improbable that it was held in common because of a belief that the land belonged to YHWH.[48] However, the Old Testament itself gives no support to the idea that land was or had been held on a communal basis. The account in Joshua of the land being divided among the tribes is a post- or late deuteronomistic composition driven by theological ideals,[49] while the story of the inheritance of the daughters of Zelophehad in Numbers 27 and 36 belongs to the very latest strata of the Pentateuch.[50] On the other hand, there are numerous references to the sale and purchase of land, and even if they do not prove exactly when such practices began (for example, is Abraham's purchase of the field and cave of Machpelah to be dated in a 'patriarchal age'?), the references indicate that the sale and purchase of private property was part of the shared world of the biblical writers/hearers and readers.

---

[45] Duchrow, '"Eigentum verpflichtet"', p. 20.

[46] A. Alt, 'Der Anteil des Königtums an der sozialen Entwicklung in den Reichen Israel und Juda' in idem, *Kleine Schriften*, vol. 3, pp. 348–72.

[47] See D. C. Hopkins *The Highlands of Canaan: Agricultural Life in the Early Iron Age* (SWBA 3), Sheffield: Almond Press, 1985, pp. 251–61.

[48] Against Alt, 'Der Anteil', pp. 348–9.

[49] V. Fritz, *Das Buch Josua* (HAT 1.7), Tübingen: Mohr Siebeck, 1994, pp. 15–57.

[50] See M. Noth, *Das vierte Buch Mose* (ATD 7), Göttingen: Vandenhoeck & Ruprecht, 1966, p. 183.

Examples include Abraham's purchase of the ground for his burial (Genesis 23.3–20), Jacob's purchase of a site for an altar in Shechem (Genesis 33.18–20), David's purchase of the threshing floor from Araunah the Jebusite (2 Samuel 24.18–25), Omri's purchase of the hill of Samaria from Shemer (1 Kings 16.24) and Jeremiah's purchase of a field in Anathoth from his cousin Hanamel (Jeremiah 32.6–15). Other narratives or laws that presuppose the existence of private property include 2 Kings 8.1–6, where a woman seeks to reclaim her house and land after an absence from it of seven years, the command not to remove a neighbour's landmark (i.e. to alter the boundary of his land, Deuteronomy 19.14 and compare Deuteronomy 27.17: 'Cursed be he who removes his neighbour's landmark') and the command in the Decalogue that one should not covet one's neighbour's house (Exodus 20.17, compare Deuteronomy 5.21).[51] To this can be added what is implied in the story of Ruth, where the plot hinges on Naomi's ability to sell the land that belonged to her husband Elimelech and from which she had been absent for an unspecified period of time (Ruth 4.3).

Returning to the question of whether all land in ancient Israel was originally commonly held and that the prophetic criticism in texts such as Isaiah 5.8–10 was directed at the breakdown or subversion of an 'old order', the likelihood is that although some land, especially that pertaining to small villages, was held in common for practical reasons, the existence of private property from the earliest times was well established, perhaps because the country also contained city states that considerably pre-dated the migrations of proto-Israelites into the area. Elsewhere I have argued that Judah and Israel derived from earlier segmentary states, that is, spheres of power and influence wielded by individuals who disposed of land and personnel, and who entered into temporary and shifting alliances with other such individuals.[52] Although the biblical accounts must be used with caution, the mention in narratives of powerful individuals such as the 'minor judges' in Judges 10.1–5; 12.8–15, Abimelech (Judges 9.1–56), and Nabal (1 Samuel 25.1b–38) not to mention David, fits this picture well. Obviously, the rise of dynastic monarchies in Israel and Judah was an important factor in the development of social arrangements, and much

---

[51] See the useful summary in F. Horst, 'Das Eigentum nach dem Alten Testament' in idem, *Gottes Recht: Studien zum Recht im Alten Testament* (TB 12), Munich: Chr. Kaiser, 1961, pp. 208–12.

[52] J. W. Rogerson, 'Israel to the End of the Persian Period: History, Social, Political and Economic Background' in J. W. Rogerson and J. M. Lieu (eds), *The Oxford Handbook of Biblical Studies*, Oxford: Oxford University Press, 2006, pp. 271–3.

attention has been focused upon 1 Samuel 8.10–18, in which Samuel's warning about what having a king will entail includes the words,

> he will take your most productive land, and vineyards and olive orchards
> and give them to those who serve him,   (1 Samuel 8.14)

together with other passages such as 1 Samuel 22.7 and 2 Samuel 9.7–13, which imply that the king had power to give and to alter grants of land.[53] However, such practice may have been nothing more than the extension of what had been done by the powerful individuals whose alliances constituted the segmentary states.

The position that I am wanting to develop here is that the prophetic critique contained in passages such as Isaiah 5.8–10 was not a protest against the breakdown or subversion of an ideal old order or of some kind of egalitarian society. Such a society never existed in ancient Israel and Judah. The prophetic critique was directed against an economic system which was amoral and which contained an inner logic that led to the accumulation of property and power by fewer and fewer individuals. The contribution of the prophets was to begin to question the morality of the amoral system from the point of view of its effects upon those who were the losers within the system.

An intriguing question, to which no clear answer can be given, is what happened to private property that was vacated by those taken into exile by the Babylonians in 597 BCE and occupied by those who were left in the land. What happened if returning exiles or their descendants wanted to reclaim their lands? Kessler has argued that post-exilic expansions of Amos, Micah, Isaiah and Zephaniah show that the editors of these books were of the view that landowners earlier guilty of the misappropriation of land should be barred from repossessing their properties.[54] However, these aspirations were not realized. Crüsemann, followed by Dietrich, suggests that the jubilee law in Leviticus 25.14–35 envisages the possibility that returning exiles should regain their lands, and is intended to make this possible.[55] This suggestion comes up against the difficulty that in Nehemiah 5.1–12, Nehemiah claims to have forced unscrupulous landowners who were exploiting their fellow countrymen to return to their owners the fields, vineyards, olive orchards and houses that had been acquired by

---

[53] See the section in Kessler, *Staat und Gesellschaft*, pp. 195–7.

[54] R. Kessler, 'Arbeit, Eigentum und Freiheit: Die Frage des Grundeigentums in der Endgestalt der Prophetenbücher' in Kessler and Loos, *Eigentum*, pp. 64–8.

[55] F. Crüsemann, *Die Tora: Theologie und Sozialgeschichte des alttestamentlichen Gesetzes*, 2nd edn, Gütersloh: Chr. Kaiser/Gütersloher Verlagshaus, 1997, pp. 330–1. W. Dietrich, 'Wem das land gehört' in idem, '*Theopolitik*', pp. 280–1.

exacting interest that could only be paid by mortgaging property and daughters to the more powerful landowners. There is no mention in Nehemiah of the legislation in Leviticus 25 (e.g. verses 35–37 prohibiting the charging of interest) that should have prevented the state of affairs that Nehemiah needed to reform. This, of course, assumes the unity of Leviticus 25, something which cannot be taken for granted. The verdict of Grabbe is that 'we are left largely in the dark about what happened to those who had continued to live in Judah during the exile and had taken over land vacated by those in captivity'.[56] The matter will be left there for the moment.

A matter of social communication concerning which Old Testament texts are unequivocal is fairness, or rather, unfairness, in matters of trading. To return to Luhmann's point about symbolically generalized media of communication and the expectations that they imply (see above pp. 92–3) an economic system that includes an element of barter is heavily dependent upon honesty and transparency in the use of weights and measures. That this was not always so in Israel and Judah is indicated by a number of texts. Deuteronomy 25.13–14 says simply

> You must not have in your bag two kinds of stone weights,
> one heavy and the other light.
> You must not have in your house two kinds of measure:
> one large, the other small.

The stone weights were most likely to be used when weighing precious metals such as silver, in an economy which lacked coins with a guaranteed value. Driver suggests that the larger or heavier ones would be used for buying, the smaller ones for selling.[57] This would have the effect of making the buyer pay more precious metal to the dishonest dealer because the latter would use the heavier weight when weighing the metal that was due to him. When the dishonest dealer bought something himself, he would weight his own payment in precious metal using the lighter stone. It is tempting to compare with this the modern practice of bureaux de change, whose clients are charged more for buying a foreign currency than for selling it! The same system would apply to the use of large and small measures, when buying and selling things such as grain and oil. Braulik sees in the deuteronomic law an amplification of the law in the Decalogue not to covet.[58] This is achieved by prohibiting the *possession* of false weights and measures, not merely their use. A passage in Leviticus 19.36 extends

---

[56] Grabbe, *History*, vol. 1, p. 206.

[57] S. R. Driver, *Deuteronomy* (ICC), Edinburgh: T. & T. Clark, 1902, p. 286.

[58] G. Braulik, *Deuteronomium II* (Neue Echter Bibel), Würzburg: Echter, 1992, pp. 189–90.

the prohibition to scales and measures of length. Among the prophetic denunciations of dishonest dealing is a passage in Amos 8.4–5.

> Hear this you who crush the poor,
> and desire to finish off the oppressed.[59]
> Who say, 'When will the new moon be over
> so that we can sell grain?
> and the sabbath, so that we can open our sacks of wheat?
> When we can make our measures small
> and our weights heavy?
> When we can deal crookedly with false balances,
> and sell the dust that remains of the wheat?'[60]

Here, unlike in Deuteronomy 25.13–14, where the command is directed not just against traders,[61] the prophet has a particular class or group in view, who take advantage of their power as traders to exploit the poor and economically powerless members of the community. From a communicative point of view their crime is not simply that they show no respect for fellow human beings, and that they take advantage of those economically weaker than themselves; it is that they abuse the whole basis of part of the communicative system that defines a community.

The social abuse that receives by far the most criticism in the Old Testament is the corruption or perversion of justice. This could take several forms, of which the most easily detectable was the giving of false evidence on the part of witnesses. This is most explicitly forbidden in Deuteronomy 19.16–19:

> If there arise a witness who intends violence by accusing another of wrongdoing the two men who are in dispute shall appear before YHWH, before the priests and the judges who hold office in those days. The judges shall investigate carefully. If the witness is a false witness who has accused his brother falsely, you shall do to him as he planned to do to his brother.

The awkwardness of the Hebrew is apparent even in translation. Most obviously, the fact that the disputants are to appear before YHWH, the priests and the judges, while only the latter are to examine them, is a clear indication that the text has been expanded more than once to reflect changing legal circumstances.[62] The view taken here is that the text originally

---

[59] vᵉlašbît provides a word-play on sabbath in the next verse. See J. Jeremias *Der Prophet Amos* (ATD 24.2), Göttingen: Vandenhoeck & Ruprecht, 1995, p. 116.

[60] Transposing 6c to the end of verse 5.

[61] Braulik, *Deuteronomium II*, p. 190.

[62] See G. von Rad, *Das fünfte Buch Mose* (ATD 8), Göttingen: Vandenhoeck & Ruprecht, 1964, p. 92.

referred to two disputants whose case would be settled by some kind of ordeal based upon an oath taken in the name of Yнwн (cf. Exodus 22.11 [Hebrew 22.10]). This was expanded by reference to an examination by judges, and the whole was given a different context by being prefaced by verse 15.

> A single witness shall not suffice against a man for any crime or wrong-doing.[63] Only the evidence of two or three witnesses will establish a matter.[64]

There is, of course, a celebrated case in the Old Testament where an innocent man was condemned and executed on the basis of false evidence, namely, Naboth in 1 Kings 21. The sequel, in 1 Kings 21.17–19, in which Elijah confronts and condemns Ahab for this crime engineered by his wife Jezebel, is meant to show, among other things, that such injustices do not go unseen or unpunished by God. The same point is made in the two slightly differing Greek versions of the story of Susanna and the Elders. Susanna, who has been falsely accused of adultery by two men that she has spurned, is rescued only when Daniel cross-questions the two men and finds their evidence to be contradictory. Daniel represents the justice of God, which will not allow an innocent and pious young woman to be wrongly condemmed.[65]

Ahab's condemnation by Elijah and Susanna's vindication by Daniel express hopes for a better world, one in which trust in the fairness of the judicial system can be unreserved. Unfortunately, as the writers of the Old Testament knew only too well, the reality was different; and their attempts to challenge this reality produced some of the most powerful passages in the whole of the Bible, only some of which can be discussed here. They will be considered under four headings: the taking of bribes by judges, the subversion of moral categories, the manipulation of the legal system to produce unjust laws, and the general feeling of powerlesness in the face of a system corrupt beyond reform.

Of the complaints about judges being susceptible to bribery, Micah 3.11 makes a simple statement about the situation in his day, probably towards the end of the eighth century BCE.

> Her heads [the rulers of Jerusalem] judge in return for a bribe.

---

[63] Omitting bᵉkol-hēt' 'ᵃšer yehᵉtā', cf. BHK.

[64] Against von Rad, *Das fünfte Buch*, p. 92, who sees the passage as an expansion of an original, 'Es soll nicht ein einzelner Zeuge gegen jemand auftreten betreffs irgendeiner Verschuldung.'

[65] Susanna and the Elders. For commentary on the Greek versions see J. W. Rogerson, 'Additions to Daniel' in J. D. G. Dunn and J. W. Rogerson (eds), *Eerdmans Commentary on the Bible*, Grand Rapids: Eerdmans, 2003, pp. 804–5.

A much more explicit and powerfully poetic condemnation comes later in the book, at 7.2–4:

> No one of integrity is left in the land,
> and honest people are no more.
> All lie in wait to commit murder,
> each hunts his brother with a net.
> They have honed their skills in wrongdoing.[66]
> The prince asks for money,
> the judge for a bribe,
> the nobleman does not hide his evil intentions.
> They twist justice.[67]
> The best of them is like a briar,
> the honest man like a hedge of thorns.

Whether or not the passage comes from Micah himself is a matter of dispute among commentators.[68] Whatever its provenance, it describes a society which is in such a state of disintegration that trust has entirely vanished. What might have preserved some semblance of order, namely, the fair administration of justice, has also become corrupted. It is perhaps a chicken and egg situation, but it is clear that judges have come to put their own interests above those of justice.

The subversion of moral categories implies that a society is still functioning together with its judicial system even if the system has become corrupt. Isaiah 5.20 condemns those who

> Say that what is bad is good,
> and what is good is bad;
> who call darkness light,
> and light darkness;
> what is bitter, sweet,
> and what is sweet, bitter,
> who acquit the wicked for a bribe,
> and deny justice to the innocent.[69]

Wildberger quotes an interesting comment from Fohrer, only to reject it as a 'modern idea'. The quotation states (in my translation) that the prophet

---

[66] Reading lᵉhāra' kappēhem hētîvū, cf. BHS.

[67] Reading yᵉ'abbtū hammišpāt, cf. BHS.

[68] Kessler, *Staat und Gesellschaft*, p. 57, notes 'wenn auch die Gründe nicht zwingend sind, dem Text Micha abzusprechen, so gibt es doch auch keine zwingenden Gründe, daß er von Micha sein müsse' [if the grounds for denying the passage to Micah are not compelling, neither are there compelling grounds for saying that it must come from Micah].

[69] Taking verses 20 and 23 together, with Wildberger, *Isaiah*, pp. 176, 195–6.

condemns 'those who "transvalue all values", who live "beyond good and evil", who redefine all accepted standards according to their own judgments and who thus create their own new view of the world'.[70] That this is certainly a modern idea is borne out by the reported statement of an aide to the administration of George W. Bush, 'When we act, we create our own reality'.[71] But was it not possible for people in power to think like this in ancient Israel and Judah? Some of the psalmists might well have agreed with Fohrer, and although there is no explicit statement in the psalms that goes as far as what he suggests, some of the complaints there are not too far removed. Psalm 36 opens with the words

> The wicked man proclaims the wickedness deep in his heart;
> there is no fear of God in his eyes.
> He flatters himself in his own sight,
> and hates his wrongdoing to be known.
> He speaks only wickedness and lies;
> he has ceased to act wisely or to do good.
> He makes evil plans as he lies abed,
> he takes his stand on a path that is not good,
> and nothing that is evil will he reject.[72]

To return to the quotation from Fohrer, readers will have noticed that it refers to two works by Nietzsche, the 'Transvaluation of all Values' and 'Beyond Good and Evil'.[73] These are the subject of the Second Excursus of Adorno and Horkheimer's *Dialectic of Enlightenment*, together with other works of Nietzsche and the *Histoire de Juliette* by the Marquis de Sade.[74] This bleak account of the logical implications of transvaluing all values, something that has found its practical embodiment in the atrocities committed by totalitarian regimes in the twentieth-century, adds a grim dimension to Isaiah's strictures against those who call what is bad, good, and vice versa. Adorno and Horkheimer quote, among other things,

---

[70] Wildberger, *Isaiah*, p. 195.

[71] F. Rich, *The Greatest Story ever Sold: The Decline and Fall of Truth from 9/11 to Katrina*, New York: Penguin, 2006, p. 3.

[72] The translations from the Psalms are taken from my *The Psalms in Daily Life*, London: SPCK, 2001.

[73] F. Nietzsche, *Jenseits von Gut und Böse* in *Friedrich Nietzsche, Sämtliche Werke: Kritische Studienausgabe* (ed. G. Colli and M. Montinari), Munich: Deutscher Taschenbuchverlag; Berlin: W. de Gruyter, 1980, vol. 5, pp. 9–243; ET *Beyond Good and Evil*, London: Penguin, 1990. *Die Umwertung aller Werte* (The Transvaluation of all Values) exists in a number of references in Nietzsche's posthumous papers. See *Sämtliche Werke*, vol. 15, p. 336 for details.

[74] T. W. Adorno and M. Horkheimer, *Dialektik der Aufklärung* in Theodor W. Adorno, *Gesammelte Schriften* (ed. R. Tiedemann), Darmstadt: Wissenschaftliche Buchgesellschaft, 1998, vol. 5; ET *Dialectic of Enlightenment*, London: Verso, 1997.

Nietzsche's claim that society is undermined not by a breakdown of values but by the presence in it of the weak and physically disadvantaged.

> 'The physically disadvantaged are man's greatest enemy, not the evil, and not the "predators". Those who are unfortunate, conquered, ruined from the start – they, the weak, are most responsible for the undermining of men's life in common; they are the ones who most effectively embitter and question our trust in life, in men, and in ourselves.'[75]

It is no coincidence that so much prophetic criticism was directed precisely at those who had no compassion for the weak and the disadvantaged and who did not scruple to exploit them whenever they could.

Perhaps the most corrosive and insidious form of the perversion of justice was the apparently legitimate use of power to frame and enforce laws that were basically unjust. In Jeremiah 8.8 is the complaint,

> How can you say 'We are wise,
> and the law of Yhwh is in our keeping?'
> In fact it has been changed to falsehood
> by the lying pens of scribes.

McKane suggests that not too much stress should be put on the reference to the 'lying pens', as though the passage refers exclusively to the development and drafting of new laws; and he allows the possibility that 'the prophet is concerned with what he regards as false rulings in connection with contemporary issues which he believes to be crucial'.[76] Perhaps this observation moves the interpretation of the passage too far in the direction of disagreement over matters of opinion. The most natural sense of the passage is that those who claim to be wise, perhaps to belong to a class of learned interpreters, are mistaken, because that on which they base their interpretations is flawed. It has been deliberately corrupted to contain material that contravenes traditionally accepted norms. The wise men may not be aware of this, in which case the insidious effects of the corruption are even worse.

Another passage which deals with the corruption of law at the point of law-making is in Psalm 94.20–21.

> Can those who cover up their wickedness have you as an ally,
> those who produce evil by passing laws?
> They band themselves against the life of the righteous,
> and condemn the innocent to death.

---

[75] Adorno and Horkheimer, *Dialektik*, p. 119, quoting Nietzsche, *Genealogie der Moral* in *Sämtliche Werke*, vol. 5, p. 368. The translation above is from the ET of *Dialectic*, p. 99.

[76] W. McKane, *Jeremiah* (ICC), Edinburgh: T. & T. Clark, vol. 1, 1986, p. 186.

The above rendering reads *m^ekasseh* – 'covers' for *kissē'* – 'throne', although this does not affect the meaning. Indeed, the traditional Hebrew 'thrones of wickedness' strongly hints at wickedness in high places. Some editors (e.g. BHK) suggest *b^elî* instead of *^elē* which would mean that the wickedness is done against, or disregarding the law, and not, as in the above translation, by means of framing unjust laws. However, most modern renderings support the view that the wickedness is perpetrated by means of the law. The NEB 'contrives a mischief under cover of law' captures the sense well. The whole psalm is quite a dark composition as it spells out a situation where justice, however it is being manipulated or ignored, is denied to those who need it most.

> They [the wicked] spout forth arrogant words;
> the evil-doers boast proudly.
> They crush your people, YHWH,
> and oppress the ones you have chosen.
> They murder the widows and strangers,
> and put the fatherless to death.
> They say 'Yah will not see.
> The God of Jacob will not notice.'
> (Psalm 94.4–7)

The kind of hopelessness expressed in this psalm is given an even stronger statement in Ecclesiastes, the more so because the implied author of the book claims to have been a king in Jerusalem, and therefore responsible for upholding law and justice. The following selection of passages makes depressing reading.

> Again I saw under the sun
> the place of justice –
> but wickedness was there;
> the place of righteousness –
> but wickedness was there.
> (Ecclesiastes 3.16)[77]

> Again, I saw all the oppressions
> that are carried out under the sun.
> I saw the tears of the oppressed,
> with no one to comfort them.

---

[77] Because of the repetition of rāša' in lines 2 and 3 some editors, e.g. BHK, propose happeša' – 'sin' for the second rāša'. However, the LXX and Targum support the Hebrew, albeit by taking the Hebrew to refer to 'the righteous man' and the 'wicked man'.

The oppressors had might on their side,
with no one to avenge them.[78]
I thought that the dead who were already dead
were luckier than the living who were still alive.

(Ecclesiastes 4.1–2)

In my futile life
I have seen everything:
a just man perishing before his time in spite of his goodness,
a wicked man growing old in spite of his wrongdoings.

(Ecclesiastes 7.15)

As has already been observed the implied author of these words claims to have been a king in Jerusalem, and he advises readers to treat kings with great respect because of their power!

Obey the king's command,
because of your oath to God.
Do not hurry to leave his presence;
do not persist in doing what displeases him,
for he does whatever he pleases.
The word of the king is sovereign.
No one can say to him 'What are you doing?'

(Ecclesiastes 8.2–3)

When these words were written (?*c.*300 BCE) the Jews had long since had no king of their own and had lately been ruled by the kings of Persia. It may be, of course, that the author of Ecclesiastes was writing in the second century and had an actual king or kings in mind, such as Antiochus III.[79] Or again, as Whybray remarks, '"king" may mean no more than a provincial governor, or alternatively the sayings about kings may be merely following a literary convention (cf. e.g. Prov. 16.14; 22.11; 25.6–7)'.[80] A difficult passage in this connection is Ecclesiastes 5.8–9 [Hebrew 5.7–8].

If, in a province, you see the oppression of the poor and denial of justice and righteousness, do not be surprised at this. Every high official has a higher one watching over him, and there are higher ones still. But best for a land is a king with lands well cultivated.

Many commentators take the enigmatic reference to the king to be a later gloss,[81] but what precedes is also far from clear. The passage appears to be

---

[78] Reading mᵉnaqēm with BHK.

[79] See the discussion in G. A. Barton, *Ecclesiastes* (ICC), Edinburgh: T. & T. Clark, 1908, pp. 60–2.

[80] R. N. Whybray, *Ecclesiastes* (OTG), Sheffield: Sheffield Academic Press, 1989, p. 21.

[81] A. Lauha, *Kohelet* (BKAT 19), Neukirchen-Vluyn: Neukirchener Verlag, 1978, pp. 103–5.

saying that oppression and injustice result from a hierarchy of officials, in which case, as Lauha observes, the sense of 'watch over' cannot be something like 'closely supervise in the interests of justice', but rather, that higher officials oppress lower ones, who in turn pass the process down to those lowest and weakest in the social order.[82] The view taken here is that there is deliberate irony in Ecclesiastes. The writer employs the fiction of having been a king, and attributes to the king a supreme measure of authority (Ecclesiastes 8.4). Yet he also says that in the place of justice, wickedness was ensconced (3.16) and that there was no one to comfort or avenge the oppressed. In this paradoxical way he drew attention to the futility of life as he saw it. Whether he thought that he was doing more than putting a message into a bottle, to quote Adorno's image (see above, p. 25), can only be surmised.

This chapter is still assuming that one way in which the biblical writers could try to bring about reform was by way of writing about the dislocations of communication within their own society, with a view to enlarging the awareness of their viewpoint. Before there is a consideration of the practical measures for reform that were proposed (which may, of course, have never been more than literary accounts of practical proposals rather than anything that was actually put into practice), a look will be taken at several narratives from 1 Kings 17 to 2 Kings 11, as provocatively commented on by Ton Veerkamp.[83] The first comment is on 1 Kings 18.2–6.

> The famine in Samaria was severe. Ahab summoned Obadiah, who was in charge of his household. (Now Obadiah feared YHWH devoutly, and when Jezebel murdered the prophets of YHWH, Obadiah had taken a hundred of them and hidden them by fifties in a cave and had fed them with food and drink.) Ahab said to Obadiah, 'Let us go[84] through the land to every spring and wadi. Perhaps we shall find grass enough to keep alive our horses and mules, and lose none of our cattle.'[85]

Veerkamp observes that the search was for food for the benefit of the king's horses, mules and cattle, not for the benefit of Ahab's subjects. In reality, of course, it is most unlikely that the king and his chief administrator would, single-handedly, divide up the whole land between themselves in their search for possible fodder. They would have officials to do this, and

---

[82] Lauha, *Kohelet*, p. 104.

[83] T. Veerkamp, *Die Vernichtung des Baal: Auslegung der Königsbücher (1.17–2.11)*, Stuttgart: Alektor, 1983.

[84] Adding na'ᵃvōr with the LXX. See C. F. Burney, *Notes on the Hebrew Text of the Books of Kings*, Oxford: Clarendon Press, 1903, p. 220.

[85] Reading vᵉlō' tikkārēt mimmennū bᵉhēmāh. See Burney, *Notes*, p. 221.

would merely give the orders. But the narrative requires that Obadiah and Ahab encounter Elijah during their travels (1 Kings 18.7–19). However, even though it is not central to the narrative, the fact that the search is for fodder for the king's animals is worthy of note. As Veerkamp writes,

> Hunger drives Ahab out of Samaria, but not because he himself is hungry. Rulers are never hungry. Neither is it because the people are hungry. In politics, the people for whose benefit everything is allegedly done take second place. Ahab is concerned for his horses and mules, the motors of his war machine and the insignia of his royal worth.[86]

In commenting on Elijah's confrontation with the prophets of Baal on Mount Carmel in 1 Kings 18.20–40, Veerkamp observes that the central point is not whether or not God exists, but whether his existence makes any practical difference to the world. It is not existence that matters, but action.[87] YHWH does not have an existence, but a name; and Veerkamp challenges readers to name the baalim that threaten their existence in today's world: the market economy, the military balance of power, the rationalization (of commerce and enterprises).[88]

The incident of Naboth's vineyard in 1 Kings 21 is one of the best-known narratives in the Old Testament. Veerkamp maintains that whatever else it is about, it has a symbolic meaning. He believes that it was written not to uphold the ancestral right to the retention of one's property in ancient Israel, but as a protest against the massive appropriation of the lands of small farmers in the middle period of the monarchy.[89] If this is correct, it could have coincided with the situation about which Micah was complaining (see above, p. 98). On this view, Naboth does not stand not for a divine law from Israel's past, but is a symbol of the future, a future in which the opportunities for such appropriations will be greatly diminished, if they cannot be abolished altogether.

Less well known than the story of Naboth is the incident which precedes it in 1 Kings 20. There is war between the king of Israel and Ben-hadad king of Damascus, which results in a great victory for the Israelites in the neighbourhood of Aphek. Ben-hadad is at the Israelite king's mercy but is spared in return for restoring to Israel the cities that Ben-hadad's father took from the father of the Israelite king. Also, the king will be allowed to establish bazaars in Damascus. Veerkamp comments that, like all peace

---

[86] Veerkamp, *Die Vernichtung*, p. 35, my translation.
[87] Veerkamp, *Die Vernichtung*, p. 44.
[88] Veerkamp, *Die Vernichtung*, p. 51.
[89] Veerkamp, *Die Vernichtung*, p. 112.

settlements, this one contains the seeds of the next war. The concessions gained relate to property and trade that will benefit royal circles, not the ordinary people who suffer and will suffer, when their rulers struggle against each other to extend their territories.[90] The incident is followed by a little-known story that is a parable, in the sense that a ruler is persuaded to make a decision that is then turned against him (1 Kings 20.35–43; cf. 2 Samuel 12.1–12, where the subject is David). A prophet persuades a fellow prophet to wound him so that he is not easily recognizable. (A colleague who refuses to do the wounding is devoured by a lion!) The wounded, and therefore disguised, prophet then sets out to meet the Israelite king on the battlefield. He puts a case before him. He had been entrusted to guard a prisoner on pain of either forfeiting his own life or having to pay a fine of a talent of silver if he lost the prisoner. He had lost the prisoner. What was his position? The king upholds the conditions of the arrangement. The prophet must either pay up or pay with his life. The prophet now reveals his identity, and the king recognizes him as one of the prophets. He delivers a judgement to the effect that because the king spared Ben-hadad, whose life should have been forfeit to God, the king's own life will be forfeit. Veerkamp's complaint against the sparing of Ben-hadad is that it is part of a game played by rulers with no thought of the effects on their ordinary subjects when war breaks out again. He contributes an interesting interpretation of the notion of *herem*, or ban, in which all the people or goods of a defeated people must be utterly destroyed and in this way 'devoted' to God (cf. Joshua 6.20–21). This practice (if it was ever more than a piece of rhetoric) is universally condemned by commentators as a relic of primitive practice abhorrent to modern sensibilities. Veerkamp argues that in fact the ban stands for a type of politics which will have no truck with the compromises devised by the leaders of nations which do nothing to change the world for the better, and simply perpetuate its injustices. The failure of the king of Israel to kill Ben-hadad and thus carry out the ban is an indication of his willing participation in the perpetuation of a corrupt and unjust world order.[91]

The whole matter is illuminated by historical criticism. In 2 Kings 6.24—7.20, a narrative that will be considered shortly, Samaria is besieged by Ben-hadad, king of Damascus. On the assumption that the books of Kings accurately narrate history, this Ben-hadad cannot be the one spared in 1 Kings 20, because a generation has passed since that incident. But the name of the king of Israel is never given in the Hebrew of 1 Kings 20,

---

[90] Veerkamp, *Die Vernichtung*, p. 100.
[91] Veerkamp, *Die Vernichtung*, p. 105.

and the insertion of the name 'Ahab' in modern translations of verse 34c is an understandable liberty taken by translators in order to make sense of the passage. In fact, it has long been recognized that the material in 1 Kings 20 to 2 Kings 11 is in some disorder and that it is likely that material relating to the son or grandson of Ahab has been transferred to Ahab's reign.[92] If this is so, then the likelihood is that the Ben-hadad who was spared by the Israelite king in 1 Kings 20 is the same Ben-hadad who besieges Samaria in 2 Kings 6—7. Veerkamp's point is even more strongly emphasized. The war games played by rulers with each other bear most heavily on the most vulnerable of their subjects.

The famine in Samaria becomes so severe that an ass's head is sold for 80 shekels of silver and the fourth part of a kab of dove's dung (either locust beans or some kind of seasoning or preservative) costs 5 shekels (2 Kings 6.25). While it is impossible to give any meaning to these prices in terms of the wealth of the people affected by the siege, the narrative intends to convey that these were outrageous prices. The point is well made that 'the market' and its 'law' of supply and demand has no room for compassion even in the most desperate situations. That communicative system we call the economy may be amoral, but it hardly commands any moral respect. The point is made even more strongly by the next part of the story in which two women appeal to the king. They had made a bargain that on one day they would eat the son of one of them, and on the next day, the son of the other woman. The first woman had carried out her side of the bargain; the second woman had hidden her son. They appeal to the king, who rends his clothes and determines to punish Elisha, whom he holds responsible for the famine. Could the king have done more? When news comes that the siege has been lifted the king suspects a trap, and sends his servants with five of the remaining horses to see if the enemy has really departed. Five remaining horses! On what had they been fed, and how many meals had the king and his household enjoyed from the ones slaughtered? The king and his retinue had not had to pay exorbitant prices for unappetizing fare, nor consider eating their own kith and kin. The news of the lifting of the siege is given by four 'lepers' who live outside the city gate (2 Kings 7.3–15). They decide to throw themselves on the mercy of the besieging Syrians but find their camp abandoned. Having eaten and drunk they conclude that they must tell the good news to the city,

---

[92] See J. W. Rogerson and P. R. Davies, *The Old Testament World*, 2nd edn, London: T. & T. Clark International, 2005, pp. 76–7; J. W. Rogerson, *Chronicle of the Old Testament Kings: The Reign-by-Reign Record of the Rulers of Ancient Israel*, London: Thames & Hudson, 1999, pp. 103–6.

otherwise punishment will overtake them (2 Kings 7.9). What is meant by 'punishment overtaking them' (Hebrew, literally, 'our iniquity will find us') is not clear. It would be good to think that precisely because they were marginalized members of the community they had a sense of solidarity with those in the city most vulnerable to the effects of the siege, and that their 'iniquity' would be failure to tell those people, rather than the king and his retinue.

The remainder of this chapter will consider the main Old Testament texts that record what may or may not have been practical steps taken to counteract the dislocations in social relationships that resulted from the amoral system of the economy. The passages have been much discussed, yet they contain critical difficulties which the present chapter will seek to negotiate. The first passage is Deuteronomy 15.1–11.

> At the end of every seven years you shall make a release; and this will be the manner of the release. Everyone who has agreed a loan will remit what he has lent to his neighbour.[93] He must not press his neighbour[94] for payment, for Yнwн's release has been proclaimed. You may press a foreigner for payment, but whatever you have agreed with your brother you shall remit.
>
> (15.1–3)

> There shall be no poor among you, for Yнwн will bless you in the land which Yнwн is giving you as an inheritance to possess, provided you diligently obey the voice of Yнwн your God to observe and perform all this commandment which I command you this day. Yнwн your God will bless you as he promised to you. You will lend to many nations but you shall not borrow. You will rule over many nations, but they will not rule over you.
>
> (15.4–6)

> If there is among you a poor man, one of your brethren[95] in any of your settlements in the land[96] which Yнwн your God is giving you, do not harden your heart and do not tighten your hand against your poor brother. You shall generously open your hand to him and lend him sufficient for his needs.[97] Take care that there is no base thought in your heart and you say,

---

[93] Taking the difficult baʿal maššeh yādō to mean that someone has made an agreement by a handshake or striking of hands. See the full discussion in F. Horst, 'Brachjahr und Schuldverhältnisse: 15,1–18' in idem, *Das Privilegrecht Jahwes: Rechtsgeschichtliche Untersuchungen zum Deuteronium* (FRLANT 45 [NF 28]), Göttingen: Vandenhoeck & Ruprecht, 1930, reprinted in *Gottes Recht*, pp. 79–103, to which reference here is made. The discussion of Deuteronomy 15.1 is on pp. 82–9.

[94] Omitting vᵉʾet ʾāhîv 'and his brother' as a later gloss.

[95] Reading mēʾaheka, cf. Horst, 'Brachjahr', p. 91, note 197.

[96] Cf. LXX and Samaritan Pentateuch. Hebrew, 'in your land'.

[97] Omitting ʾašēr yehsar lō, cf. BHK.

'the seventh year, the year of release is close', and you become hostile to your brother and give him nothing. If he appeals to Yʜwʜ against you, it will be counted as a sin against you. You must give generously to him and not be grudging when you give to him. If you give generously Yʜwʜ your God will bless you in all that you do and undertake. The poor will always be in the land; therefore I command you to open your hand generously to your brother, to the needy and to the poor in your land.   (15.7–12)

It is generally agreed that Deuteronomy 15.1 refers back to Exodus 23.10:

For six years you shall sow your land and harvest what it produces. But the seventh year you shall let it rest and not tend it.

Although the interpretation of this passage is not the main concern here, there is one issue that needs to be addressed. Whatever the origin of the sabbatical year (according to Albertz it had its roots in ancient tabu practices which were believed to ensure the fertility of the land in future years)[98] there has been agreement that the sabbatical year was not observed simultaneously throughout the land, but that it was applied individually by farmers, at differing times.[99] Dietrich is typical of those who argue that it would have been impossible for the whole country to observe a sabbatical year simultaneously, and he also assumes that one of its purposes was to allow the land to recover its fertility.[100] However, Hopkins has shown that land was fallowed every other year in the highlands of Canaan, and he also produces a scheme to show how a country-wide sabbatical year could fit in with the process of biannual fallowing.[101] The fact that it was possible for there to be a country-wide sabbatical year applied to the land does not, of course, mean that it was observed, or that this is what Exodus 23.10 envisages. But the disposal of the argument that it was not possible removes one puzzle, namely, why an agricultural practice that was staggered was later extended to cover loans simultaneously on a country-wide basis.

Deuteronomy 15.1, then, looks back to Exodus 23.10, but it is extended to apply to loans. How it was applied to loans is another matter of disagreement. The two possibilities are, first, that no interest or repayment instalment was taken in the seventh year and, second, that the whole

[98] R. Albertz, 'Sabbatjahr' in M. Görg and B. Lang, *Neues Bibel-Lexikon*, Zurich: Benzinger, 1998, vol. 3, pp. 394–5.
[99] So, for example, Albertz, 'Sabbatjahr', p. 394; W. Dietrich, '. . . den Armen das Evangelium zu verkünden'. Vom befreiendem Sinn biblischer Gesetze' in idem. '*Theolpolitik*', p. 189.
[100] Dietrich, '. . . den Armen', pp. 190–1.
[101] Hopkins, *Highlands*, pp. 200–2.

outstanding debt was remitted in the seventh year.[102] An interesting observation by Dietrich is that if the text originally required only a moratorium on payments, verses 7–10 were added to make it clear that a full remission of the debt was required.[103]

From the communicative point of view the most significant verse is Deuteronomy 15.9, in which potential lenders are warned not to be deterred from making a loan because the year of release is near. The implication is that the nearer a loan was made to the beginning of the seven-year period, the greater the likelihood that it would be repaid. A reluctance to make a loan shortly before the year of release is understandable. As was observed above (p. 104), the system of loans helped to keep people from starvation. Any regulations that prevented lenders from receiving their loan back would simply result in there being no loans, with the obvious consequences for those who needed assistance. The system was amoral, and for good reason. There is also the point that if people could get loans which they had no intention of repaying, by taking them out close to the year of release, this would institutionalize a shirkers' or spongers' charter. Indeed, these considerations raise the question why there should have been a year of release at all, given that it introduced a rationality that threatened to undermine the system of loans.

The first answer to this question is presumably that those who proposed the year of release were extending to the sphere of monetary exchange a law that governed the usage of land. Of course, the terminology 'monetary exchange' is not exact because there was no coinage in Judah at the presumed time of the composition of the deuteronomic text (i.e. *c.*sixth to fifth centuries BCE) and loans could be made in kind, e.g. in quantities of cereals, oil and livestock. It may also be the case that if the regulation was proposed after the so-called return from exile, it had been adapted to the fact that Judah was now a comparatively small area without extensive landholding. It is to the spirit of the law limiting the use of land that we have to look, in order to take the matter further. Whatever the origins of the law about the sabbatical agricultural year (see above p. 122) its rationale seems to have become that there should be a limit to the exploitation of the natural resource of the land. This may well have been far more meaningful to a people whose closeness to the land (unlike that of most Westerners in today's world) gave them a great respect for its contribution to their survival. Furthermore, later additions to the law of the sabbatical

---

[102] The alternatives are discussed by Horst, 'Brachjahr', pp. 87–8, who favours the view that the entire loan was written off.

[103] Dietrich, '. . . den Armen', p. 188, note 16.

year in Exodus 23.11 linked its observance to providing for the poor and needy, who were deemed to have a prior claim on what the land produced in the seventh year.

There is also another factor, that of interest charged on the loans. There is, in fact, no mention of interest in Deuteronomy 15.1–11, but the commentators assume that it was involved. One view of the nature of the year of release, as has already been mentioned, is that it involved a moratorium on the charging of interest rather than the liquidation of the entire loan.[104] Driver, summarizing this view, notes an important analogy:

> the interest, or annual produce of money, corresponds to the harvest, the annual produce of the land: money, like land, was to be unproductive every seventh year.[105]

The view taken here is that this analogy helps to explain why there was a year of release, without specifying its exact nature. There was a perceived correspondence between specifying that land was to be fallowed every seventh year and that loans (which produced interest) should be unproductive every seventh year. However, the tradition that the poor should benefit from the sabbatical agricultural year was applied to the year of release by decreeing that the loan should be extinguished entirely. If all that was to be remitted was the interest on a loan, it is hard to see why the text needed to warn potential lenders not to be reluctant to lend when the year of release was close. The reluctance would be much more understandable if the lender stood to lose the whole loan rather than one year's interest. If, as seems likely, those scholars are correct who draw an analogy between the land producing food and loans producing wealth in the form of interest, the Old Testament went in the opposite direction compared with Greek thought, as represented by Aristotle. In *The Nichomachean Ethics* Aristotle argued that money did not exist 'by nature' and that therefore it should not grow or increase by interest being charged on it.[106] This view profoundly affected Christian attitudes to the charging of interest, until it was ridiculed by Calvin in the sixteenth century.[107]

It remains to comment on the role assigned to Yhwh in Deuteronomy 15.9. He is the guarantor of the year of release (which is called 'Yhwh's

---

[104] See the discussion in Driver, *Deuteronomy*, pp. 179–80.

[105] Driver, *Deuteronomy*, p. 180.

[106] Aristotle, *The Nichomachean Ethics* (ed. H. Rackham; Loeb Classical Library), London/ Cambridge, Mass.: Heinemann/Harvard University Press, 1956, 5.9–11 (pp. 283–5).

[107] J. W. Rogerson, *According to the Scriptures? The Challenge of Using the Bible in Social, Moral and Political Questions*, London: Equinox, 2007, pp. 96–7. K.-H. Brodbeck, *Die Herrschaft des Geldes: Geschichte und Systematik*, Darmstadt: Wissenschaftliche Buchgesellschaft, 2009, pp. 934–46.

release' in verse 2), and will regard it as a sin if the nearness of the year of release deters anyone from helping their fellow Israelites. This role can be understood in at least two ways. It can be seen as a form of intimidation, with the intention that potential lenders will be sufficiently worried about the misfortunes that might follow their reluctance to act, that they will make loans, however unwillingly. Not necessarily contradicting this view is the approach that sees behind the introduction of Yhwh a desire to create a society that reflects divine graciousness, and which is not subject merely to the amoral processes of the 'logic' of the market. This desire becomes increasingly strongly expressed, in what follows in Deuteronomy 15 and what comes in Leviticus 25.

Deuteronomy 15.12–18 reads as follows:

> If your Hebrew brother (or Hebrew sister) sells himself[108] to you he shall serve you for six years, and in the seventh you must let him go free from you. And when you let him go free you must not send him away empty-handed. You must lavish upon him[109] provisions from your flock, your threshing-floor and your winepress. Because Yhwh your God has blessed you, you must be generous to him. You must remember that you were a slave in the land of Egypt and Yhwh your God set you free. Therefore I am giving you this commandment today. If he says to you, 'I do not wish to leave you', because he loves you and your household, and fares well with you, you shall take an awl and pierce it through his ear to the door, and he will be your slave for life. You shall do likewise to your slave-woman. You must not begrudge setting him free. His service for six years has been worth twice that of a hired servant; and Yhwh your God will bless you in all your endeavours.

That this law is dependent upon, and expands and modifies, Exodus 21.2–11, needs no justification. The important differences are that in Exodus 21 no rights are granted to women slaves, unless they marry into their master's family. Although the references to women in Deuteronomy 15.12 and 17 are clearly later additions, they are nonetheless indications that the underlying thought is moving in a progressively humanitarian direction. The second difference is that the released slave is to be equipped with the wherewithal to resume his (or her) place in the community. Another difference is that in Exodus 21 the slave is bought, whereas in Deuteronomy 15 he sells himself. This difference is further emphasized by him being called a brother. One is reminded of the story of the young Scottish lad who used to carry his lame younger brother to school each

---

[108] Taking the Niph'al form of the verb as reflexive; with NEB and against RSV and NRSV text, which have the passive.
[109] Literally, 'bejewel him'.

day. When someone remarked what a heavy burden he had to carry, he replied that it wasn't a burden, it was his brother. Finally, the act in which a slave, who does not wish to be released, gives up his freedom, is a publicly witnessed, possibly sacral act in Exodus 21.6, but privately carried out in Deuteronomy 15.17.

The striking thing about Deuteronomy 15.12–18 is that its genre is preaching, rather than law.[110] It does not specify how many sheep or how much grain or oil must be given to the departing former slave, it appeals to the generosity of the master, together with a reminder that YHWH set him (and by implication, his people) free from slavery in Egypt. There is no suggestion that slavery is wrong. There is an implied acceptance that it is a necessary mechanism in a society subject to market forces, and that it has the function of helping people who, for various reasons, have become victims of 'market forces' to get help and support. The right of the master to have control of the freedom of such unfortunates, albeit for six years, is not disputed. However, what is also clear from the passage is that the disruption of communication that occurs when 'brothers' become master and slave, cannot be tolerated indefinitely. There is an obligation upon a master not only to set his brother free, but to ensure that he (and she!) is once more in a position to be equal in the various communicative systems that constitute a society. All this derives not merely from humanitarian or national solidarity, but from divine graciousness as expressed in the cultural memory of the redemption from slavery in Egypt.

The thrust, or trajectory, that can be discerned when Exodus 21 and Deuteronomy 15 are compared, that is, a trajectory towards a society whose 'symbolically generalized media of communication' are increasingly expressive of divine graciousness and therefore of greater humanity, reaches its high point in Leviticus 25. If, in Deuteronomy 15, the institution of slavery has been humanized as far as possible, in Leviticus 25.35–43 it is virtually abolished. The passage reads thus:

> If your brother falls into poverty and lacks the power to sustain himself, you must support him and let him live with you.[111] Do not take any interest from him in any form[112] but fear your God, and let your brother live with you. You shall not deduct interest when making him a loan and you shall not add a charge when supplying food or credit. I am YHWH your God who brought you from the land of Egypt, to give you the land of Canaan and to be your God.

---

[110] Von Rad, *Das fünfte Buch*, p. 76.
[111] Omitting gēr vᵉtōšāv, cf. BHK.
[112] Literally 'deduction [in advance from the sum loaned]' or 'increase [above what is loaned]'.

> If your brother falls into poverty and sells himself to you, you shall not make him serve you as though he were a slave. You must treat him as a hired worker or a temporary resident. He shall work for you until the Jubilee year, and then he will leave your service together with his children, and return to his family and to his ancestral land. For they are my servants whom I brought from the land of Egypt. They shall not be sold as slaves are sold. You shall not rule him harshly, but you shall fear your God.

Although this passage (which is treated by many commentators as two units: Leviticus 25.35–38 and 39–46 – the above translation stops at verse 43) occurs in the context of the Jubilee year, and contains a reference to the Jubilee in verses 40–41, the view taken here is that it should be considered as independent from the Jubilee regulations and that verses 40–41 are editorial additions arising from the inclusion of the passage in its present context. As commentators have observed, the injunction in verse 41, that the poor brother must be set free in the Jubilee year, creates two problems. The first is that the whole point of the passage is that the poor brother should not lose his freedom in the first place, and therefore does not need to regain it! Second, if his freedom has been lost, the Jubilee law puts him in a worse position compared with what is enjoined in Exodus 21.2 and Deuteronomy 15.12. There, the period of slavery is six years; here, it can be anything up to 49 years![113] There is a further difficulty that, on being freed, the poor brother can return to his family (*mišpāchāh*) and ancestral lands, whereas his family should have supported him in the first place, according to Leviticus 25.25.

If verses 40b–41 are disregarded, a clear picture of the proposals emerges. The 'brother' who has fallen into poverty is not necessarily a member of the family of the one who is to help him. He is a fellow-member of the people created by God by means of the redemption from slavery in Egypt, and it is therefore not right that circumstances should force him into slavery. The one who has the means to help must adopt him into his family and treat him no worse than he would a *tōšāv*, that is someone alienated from his own kin group and residing temporarily with him. This is a call for the creation of new kinds of families, families based not upon kinship, but upon common membership of the people created by God. This in turn implies a new vision of what it means, practically and socially, to be God's people. Nothing is said about how long this arrangement is to last, and this could well be the reason why the editor(s) of Leviticus 25 added the reference to the Jubilee in verses 40b–41. But presumably, there is no need for

---

[113] For a recent discussion of the whole passage see E. Gerstenberger, *Das dritte Buch Mose: Leviticus* (ATD 6), Göttingen: Vandenhoeck & Ruprecht, 1993, pp. 353–7.

time limits under the arrangements that are proposed. The poor brother does not lose his freedom but finds himself embodied in a new and supportive social network, from which he can gain his independence at any time. The power of the 'market' to turn misfortune into degradation has been completely neutralized.

If Leviticus 25 envisages the neutralization of slavery, it also envisages the neutralization of the ability of powerful landowners permanently to acquire the property of landholders who have fallen on hard times. The relevant passage is Leviticus 25.13–17:

> In this year of Jubilee each one of you shall return to his property. If you sell to your fellow countryman or buy from your fellow countryman, neither of you shall drive a hard bargain. What you pay your fellow countryman will depend on how many years have passed since the Jubilee; what you get in return will be the produce for the remaining years. If there are many the price will be higher; if fewer the price will be lower, because he is selling you the produce for a period of years. No one shall drive a hard bargain against his fellow countryman, you shall stand in awe of your God. I am YHWH your God.

What is envisaged here is that land can never be purchased. The 'buyer' in such cases is purchasing the right to enjoy what the land produces, from the time of the agreement to the end of the 49- or 50-year period. What he pays for this privilege depends upon the number of years between the time of the agreement and the arrival of the Jubilee year. If there are many years to run, a higher price is paid than if there are fewer years. This proposal has a logic about it which is immediately obvious, and transparently fair. Yet it is a logic which goes against what usually happens in the 'market'. In the 'market' the debtor is the weaker party, the creditor is the stronger one. Depending on how desperate the debtor is, the creditor can impose terms that are increasingly to his (the creditor's) advantage. This is not strictly immoral. Some would describe it as the 'law' of 'supply and demand', the kind of 'law' that demanded such high prices for trivia in the siege of Samaria in 2 Kings 6.24—7.20 (see above, p. 120). In Leviticus 25.13–17, the injunction that a hard bargain should not be driven when land is being 'bought' and 'sold' is backed up with a practical measure which in effect is a form of price control based upon a principle that is transparently fair. The 'buyer' must pay the estimated cost of the number of harvests that he will enjoy until the Jubilee year comes.

In Leviticus 25.25–28 there is another proposal relating to the sale of land. In some ways it overlaps with 25.13–17, yet it seems to come from a different stream of tradition. It is noteworthy that whereas Leviticus

25.13–17 consistently uses the term *ʿāmît* – fellow countryman – verses 25–28 use the terms *ʾāh* – brother – and *ʾîš* – man. The passage reads as follows:

> If your brother falls into poverty and sells some of his property, his kinsman who is close to him must come and redeem what his brother has sold. If a man has no such close relative, and later finds himself in a position to redeem what he sold, he must reckon how many years have passed since the sale, and pay the remainder to the man to whom he sold the land, and he can take possession of his property. If he is not in a position to pay what is outstanding, the property will remain in the possession of the buyer until the Jubilee. In the Jubilee it will be released and he can regain its possession.

The first question that naturally arises is why the earlier passage (Leviticus 25.13–17) makes no mention of the duty of the next of kin to assist someone who needs to sell his land or part if it. Second, verse 27, which speaks of reckoning how many years have passed since the sale of the land in order to work out now many years remain, is an unnecessary provision if the Jubilee periods were fixed and observed country-wide. Verse 27 only seems to make sense if the periods of 50 years limiting the time that land could be held by a purchaser were specific to each transaction, and not observed country-wide. There is, of course, an example of land being bought by a next of kin in Jeremiah 32.6–15, when Jeremiah purchases a field in Anathoth from his cousin, Hanamel. The beginning of the chapter, Jeremiah 32.1, gives a date, namely 588 BCE. Assuming that the date applies to the narrative of the sale, and that the biographical nature of the story assures its genuineness in the life of Jeremiah, it could be concluded that the practice proposed in Leviticus 25.25 dated at least from the early sixth century. However, doubts about the historical veracity of the incident have been raised[114] and in any case, it would be perilous to assume that there was standardized legal practice with regard to the sale of property throughout Israel and Judah and that it was subject to unilinear development. The temptation to see Leviticus 25.13–17 and 25–28 as respectively earlier or later forms or proposals of practice, must be resisted. The substantive point is that both passages have the practical aim of ensuring that property is never sold. The 'purchaser' buys only the right to enjoy its produce for a fixed period which is determined by the date of the 'sale' in relation to the advent of a or the Jubilee.

Before this is commented on further, it has to be said in fairness that if Leviticus 25 is envisaging a blueprint for a new society, it is not proposing a blueprint for a new world. Leviticus 25.44–46 allows the Israelites to buy

---

[114] See the discussion in McKane, *Jeremiah*, p. 841.

slaves from neighbouring countries or from the families of (presumably) non-Israelites who are settled in the land. There are no provisions about freeing them, and they can be passed from father to son. There are also other proposals that repeat in various ways the passages already considered above, and because they add nothing substantially new to the points that have been made, they will be passed over here.

From where did the idea of the Jubilee come? Crüsemann links it to the end of the exile and the period of the restoration while, in the same vein, Dietrich sees it as an answer to the question to whom the land belonged when exiles returning to Palestine, after their families had spent 50 years in Babylon, found their properties occupied by others (see above, p. 108).[115] The view taken here agrees with Albertz, that the Jubilee was an attempt to deal with the dispossessions of small landowners and the enslavement of free men and women that occurred in post-exilic Judah, as indicated in Nehemiah 5.1–12.[116]

> There was a great outcry from the people and their wives against their fellow Jews. Some said, 'We are pledging[117] our sons and daughters so that we can get grain in order to live.' Others said, 'We are mortgaging our lands, our vineyards and our houses in order to get grain to live.' Yet others were saying, 'We are borrowing money to pay the king's tax.[118] There is no difference between us and our fellow Jews, nor between our children and theirs, yet we are compelling our sons and daughters to become slaves, and some of our daughters have been taken by force. We are powerless to do anything, for our lands and vineyards belong to the wealthy.'[119] I was extremely angry when I heard their outcry and their story. I was beside myself and I took issue with the nobles and those in charge, accusing them of laying a heavy burden[120] upon their fellow Jews. I convened a general meeting and said to them, 'We have bought back our fellow Jews who had been sold to foreigners, as many as we were able, whereas you have sold your fellow Jews, so that they can be bought back by us!' They were speechless, and would say nothing. I said, 'What you are doing is wrong. You should live in awe of our God, and be free from the disdain of our foreign enemies. Furthermore, I, my family and my officials are lending them money and grain. Let us leave off charging this interest. Return to them this very day their lands, vineyards, olive orchards and houses and the

---

[115] Crüsemann, *Die Torah*, pp. 330–1; Dietrich, 'Wem das Land gehört', p. 281.

[116] R. Albertz, 'Jobeljahr' in *NBL*, vol. 2, pp. 346–7. See also K.-D. Schunk, *Nehemiah* (BKAT 23), Neukirchen-Vluyn: Neukirchener Verlag, 2001, p. 152.

[117] Reading ʿōrᵉvîm, cf. BHK.

[118] Omitting sᵉdōtēnū ūkerāmēnū, cf. BHK.

[119] Reading lahōrîm, cf. BHK.

[120] Reading massāʾ.

exaction[121] of money, grain, new wine and oil which you have been charging them.' They replied, 'We will return them, and seek nothing from them in return. We will do what you say.' So I called the priests, and made them take an oath that they would do what they had promised.

What is striking about this passage is the complete absence in it of any recognition of any of the provisions that have been discussed so far in this chapter with regard to the amelioration of slavery, the remitting of debts or the 'sale' of property. Of course, this does not mean that such provisions were unknown in the time of Nehemiah (in the second part of the fifth century BCE). It could be that they were being blatantly and deliberately ignored. Perhaps, also, we should not press the fact that Nehemiah, in condemning the abuses, did not appeal to any Old Testament legislation which may have been contravened. Yet it is hard to escape the conclusion that it was precisely to counteract such abuses that some, at any rate, of the material in Leviticus 25 was composed. In other words, the Jubilee proposals were produced by the kind of situation in post-exilic Judah that is described in Nehemiah 5. A possible pointer in this direction is verse 10. If it seems that Nehemiah and his entourage had been charging interest on what they had been lending, then they were either violating what is proposed in Leviticus 25.36–37, that no interest should be exacted from one's fellow countrymen (see above pp. 126–7), or this proposal had not yet been formulated. The latter conclusion seems to be the more likely.

It is time to come to a conclusion and to outline a direction of thought that goes in the totally opposite direction compared with that of older, classical, Old Testament scholarship. This 'classical' view was expressed by Alt in the following words:

Alle Wahrscheinlichkeit spricht dafür, daß diese kleinbäuerliche Gesellschafts- und Wirtschaftsordnung bis in die Frühzeit des Lebens der israelitischen Stämme auf dem Boden des Kulturlandes von Kanaan zurückgeht und insofern eine entscheidende Grundlage für die ganze weitere Entwicklung bildet.[122]

By the smallholding social and economic order, Alt meant a view of things in which YHWH was the ultimate owner of the land, and in which land was held in trust by the extended family, which had a duty to retain it for this kin group by assisting any individual or individual family which found

---

[121] Reading ūmaššʾat.

[122] Alt, 'Der Anteil', p. 349. 'In all probability this smallholding social and economic order goes back to the early times of the existence of the Israelite tribes in the cultivated land of Canaan and thus provided the decisive basis for the whole subsequent development' (my translation).

itself in difficulty. On this view, actions such as those condemned in Micah 2.1–11 or Isaiah 5.8–10 were breaches of the social and religious order that had been established when the Israelite tribes achieved their conscious political and religious unity after their settlement in Canaan. This approach was complemented, whether consciously or not, by the theory that Israel had emerged in Canaan as an egalitarian segmentary society, whose ideology had been betrayed by the subsequent development of monarchy and all that flowed from it.[123] The view taken here is that the development went in entirely the opposite direction, that is, from the importance of private property to the gradual realization that this was a major cause of social injustice, and thus to attempts to argue that all property belonged to YHWH, and that any attempt to buy or sell it must be strictly regulated from a humanitarian perspective.

It was argued that the 'states' of Israel and Judah emerged from segmentary states, that is, from social arrangements in which powerful individuals whose power was based upon their ownership of land and other resources, including military resources, entered into unstable and shifting alliances until one was able to consolidate power over the others, and establish a dynasty. The book of Judges contains cultural memories of such individuals, as do the traditions surrounding Saul and David. With the consolidation of what we call Judah and Israel the process of shifting alliances became more stable, although the traditions of revolts against David's rule (2 Samuel 13—20), and of changes of dynasty in the northern kingdom, Israel, show that complete stability was not achieved. During the history of these small monarchies, there was a gradual extension of influence from the administrative centres of power to the small villages that practised subsistence agriculture, the whole process being exacerbated by wars between Judah and Israel, wars between Israel and Syria, and the periodic invasions of the land by the neighbouring empires of Egypt, Assyria and Babylon. In this situation, the seizure of land complained of by Micah and Isaiah, for example, and dealt with by Elijah and Elisha, were not breaches of a political and religious order reaching back to the time of Israel's origins in Canaan. They were partly responses to military threats (as in Micah 2.1–12; see above p. 98) and partly the result of the fact that it belongs to the nature of property and power, that those who possess them desire to have more, and are not hindered by moral scruples in

[123] See N. K. Gottwald, *The Tribes of Yahweh: A Sociology of the Religion of Liberated Israel 1250 to 1050 B.C.E.*, New York: Orbis, 1979; F. Crüsemann, *Der Widerstand gegen des Königtum: Die antiköniglichen Texte des Alten Testaments und der Kampf um den frühen israelitischen Stadt* (WMANT 49), Neukirchen-Vluyn: Neukirchener Verlag, 1978.

attaining their goals. The Old Testament prophets who condemned their actions were motivated not by a desire to uphold sacred law that was long since established. They were inspired by a progressively sharpened sense of moral insight that derived from their religious convictions.

The débacle of the fall of Jerusalem in 587 BCE delivered a temporary shock to the whole system of private property and land tenure; but it was only a temporary shock. Whatever happened to the property of those who were exiled to Babylon in what was probably the greater deportation, in 597,[124] and whatever happened when returning exiles or their descendants found their land occupied by strangers, Nehemiah indicates that the regime of the possession of private property and the social evils that accrued therefrom had reasserted themselves by the late fifth century, and probably earlier.

The view taken here is that the material collected into Leviticus 25, whether originally associated with the Jubilee or not, represented attempts to curb the kind of social injustice described in Nehemiah 5, and to deal with their underlying cause, namely, the ownership of private property. This was done, as described earlier in this chapter, by proposing in effect the abolition of slavery, and by declaring that land could not be bought, only enjoyed for a limited period. These visions of reform were grounded theologically in the cultural memory of the exodus from Egypt, which supplied the moral justification for what was envisaged. Because God had freed his people from slavery, the notion was abhorrent that Israelites could enslave each other, even if this moral insight did not reach as far as the treatment of non-Israelites (Leviticus 25.42–46, 55). The declaration that the land was ultimately owned by YHWH reinforced the attempt to undermine the idea of private property. A case could also be made for seeing in those parts of the book of Joshua where the land is apportioned to the tribes, another post-exilic attempt to oppose the idea of private properties. These narratives also declare that the land belongs to YHWH, because the Israelites gain it only by the type of conquest that involves obeying God's instructions. The subsequent apportionment emphasizes that the land is a gift, as do the warnings that this gift will be withdrawn if the Israelites turn to other gods (Joshua 23.6–16).

If this is a plausible reconstruction of the development of attitudes to private property in the Old Testament[125] it remains to explain it theologically.

---

[124] See Jeremiah 52.28–30. The passage is discussed fully by McKane, *Jeremiah*, pp. 1381–5.

[125] For similar ideas see Gerstenberger, *Leviticus*, pp. 349–50; Albertz, 'Jobeljahr', p. 346; Dietrich, 'Wem das Land gehört', p. 286 and his observation, 'Gerne hat man diesen Gedanken als den uralten Grundsatz des israelitischen Bodenrechts betrachtet. Das geht nicht an' [This view has been regarded as the ancient basis of Israelite law relating to property. This is not tenable].

In his *The Two Moralities*, A. D. Lindsay contrasted what he called the Morality of Grace with what he called the Morality of my Station and its Duties.[126] The Morality of Grace was, for Lindsay, particularly expressed in the Sermon on the Mount, with its imperatives that flatly contradicted some of the basic principles of laws governing society. But he also argued that the Morality of Grace represented a moral tradition that was constantly ahead of what was accepted in society, a tradition whose insights and proposals broke new ground, albeit new ground that could, and did, later become part of the Morality of my Station and its Duties. The following quotation sums up the essence of Lindsay's thought on this matter:

> Grace is not a thing which can be measured and calculated. There is in it, indeed, a certain extravagance . . . The morality of grace cannot be codified. There is always a touch of the infinite about it . . . The contrast between the two moralities in this matter is almost this . . . In the morality of my station and its duties the station presents us with the duty, and we say 'Yes' or 'No.' 'I will' or 'I will not'. We choose between obeying or disobeying a given command. In the morality of challenge or grace the situation says, 'Here is a mess, a crying evil, a need! What can you do about it?' We are asked not to say 'Yes' or 'No' or 'I will' or 'I will not', but to be inventive, to create, to discover something new. The difference between ordinary people and saints is not that saints fulfil the plain duties which ordinary men neglect: the things saints do have not usually occurred to ordinary people at all.[127]

In further delineating the difference between the two moralities, Lindsay argued that 'the morality of challenge or grace is normally, though not invariably, connected with religion'. He went on:

> Its demands are not thought of as our demands, nor as the demands of society . . . its demands and its challenge are the challenge of God.[128]

The view taken in the present work is that Lindsay's account of the morality of challenge or of grace can be applied to that material in the Old Testament that challenged the acquisitiveness of those who had land and power, and who used unscrupulous means to enlarge what they had. The proposals found in Deuteronomy 15 and Leviticus 25 were likewise attempts to formulate visions derived from a morality of grace that was grounded in a particular understanding of the cultural memory of the exodus. While this particular understanding of the exodus had not risen

---

[126] A. D. Lindsay, *The Two Moralities: Our Duty to God and to Society*, London. Eyre & Spottiswoode, 1940.

[127] Lindsay, *Two Moralities*, pp. 48–9.

[128] Lindsay, *Two Moralities*, pp. 51–2.

above certain xenophobic elements in the cultural memory, so that the generosity accorded to fellow Israelites was not extended to foreigners, it nonetheless saw in the memory of the freeing of a slave people that which made inconceivable any forms of slavery or exploitation within the redeemed community. What Lindsay wrote about saints applies equally to the prophets and writers of the Old Testament who thought the unthinkable and proposed the impractical with regard to the communicative system that we call the economy.

There was, in a sense, a 'progressive revelation' in the matter of property, a movement from its acceptance as a basic fact of life and the economy, to seeing it as one of the roots of distorted communication, so that ways needed to be found of neutralizing its disruptive effects and of creating communicative harmony. It is in this respect that this Old Testament material has something to say to today's world.

'Progressive revelation' or 'progressive education' as it was also called, was one of the concepts used by nineteenth- and twentieth-century scholarship to rescue the Old Testament from condemnation as the annals of a barbaric Semitic tribe.[129] The moral crudities of Joshua's slaughter of the Canaanites or Abraham's readiness to sacrifice his son Isaac were seen as remnants of a primitive stage in ancient Israel's understanding of God and the nature of humanity, a primitive stage from which God had delivered the Israelites as he led them to higher conceptions of the divine and the human. This school of thought concentrated upon the moral aspects of life, something where they believed they had a moral superiority over the Old Testament writers and could (patronizingly) applaud a development from the lower to the higher. They would have done better to consider the social and economic aspects of the Old Testament, for here, there is no moral superiority from a modern perspective.

At the time of writing this chapter the Western world is in the grip of a financial crisis caused by private property. The peer pressure for people to own their own homes has generated a growth in house prices out of all proportion to the growth in average incomes. In Britain and the United States people have been encouraged to take out mortgages that they could not afford, which debts have then been represented to other financial institutions as gold-plated investments. The bubble has burst, house prices have begun to fall, and not a few people find themselves in the position of having a mortgage they cannot afford for a house whose value is declining.

---

[129] See J. W. Rogerson, 'Progressive Revelation: Its History and its Value as a Key to Old Testament Interpretation' (the A. S. Peake Memorial Lecture 1981), *Epworth Review* 9 (1982), pp. 73–86.

Repossessions are mounting in number – the modern equivalent of Israelites being ordered off their own land when they could not repay their debts. So far, the only solution that has been proposed is that governments and central banks should shore up the corrupt system that has caused the problem, by massive injections of funds.

The Old Testament challenges us to ask whether more practical steps need to be taken – whether the whole system of mortgages and indebtedness is not an insipid modern form of slavery, a system that enables the rich and powerful to exploit the weak and vulnerable. Whether or not the material in Leviticus 25 was ever put into effect in Judah, it retains its power to challenge current economic practice in the so-called developed world.

It is unlikely that the content of this chapter will come to the attention of anyone who has the power to try to alter the economic systems that shape today's world, and even less likely that they would feel moved to do anything if they did happen to read it. Perhaps this situation is no different from that faced by those who put together the materials from the Old Testament that have been discussed in this chapter. Did they have any realistic hopes that their visions, of a humane and compassionate nation, would have any effects? We do not know. Did they think that they were doing anything more than putting a message in a bottle? Again, we do not know. What is remarkable, however, is the fact that their words have somehow survived to become a part of our world. They have become a communicative factor in our world, a world of breakdowns in the systems that ought to bind us together, but which separate and divide us. They are one of the many reasons why we cannot ignore what the Old Testament has to say to us.

5

Disrupted communication: divine–human relationships

The Old Testament devotes a great deal of space to failed communication between humanity and God. In the psalter, by far the largest class of psalms according to modern classifications is laments. Roughly 34 are reckoned to be individual laments and 11 to be laments of the nation – taken together, nearly one-third of the whole psalter.[1] They give expression to complaints about the oppression of the nation by foreign enemies, or to the plight of individuals who are suffering from sickness or from persecution at the hand of fellow Israelites. In the books of Exodus and Numbers there are frequent complaints, both by Moses and the Israelites, about the state of things in the wilderness and God's apparent desire to destroy the people either through negligence or direct hostile action. Job, in the book of Job, complains that he cannot get a hearing before God. His plight is not simply that he believes himself to be suffering far in excess of any punishment he might reasonably deserve. His plight is that God is avoiding him and seems indifferent to Job's desire to lay his complaint before God. The book of Lamentations contains heart-rending pleas to God for him to reverse the conditions in which the people find themselves. These pleas are backed by vivid descriptions of the extremities of human degradation to which war and its aftermath have brought the lamenting community. Even books such as Nehemiah (Nehemiah 9.32–37) and Daniel (Daniel 9.4–19) contain moving laments addressed to God. A series of poems in Jeremiah, often called the Confessions of Jeremiah, contain sentiments that go so far as to accuse God of deceiving Jeremiah by calling him to be a messenger of God's word (Jeremiah 20.7–18).

But there is another side to this, less prominent in the Old Testament, but important nonetheless, namely, passages in which God complains about the inability or unwillingness of the people to listen to him. A standard formula is found in Jeremiah 35.15:

---

[1] A. A. Anderson, *Psalms* (NCB), London: Oliphants, 1972, vol. 1, pp. 38–9.

I sent to you all my servants the prophets[2] saying, 'return each of you from his evil way and make good your deeds, and do not go after other gods to serve them . . .' but you did not incline your ear and did not listen to me.

But under this heading these are not only complaints from the side of God about the obtuseness of his people. There are passages that express a desire to lavish love abundantly upon them. We are entitled to see in such passages a divine frustration, as the extended love is either not comprehended, or is spurned. The following words in Hosea 14.4–7 [Hebrew 14.5–8], which express God's love and blessing –

> I will heal their apostasy,
> I will love them unreservedly,
> for my anger has turned away from them.
> I will become like dew to Israel,
> and he will blossom like the lily,
> strike roots like the forest of Lebanon.
> His shoots will spread out
> so that his beauty is like an olive,
> his scent like frankincense.[3]
> They shall dwell again in my shadow.[4]
> They shall grow grain
> and produce abundant vines,[5]
> whose fame will be like the wine of Lebanon.

– are followed by a verse that expresses an element of frustration:

> Why does Ephraim still concern himself with idols?[6]
> I am the one who answers and assures him.[7]
> I am like a luxuriant pine-tree.
> Your fruit comes from me!

The aim of this chapter is to examine passages from the Old Testament that resonate with modern experiences of disrupted communication with God to see whether they enable the Old Testament to say anything to our situation. In his recent biography of the late Cardinal Basil Hume, Anthony Howard relates that during his final illness, the Cardinal confided to a younger colleague that he could no longer read or pray, and that he

---

[2] Omitting haškēm vᵉšālōah with LXX and Vulgate, cf. BHK.

[3] Reading lᵉvōnāh, cf. BHS.

[4] Reading bᵉṣillî.

[5] Reading vᵉyafrîhū, cf. BHS.

[6] Reading lō with LXX, cf. BHS.

[7] Reading vaʾᵃšōrennū, cf. H. W. Wolff, *Hosea*, 2nd edn (BKAT 14.1), Neukirchen-Vluyn: Neukirchener Verlag, 1963, p. 302.

had to content himself with holding a crucifix and reflecting on Christ's sufferings.[8] He also spoke of a curtain having come down between him and God. This sounds not unlike complaints in the psalms in which a combination of illness and weakness seems to hinder the psalmist from a sense of the presence of God.

Another factor that causes disruption in the communication between God and humans is the intellectual difficulty of the apparent ascendancy of wickedness in the world and the apparent ultimate futility of goodness. The matter has been touched upon already in this book (see p. 90). This difficulty ceases to be simply the intellectual difficulty of individuals, and becomes a matter of survival, in those psalms which speak of the taunts directed by the wicked and cynical members of the community against those who try to maintain their honesty and integrity. In the book of Job, the intellectual difficulty is exacerbated by the attempts of Job's friends to convince him that he has completely misunderstood the nature of his situation. A further aspect of this difficulty is explained in texts such as Lamentations. Here, the full horror of the results of inhumane behaviour is laid bare, especially that driven by war, and the question is raised as to how, if at all, faith in God can provide any hope.

The first text to be considered is Psalm 88, the saddest and bleakest psalm in the whole psalter. It reads as follows:

> Yʜwʜ my God,
> my plea by day,[9]
> and my cry by night come before you;
> let my prayer come into your presence;
> bend your ear to my fervent plea.
> For my soul has had its full share of troubles
> and my life has come close to death.
> I am thought to belong with those who go down to the pit;
> I have become a man who can no longer be helped.
> People include[10] me with the dead,
> like the slain who lie in the grave,
> whom you remember no longer
> and who are cut off from your hand.
> You have put me in the lowest pit;
> in dark places and in watery depths.

---

[8] A. Howard, *Basil Hume: The Monk Cardinal*, London: Headline, 2005, p. 310.

[9] Reading ᵓᵉlōhai šivʿātî yōmām, cf. BHK.

[10] Reading nehšavtî with Wellhausen. See Gunkel, *Die Psalmen*, Göttingen: Vandenhoeck & Ruprecht, 1929, p. 382.

Your anger lies heavily upon me
and all your breakers have buffeted me.
You have removed my friends far from me,
and made me an abomination in their sight.
I am imprisoned and cannot get free.
My eyesight fails because of my troubles.
I have called to you, YHWH, day by day;
I have stretched out my hands to you.
Do you work miracles for the dead?
Do the shades rise again and praise you?
Is your unfailing love spoken of in the grave,
or your faithfulness in the place of destruction?
Are your miracles made known in the darkness,
or your saving acts in the land where all is forgotten?
As for me, I will cry to you, YHWH,
and my prayer will come before you in the morning.
Why, YHWH, do you spurn me?
Why do you hide your face from me?
I have been plagued with troubles and wearied from my youth.
I have borne your terrors and am at my wits' end.
Your fierce anger has come upon me,
your terrors have destroyed me;
they have encircled me like a flood all day long;
they have surrounded me on every side.
You have removed far from me those I love;[11]
Instead of companions I have only darkness.

It is natural that we should wonder about the origins of this psalm – who composed it and in what circumstances. Jewish interpretation, as represented by the Targum and the mediaeval commentators Rashi and Qimhi, related it to Israel during the Babylonian captivity.[12] However, most modern commentators see it as the response of an individual to intense suffering, most likely some kind of illness. A possible candidate for this condition has been sought in King Uzziah, who, according to 2 Chronicles 26.20–21, was smitten with leprosy and confined to a separate house for the remainder of his life.[13] But recent work on the psalms has emphasized that they have been decontextualized, that is, if they ever did contain material

---

[11] Omitting vārēʿai with LXX, cf. BHK.

[12] A. Cohen, *The Psalms*, Hindhead: Soncino Press, 1945, p. 285. See also Qimhi, in R. David Qimhi, *Haperush Hashalem al Tehillim*, Jerusalem: Mossad Harav Kook, 1971, pp. 193–4.

[13] A thorough survey of the history of interpretation of the psalm is given in L. Jacquet, *Les Psaumes et le coeur de l'homme: Étude textuelle, littéraire et doctrinale*, n.p.: Duculot, 1977, vol. 2, pp. 670–4.

that would make the identification of their circumstances of composition reasonably certain, these traces have been removed in order to impart to the psalms a certain timelessness that has enabled them to be used by many different people in later generations and circumstances.[14] This point is of particular importance for Psalm 88. Whoever may have composed it, and for whatever reason, the compilers of the psalter included it because they felt that it would meet the needs of those for whom communication with God seemed to have broken down completely. To put it another way, Psalm 88 is not meant to be a one-off composition, but something representative within the Old Testament experience of God. It has to be recognized, however, that just as people with different needs can feel that a psalm such as 88 can communicate something to them, so it can be read and interpreted in different ways. In what follows, Psalm 88 will be read from a communicative point of view. The main argument will be that only the closest type of relationship between a person and God can produce such a sad and apparently negative psalm, or, to put it in communicative terms, the more intimate communication is within a relationship, the more catastrophic its breakdown will seem.

This approach will be justified on the basis of verses 10–12:

> Do you work miracles for the dead?
> Do the shades rise again and praise you?
> Is your unfailing love spoken of in the grave,
> or your faithfulness in the place of destruction?
> Are your miracles made known in the darkness,
> or your saving acts in the land
> where all is forgotten?

The assumption here is that there is a limit to God's power, and that this power is exercised only within the sphere of the living. It does not extend into the realm of death, to Sheol, where human existence is a mere shadow of what it was previously in life (cf. Job 3.16–19). This, of course, is not the only view of the matter in the Old Testament. Psalm 139.8 states that the psalmist cannot escape from God's presence even in Sheol. However, let us stay with Psalm 88 and its apparent view that God's writ does not run in the land of the dead. What does this mean in the context of the psalm? A view that has been championed recently by Bernd Janowski is that the psalmist is challenging God to prove that he *is* God. He is pointing out God's limitations to him in order to provoke him into stronger

---

14 See B. S. Childs, *Introduction to the Old Testament as Scripture*, London: SCM Press, 1979, pp. 522–3.

action.[15] The view taken here is that the psalmist is pointing out that God's writ does not run in Sheol because he wants to remind God that once the psalmist enters that realm, he will be cut off from God. What he fears most about dying is not that it will deprive him of life but that it will sever his relationship with God. This is the cause of the sadness that permeates the psalm. Death will involve the loss of a relationship that was fundamental to life, and which shaped it profoundly.

If this view is taken back to the rest of the psalm its pessimism can be seen in a different light. The psalmist attributes everything that had happened to him in life to God, including the bad things.

> I have been plagued with troubles and wearied from my youth.
> You have removed my friends far from me,
> and made me an abomination in their sight.
> You have removed far from me those I love.

The psalmist's problem had not been an absence of God in his life, but too much involvement on the part of God! If he now felt himself to be on the threshold of death with the prospect, as he saw it, of being deprived of God's presence, he felt betrayed by God, rather than relieved at the prospect of escaping from his awareness of God. During his lifetime he had gained strength from the belief that God was directing many aspects of his life, even if there were dark sides as well as good sides to the process. From the perspective of the ending of his life, the thought of facing the future, whatever that might be, without the sense of God's presence, caused the psalmist to pour out his bitter complaint. Just as we may feel bitter when a close friend lets us down at the moment when we most need his or her help, so the psalmist felt let down at the prospect of entering a realm where he would have no sense of the presence and companionship of God.

This line of thinking will now be pursued further by considering whether the almost offensive language addressed to God in psalms of lament was not, in fact, the result of the intimate relationship which the psalmists believed that they enjoyed with God. It is easy to imagine situations in which things can be said to a person only because of the existence of an intimate relationship. A high court judge, for example, may have teenage children who regard him as an out-of-touch and square fuddy-duddy who has no conception of what they understand as 'real life'. They may express their opinions of him in no uncertain terms, urging him to 'get real'. Yet this is a man who is used to being treated with great honour and respect,

---

[15] B. Janowski, *Konfliktgespräche mit Gott: Eine Anthropologie der Psalmen*, Neukirchen-Vluyn: Neukirchener Verlag, 2003, pp. 244–9.

and who has in his court the power to send people to prison for contempt of court, that is, for language and behaviour in court that he regards as insulting. Only his teenage children are in a position to say to him the things they do, and this is because of the relationship between them. Is something analogous going on in Psalm 88 and the psalms of lament? The question needs to be asked because it raises the whole question of how we approach the psalms. In communicative terms, it affects the shared assumptions that determine the character of the communication.

There is all the difference between approaching Psalm 88 as the expression of someone who feels let down by a God who had been trusted throughout a lifetime, and approaching it as the expression of the frustration of someone for whom God was an abstract idea, a factor that became important as a last resort in situations where all else had failed. It is arguable that when we read the psalms of lament today, we do so as people who most of the time get on perfectly well without any idea or sense of God, and who turn to him, if at all, only in times of crisis or anxiety. I suspect that we read them as people who would not particularly notice if any contact at all that we had with God ceased to exist. These may, of course, be mistaken ideas, just as the approach may be mistaken that takes Psalm 88 to be an expression of apprehension at the idea of losing contact with God's presence. However, raising these questions about the psalms of lament addresses questions to our own perceptions or non-perceptions of God, and how we approach sacred texts. If what I have said about Psalm 88 is correct, we may ask how it had become possible for individuals in ancient Israel to enter into such a close relationship with God. We may find that our spiritualities, such as they are, are deeply challenged. We may find that the psalms of lament do not simply resonate with our feelings of despair in the face of an inexplicable world and an inexplicable God, assuming that they do that. We may find that they give us a desire to seek for the kind of relationship with God that is at the base of the complaints about the apparent loss of that relationship.

But why is that relationship apparently lost? Why is the communication disrupted? It may be a function of human frailty, something akin to the curtain that Cardinal Hume felt had come down between him and God in his last illness. It may also have something to do with the nature of God himself. If I can go back to the example of the high court judge and his teenage children, there must be occasions when even they have no possibility of access to him, occasions when he might appear to be frighteningly withdrawn and unapproachable. This is another way of saying that communication is not a one-way process, and that if it is, then one of the parties is merely a tool for the other, and not a genuine partner. In human, not to mention divine–human communication, each partner is an 'other' with its own integrity, or at least this is how it should be, even though it is often not the case. The psalms contain much material about the awesome majesty of God, and this has to be placed alongside those psalms that seem to address God in an almost insolently intimate way. Here are a few examples:

> Ascribe to YHWH you heavenly beings,
> ascribe to YHWH glory and might.
> Ascribe to YHWH the glory of his name.
> Do obeisance to YHWH in festal array.
> The voice of YHWH thunders upon the waters,[16]
> YHWH upon many waters.[17]
> The voice of YHWH is powerful,
> the voice of YHWH is majestic.
> The voice of YHWH breaks the cedars,
> the voice of YHWH shatters the cedars of Lebanon.
> (Psalm 29.1–5)

> YHWH speaks and the earth is filled with awe,[18]
> from the rising of the sun to its setting.
> Out of Zion, perfection of beauty,
> God shines out.
> He comes,[19] he is not silent.
> Devouring fire precedes him,
> a mighty tempest surrounds him.
> He calls to the heavens above,
> and to the earth, to judge his people.
> 'Gather to me my loyal ones,
> who have entered my covenant with sacrifice.'
> Let the heavens declare his justice,
> for he is a God of judgement.[20]
> (Psalm 50.1–6)

Granted these, and other passages that could be cited not only from the psalms but the prophetic books, it can be said that if God is to be himself (whatever that may mean) in communication, and not simply a tool in a one-way communication from the human side, then there will be what, from the human perspective, appears to be a dark side of God, a side that

---

[16] Adding hir'îm, cf. BHK.
[17] Omitting 'ēl hakāvōd, cf. BHK.
[18] Omitting 'ēl 'elōhîm and reading tîrā', cf. BHK.
[19] Omitting 'elōhēnū, cf. BHK.
[20] Reading 'elōhē mišpāt, cf. BHK.

will be puzzling because it does not conform to human preconceptions of what God should be like. It may appear to associate God with evil, in the sense of God apparently allowing natural disasters and the ravages of war to afflict the world in general and ancient Israel in particular. Difficult as this may then become for faith, it may well be a necessary part of the divine–human relationship, without which God will certainly only be a tool in a one-sided relationship.

I now propose to apply this thinking to several key passages in the Old Testament, beginning with Psalm 22.

> My God, my God, why have you forsaken me?
> Why do my words of groaning bring no deliverance?
> I[21] have cried to you by day and got no answer,
> and by night and gained no respite.
> Yet you are the Holy One,[22]
> enthroned on the praises of Israel.
> It was in you that our fathers trusted –
> trusted, and you delivered them.
> It was to you that they cried and you delivered them;
> it was you that they trusted and were not put to shame.
> As for me, I am a worm, not a man,
> a scorn of men and despised by the people.
> All who see me laugh scornfully at me;
> they gape at me and shake their heads:
> 'Let him lean on Yнwн – he will deliver him!
> He will rescue him, for he is his favourite!'
> But it was you who helped me burst from the womb,
> and laid me[23] upon my mother's breasts.
> I have depended on you since my birth,
> and you have been my God from my mother's womb.
> Do not desert me, for trouble is at hand
> and there is no one else to help.
> I am surrounded by many wild oxen;
> strong bulls of Bashan encircle me.
> They gape at me with open mouths
> like lions that tear their prey and roar.
> I am like water poured on the ground,
> and all my bones are out of joint.
> My heart is like wax
> melting into my bowels.

---

[21] Omitting ʾelōhai, cf. BHK.
[22] Reading haqādōš, cf. BHK.
[23] Taking the verb bth from the second stem; cf. *SDCH*, vol. 2, p. 141.

My mouth is dry like a piece of clay pot,
and my tongue is glued fast to my gums.
You are laying me in the dust of death.
For dogs have come at me from all sides,
a band of wrongdoers has surrounded me;
my hands and my feet are like a lion's.[24]
I can count all my bones;
my enemies look up and stare at me.
They parcel out my garments among them
and cast lots for my clothes.
As for you, YHWH, do not be absent;
you, my helper, come to my aid!
Save me from the sword,
my life from the power of the dogs.
Deliver me from the mouth of the lion,
and from the horns of the wild oxen.
You have answered me!
I will tell stories of your renown to my brethren;
I will praise you within the congregation.
Praise YHWH, all you who fear him,
honour him, all you seed of Jacob,
be in awe of him, all you seed of Israel!
For he has not abhorred or despised
the affliction of the poor;
he has not hidden his face from him,
but has heard when he cried to him.
Because of you I can praise you in the great congregation;
I shall perform my vows in the presence of all who fear you.
The poor will eat and be satisfied;
those who seek YHWH will praise him.
May their hearts live for ever.
All the ends of the earth will remember
and will return to YHWH,
and all the families of the nations
will fall down in worship before him.
For kingship belongs to YHWH,
and he rules over the nations.

---

[24] For the rendering 'they pierced my hands and my feet' and various attempts to emend the text, see H.-J. Kraus, *Psalmen*, 2nd edn (BKAT 15.1), Neukirchen-Vluyn: Neukirchener Verlag, 1961, pp. 175–6, 181; Anderson, *Psalms*, vol. 1, p. 190. The rendering given above follows the traditional Hebrew text and assumes that the hands and feet of the complainant had taken on gigantic and grotesque proportions as his body wasted away. This phenomenon can be seen from photographs of the victims of concentration camps and was confirmed to me by a colleague who had been a Japanese prisoner of war.

The fat ones of the world[25] will also fall down in worship before him;
those who go down to the grave will kneel before him
and will not save their own lives.[26]
Posterity will serve him;
stories will be told of the Lord to future generations.
They shall come and recount his saving deeds
to a people not yet born,
that he, Yнwн[27] has done it.

Bearing in mind what was said above about the psalms being decontextualized (p. 140) so that they could apply to many different situations, Psalm 22 seems to bear unmistakable traces of the experience or language of someone suffering from an illness that has brought him seemingly close to death. The phrase

I am like water poured on the ground

can be compared with the statement in 2 Samuel 14.14

For we must all certainly die and be like water that is spilled on the ground and cannot be gathered up again.

The next phrase,

all my bones are out of joint

is reminiscent of the famous vision of the valley of dry bones in Ezekiel 37, where disjointed bones have to be put together before the corpses can be brought to life. The phrase

you are laying me in the dust of death

seems to be an explicit reference to a perception of the imminence of death. The behaviour of the psalmist's enemies implies that they, too, expect the imminent demise of the psalmist. Even while he lives they notionally divide up his garments among themselves. Their motivation is that the psalmist has become emaciated. He is so skeletal that he can see and count his bones. In comparison to his shrunken body his hands and feet seem grotesquely large and claw-like.

There seems to be no sense in the psalm that there is a continuation of life after death in which the presence of God will be a factor. There is a reference to the afterlife, of course, at the end of the psalm, but it is to the

---

[25] Reading ʾak lō, cf. BHK.
[26] Hebrew 'his life'.
[27] Adding Yнwн with LXX and Peshitta, cf. BHK.

gloomy after-world familiar from other parts of the Old Testament, from which even the 'fat ones' of the world will not be able to escape. If the psalmist has a hope, it is in the lives of those who will be born after him, and who will continue to bear witness to the saving deeds of Yʜwʜ.

If this analysis is correct, then Psalm 22 is similar to Psalm 88 in that the immanence of death fills the complainant with dismay, not at the prospect of losing life, but at the prospect of losing touch with God. He speaks in intimate terms of God's involvement in his life from its very beginning. He can use the appellation 'my God', denoting God not as a proposition or idea, but as a factor that was determinant of life. As with Psalm 88, so here in Psalm 22, we who read the psalms as people for whom God is a good deal less than determinant in our lives, are left to wonder at how the psalmist could have known such closeness to God, and how this worked out in practice.

Part of the answer to this may be contained in the second part of the psalm. The abrupt change from complaint to praise has, of course, led some commentators to suggest that two psalms have been put together one after the other.[28] Again, the translation of verse 21 is disputed. The psalter of the Book of Common Prayer rendered it

> thou hast heard me also from among the horns of the unicorns,

while the Authorized Version had the similar

> for thou hast heard me from the horns of the unicorns.

The RSV emends the verb translated 'thou has heard me' to a word meaning 'my afflicted soul'. This tradition is followed, for example, by the NEB, which has 'my poor body'. The view taken here is that the Hebrew 'you have answered me' makes the transition between the complaint of the first half of the psalm and the praise of the second part.[29] What occasioned the transition from the complaint that the psalmist had 'got no answer' at the beginning of the psalm to the assertion 'you have answered me' (assuming that the psalm is speaking of someone's experience, as opposed to the transition being a literary phenomenon) cannot be said. But the difference between the two sections is that in the first, the psalmist is surrounded by people who gloat over him and wish him no good, whereas in the second part he seems to be surrounded by people who share his faith in Yʜwʜ and whom he can call upon confidently to celebrate Yʜwʜ's kingship. The

---

[28] See Anderson, *Psalms*, vol. 1, p. 184.

[29] See Kraus, *Psalmen*, p. 182; Janowski, *Konfliktgespräche*, p. 351; S. R. Driver, *The Parallel Psalter*, Oxford: Clarendon Press, 1898, p. 57.

answer to the question how and from whom the psalmist gained his sense of the presence of God may well be that it came from his belonging to a group of people who shared, sustained and communicated this awareness of God. We may find this difficult to grasp in our individualistic Western world, where much religion is individualistic and intellectualized, and where the building of faith communities can easily be subverted into the creation of sects that demand total control over the lives of their adherents. Psalm 22 may well challenge our so-called spiritualities in this regard.

If what has been argued here is correct, that Psalm 22 is about an awareness of God that drew its strength from some sort of membership of a community of faith, the same may well not be true of what lies behind a fragment from the book of Jeremiah which can be rendered as follows.

> You have deceived me, YHWH, and I was deceived;
> you were stronger than me,
> and so prevailed.
> I have become a laughing-stock the whole time,
> everyone jeers at me.
> Whenever I speak, it is in anguish,
> crying out about violence and destruction.
> The word of YHWH has become to me
> a source of reproach and derision.
> If I say 'I will not think of it,
> I shall no longer speak in his name'
> it becomes like a burning fire within me,
> it is shut up in my very being.
> I become worn out trying to contain it,
> and am not able to do so.
>
> (Jeremiah 20.7–9)

The fragment is part of the so-called Confessions of Jeremiah, passages that include 11.18–23; 12.1–6; 15.10–21; 17.12–18; 18.18–23 and 20.7–13. Their similarity to the psalms of lament has often been commented upon.[30]

To what extent the fragment can be traced back to an historical Jeremiah and can give access to the most intimate experiences of the prophet of that name, is a matter of dispute. The fact that the fragment begins with a first-person address to YHWH but then continues in the third person (i.e. 'the word of YHWH' rather than 'your word') must give pause for thought.

---

[30] For what follows see the analysis of McKane, *Jeremiah*, vol. 1, pp. 467–75; also R. Davidson, *The Courage to Doubt: Exploring an Old Testament Theme*, London: SCM Press, 1983, pp. 136–9.

Whatever view is taken on the matter, there is no doubt that the tradition connects it with the ministry of Jeremiah.[31]

What was the nature of the 'deception' complained of in the opening line, and how does it relate to the conclusion of the fragment, which describes the impossibility on the part of the speaker to be silent? The view taken here follows a line of thought derived from McKane,[32] which sees the 'compulsion' felt by the prophet not in terms of a supernatural process imposed upon the individual from without, but rather in terms of feelings of outrage that arise from within when confronted by situations that are perceived to be corrupt and immoral. In modern terms, and running the danger of trivializing the matter, the example could be quoted of someone working for a government department or multinational organization, who becomes aware that financial accounts are being falsified, or that evidence is being skewed or misrepresented so that policies can be implemented that are fundamentally dishonest and unjust. It is difficult to avoid thinking about how the governments of Britain and the United States misrepresented the evidence for Saddam Hussein possessing weapons of mass destruction, and how the British Prime Minister stated publicly that these weapons could be deployed against his country in 45 minutes. Anyone who had an alternative view based on contrary evidence had a hard time in opposing what the leaders of Britain and the United States had already decided to do, namely, to invade Iraq. There was at least one victim, the expert Dr David Kelly, who took his own life; and one wonders how close he came to something like what is described in Jeremiah 20.7–9 – a feeling of outrage at the deception that was being publicly sponsored, and the personal suffering that he endured when he tried to speak out against the deception.

Is God to be blamed for such situations in which people may find themselves, and in what sense could the complainant in Jeremiah 20.7–9 be said to have been deceived and overpowered by Yнwн? Because the attempt has been made here to explain the fragment in terms drawn from secular experience, it could be fairly argued that God has nothing to do with such matters. But this is not the view of the fragment, and an attempt must be made to spell out its implications. The attempt will almost certainly have to go beyond how the matter could have been understood by the authors of the tradition.

---

[31] For an interesting set of reflections on the relationship between the prophet Jeremiah and the traditions about him see A. R. P. Diamond, 'Jeremiah', in *Eerdmans Commentary*, pp. 534–48.

[32] McKane, *Jeremiah*, p. 474.

The first step will be to see the individual embedded in a subculture whose values and ideals are those of a community of faith for whom God is the upholder of justice and the defender of the weak and oppressed. The values of that subculture may come into conflict with those of other sub-cultures in the wider community, or the subculture may itself, for reasons of expediency, become untrue to its own values. The individual not only feels affronted by those clashes; he sees them not simply as matters of prin-ciple. He sees them as a slight upon the integrity of God. He feels that if the integrity of God is called into question, then he is living in a different world from the one he hoped he was living in – one in which justice would have the last word. The call to be a prophet, therefore, is an inner convic-tion that the integrity of God must be upheld, because the mechanism by which this is done includes the readiness of individuals to put their own interests aside and to speak out in God's name about the evils that they discern. In the case of the fragment from Jeremiah, the outcome is not that people take notice and amend their ways, but that they mock and deride the speaker. The individual is caught between two types of suffering, from neither of which there is any escape. On the one hand is the abuse and mockery of those who do not want to hear what is proclaimed. On the other hand is the impossibility of remaining silent when confronted by manifest injustices. Is God indifferent to this? Does he create communities of faith and impart to members within it the moral insights that will bring them pain and suffering? Christian tradition has been reluctant until com-paratively recent times to envisage the idea of God suffering.[33] Early Jewish tradition was more ready to do this,[34] and in the 1930s A. J. Heschel devel-oped a theory of divine 'pathos'.[35] The view taken here is that any notion of an impassible God whose involvement with humanity causes them, but not him, pain and suffering, is immoral. The fragment in Jeremiah 20.7–9 interpreted theologically brings us close to the being of God, expressing as it does a paradox of existence. In terms of the subject of the present chap-ter it implies that disrupted communication with God is not, in fact, an absence of the divine, but an encounter with God that invites reflection to go beyond human logic and into the heart of the phenomenon of divine suffering, as an attempt to create good out of evil. This account of things may seem irredeemably reductive; but at least it is an attempt to avoid the

---

[33] M. Sarot, 'Apathie' in *RGG*, p. 583.

[34] S. Lauer, 'Leiden II' in *TRE*, vol. 20, p. 676.

[35] A. J. Heschel, *The Prophets*, New York: Harper & Row, 1962, Part II, pp. 5–11. See Part I, pp. 113–14 for a discussion of Jeremiah 20.7–9; and E. K. Kaplan and S. H. Dresner, *Abraham Joshua Heschel: Prophetic Witness*, New Haven: Yale University Press, 1998, pp. 163–71, for the biographical background.

obfuscating language of piety and to bring the matter within reach of our own experiences, for all that we are no doubt far from the intensity of conviction that the fragment expresses.

I now propose to consider aspects of the book of Lamentations, a work of five chapters, four of which (1 to 4) are constructed on the acrostic principle of each verse (with some variations) beginning with successive letters of the Hebrew alphabet. In fact, the title 'Lamentations' is misleading, suggesting, as it does, that the book's chapters are laments, similar to the psalms of lament. While some of the material has some similarity with psalms of lament (e.g. 3.42–66; 5.1–22), the bulk of the book can better be described as commentary or reflection upon the misfortunes of the nation. The verdict upon the genre of the chapters affects theories about why the book was composed and how it was used. Kraus, for example, represents those who think that the poems were composed for liturgical use in the ruined temple in Jerusalem.[36] The view taken here is that this was most unlikely, given the highly elaborate literary devices used in the composition of the poems, and the likelihood that some chapters are dependent, from the literary point of view, on other chapters.

The opinion is currently strongly represented in scholarship that the earliest of the poems is that in chapter 2, while the poem in chapter 1 is dependent on that in chapter 2, and the poem in chapter 4 is dependent upon both chapters 2 and 1.[37] While it could be argued that biblical books should be read and interpreted in the order in which we find them rather than an order based upon scholarly hypotheses, what follows will begin with chapter 2, the opening verses of which read as follows:

> How terribly[38] the Lord[39] has put to shame[40]
> the daughter of Zion.
> He has thrown down from heaven to earth
> the beauty of Israel,
> disregarded his footstool
> on the day of his anger.
> The Lord has engulfed without mercy
> all the dwellings of Jacob,

[36] H.-J. Kraus, *Klagelieder*, pp. 13–14.

[37] Kaiser, *Klagelieder*, pp. 95–111 and *passim*. See most recently C. Diller, *Zwischen JHWH-Tag und neuer Hoffnung: Eine Exegese von Klagelieder 1* (ATSAT 82), St Ottilien: EOS, 2007, pp. 487–92.

[38] The Hebrew ʾēkhāh stands at the beginning of chs 1, 2, and 4 and gives its name to the book in the Hebrew canon.

[39] The divine name varies between ʾadōnāi – Lord – and Yhwh – Lord.

[40] See Kaiser, *Klagelieder*, p. 130, note 1.

broken down in his wrath
the fortresses of the daughter of Judah.
He has abhorred the land[41]
and dishonoured the kingdom and its rulers.
In his fury he has cut off
the whole horn of Israel,
turned back Israel's power[42] from before his enemy,
and burned against Jacob like a flaming fire,
consuming all around.
He strung his bow like an enemy,
like a foe took up position.[43]
His right hand slew all of which one could be proud.
He poured out his anger like fire,
in the tent of the daughter of Zion.
The Lord has become like an enemy;
he has overwhelmed Israel,
overwhelmed all its palaces,
destroyed its fortresses.
He has heaped sorrow upon sorrow
for the daughter of Judah.
He has done violence like an intruder[44] to his booth,
destroyed the place of assembly.
In Zion Yнwн has blotted out all memory
of appointed feast and sabbath,
has spurned in the fury of his anger
both King and priest.
The Lord has despised his altar,
spurned his sanctuary.
He has delivered into the hands of the enemy
the fortifications of Zion's palaces.
There have been enemy shouts in the house of Yнwн
as though it were a day of festival.
Yнwн set out to destroy
the walls of the daughter of Zion.
He extended a measuring line
and did not restrain his hand from destruction.
He made both outer and inner wall lament;
together they languished.

---

[41] Reading higʿil 'erets.
[42] Taking yᵉmînō – 'his hand' – to mean Israel's power.
[43] Transposing yᵉmînō after vᵉyahᵃrōg.
[44] Reading kᵉgannāv, cf. BHK.

Her gates have subsided to the ground,
their bars destroyed.[45]
Her king and rulers are among the nations;
there is no law.
Her prophets also obtain no vision from YHWH.
The elders of the daughters of Zion
sit silent on the ground.
They have put dust on their heads
and sackcloth on their bodies.
The maidens of Jerusalem
have bent their heads to the ground.

These first ten verses of the poem describe the state of things after the destruction of Jerusalem by the Babylonians in 587 BCE. They imply a city whose defensive walls and gates have been torn down, whose rulers have been taken into exile, whose priests, prophets and elders have ceased to function, and whose young women are in mourning. Because of this the poem has been dated in the period 587 to 540 or later, at any rate to the time before the rebuilding of the temple in 515, if it was rebuilt then. Kaiser convincingly draws attention to the highly developed style of the reflection and language, and places the *terminus a quo* of the poem in the last third of the sixth century.[46]

What is remarkable about the poem is that there is no mention of the Babylonians, who were the immediate cause of the catastrophe. There is only one person responsible, and that is YHWH, who has initiated what appears to be a massive breakdown in his relationship with his people. But is it a massive breakdown? It depends on how one conceives of the relationship and its breakdown, of course; but it is only a breakdown if the view is taken that the relationship must always yield positive results and must never have any dark side. The same problem is encountered in modern discussions of theodicy – the attempt to justify God in a world plagued by evil and disaster. This, too, assumes that God must always be the author of good and never of bad, and that the occurrence of the latter constitutes a fatal case against God. In a way, this is flattering to God to the extent that it conceals or implies a desire for a God who transcends our human moral weaknesses. But theodicy is a modern not an ancient problem,[47]

---

[45] Omitting šibbar and taking the subject of ʾibbad as impersonal to express the passive.

[46] Kaiser, *Klagelieder*, p. 136.

[47] See M. Sarot, 'Theodicy and Modernity' in A. Laato and J. C. de Moor (eds), *Theodicy in the World of the Bible*, Leiden: E. J. Brill, 2003, pp. 1–26. The essay on Lamentations in this volume by J. Renkema (pp. 410–28) goes too far in trying to argue that the poems do not consider YHWH to be responsible for the disaster.

stemming from the understandable desire to define God according to our own concepts.

Returning to Lamentations, the striking thing about the opening ten verses of chapter 2 is the constant naming of God as the one responsible for the catastrophe. This point is made even stronger if it is accepted that in verses 1, 2 and 5 the text should be read as Yнwн and not Adonai, in accordance with a number of Hebrew manuscripts.[48] If this is correct, the blame (if that is what it is) is laid fairly and squarely upon Yнwн. There is no mention up to this point of any guilt on the part of Jerusalem and Judah.

In verse 11 the poet allows himself to speak:

> My eyes can see no more because of tears,
> my bowels pain me;
> my liver is as though thrown on the ground,
> because of the shattering of the daughter of my people,
> as children and the newly born faint away
> in the open places of the city.

Similar expressions of despair at what is observed follow, culminating in verse 17:

> Yнwн has done what he planned,
> has completed what he said
> when he commanded long ago.
> He has destroyed without pity,
> made the enemy exult over you,
> exalted the horn of your foes.

For the first time in the poem there is a hint that what Yнwн has done has not been an act of arbitrary malevolence. It has been in accordance with a plan, a plan linked to Yнwн's desire for obedience to his laws. Had he not acted, we may infer, he would have betrayed all that was meant by giving laws and by the witness of the prophets.

It is only now that the poem begins in any way to resemble a lament, as the writer calls upon the city to cry aloud to Yнwн[49] and asks him whether the awful situation, in which women are forced to eat their children (verse 20) and the open spaces are filled with the bodies of slain young men and women (verse 21), are conditions that can be tolerated.

The fact that this can be done, that the writer can call upon the personified city to pour out its pleas before Yнwн, is an indication that the

---

[48] See BHK.
[49] So a number of Hebrew manuscripts.

communication has not been entirely cut off. Had it been, there would be no point in continuing to pray. As Kaiser remarks about Lamentations generally,[50] the poems do not allow the catastrophe of Jerusalem's fall to be seen as the result of chance or fate (*blindes Verhängnis*), or, it could be added, as an instance of the violence and inhumanity of humans towards each other (although it is that). The fact that Yнwн is believed to be implicated is a ground for hope, strange and bewildering as this may seem to our modern, sanitized ideas of how we should like God to be.

The opening chapter of Lamentations begins by adopting the tone present in chapter 2. The first nine verses are by way of a report, beginning as follows:

> How terribly lonely sits the city
> once full of people.
> Once great among the nations,
> she has become a widow.
> Once a princess among provinces,
> she is now put to forced labour.
> She weeps bitterly in the night,
> the tears run down her cheeks.
> She has no one to comfort her
> from among her former lovers.
> All her neighbours have betrayed her
> and become her enemies.
> Judah is stripped naked[51] by affliction
> and hard labour.
> She dwells among the nations
> but finds no place to rest,
> all who pursue her have overtaken her,
> amidst her troubles.

However, beginning in verse 5, there is the recognition, in language reminiscent of Isaiah 40.2, that Jerusalem's wrongdoings are the cause of the downfall.

> Her foes have gained the upper hand,
> her enemies prosper,
> because Yнwн made her suffer
> on account of her excessive wrongdoings . . .
> Jerusalem sinned grievously,
> became impure.[52]

---

[50] Kaiser, *Klagelieder*, p. 111.
[51] Reading the puʿal, gullᵉtāh.
[52] Omitting ʿal kēn, cf. BHK.

> All her admirers despised her,
> for they saw her lewdness.
> She herself groans in distress,
> and turns her face away.
>   (Lamentations 1.5, 8)

As the third-person narrative turns to first-person testimony (finally in verse 11c), the speaker initially names Yʜwʜ as the cause of the disaster.

> Come, all who pass by;[53]
> look and see.
> Is there any pain like my pain
> which has been brought on me,
> with which Yʜwʜ has afflicted me
> on the day of his fierce anger?
>   (Lamentations 1.12)

This naming of Yʜwʜ, however, leads to the acknowledgement that Yʜwʜ was justified in what he did.

> Yʜwʜ is the one who is in the right,
> for I rebelled against his words,
>   (Lamentations 1.18a)

and finally passes into direct address:

> Look, Yʜwʜ, for I am distressed,
> my bowels pain me,
> my stomach is upset,
> for I have been incorrigibly rebellious,
>   (Lamentations 1.20)

– direct address which also asks Yʜwʜ to punish those who have gloated over Jerusalem's distress and have sought to take advantage of it.

> Let all the evil they have done
> come to your notice,
> and take action against them,
> as you have acted against me,
> because of all my wrongdoing.
>   (Lamentations 1.22a–b)

This is not a desire to see others suffering because the speaker is suffering, and will feel better if the same fate overtakes others. It is a cry for justice based upon a sincere acknowledgement of responsibility for the punishments

---

53 Reading lᶜkū kōl. See the discussion in Diller, *Zwischen JHWH-Tag*, pp. 35–9, similarly Kaiser, *Klagelieder*, p. 115. The traditional rendering 'Is it nothing to you, all you who pass by' has been used in Christian worship on Good Friday.

that have been administered. Without such reciprocity, the speaker would be living in an unjust world. This is not to say, of course, that in the real world people always get what they deserve. The Old Testament writers are too honest and realistic to think this; but the hope that this should be so is a way in which it is possible to grasp an ideal or transcendent world and to use what is grasped to cope with, and if possible, to transform the world as it is.

Chapter 4 of Lamentations adds substance to what precedes it in chapters 1 and 2. Cast again in the form of comment or report, it describes the anguish of the nation in more graphic detail than the earlier chapters. Those who were killed in battle are deemed more fortunate than those who survived, and who experience hunger and starvation (Lamentations 4.9). Any leaders who escaped have seen their pampered lifestyle become so desperate that they cannot be recognized when people meet them, so changed and shrunken have they become (Lamentations 4.7–8). The priests who survived were so drenched in blood that people treated them as lepers, a just reward for the way in which they were believed to have shed innocent blood during the abuse of their term of office (Lamentations 4.13–15).[54] The chapter ends unexpectedly, with an ironic warning to Edom to rejoice, but to be ready to drink the same bitter cup that Jerusalem has drunk, and with the promise to the daughters of Zion that the punishment of her wrongdoings is at an end (Lamentations 4.21–22). The similarity of this language to that in Isaiah 40.2 has been a prime reason for dating the chapter in the late exilic or early post-exilic period.[55]

Chapter 5 differs from the earlier chapters in at least two respects. First, although it contains 22 verses, the number of the letters of the Hebrew alphabet, it is not an acrostic composition. Second, it corresponds closely to psalms of national lament such as 74, 79, 80 and 83. It is an especially moving and poignant example of this genre, and describes graphically the situation of an occupied people turned out of their houses to accommodate the visitors, and subject to many hardships imposed upon them. If, in the present chapter, little is said about the passage, it will be because it adds little to the discussion, for all that it is one of the most moving descriptions in the Old Testament of the effects of war and occupation, and of human inhumanity. It has, not surprisingly, become a key text in the liberation theology of Latin America.[56]

---

[54] See Kaiser, *Klagelieder*, pp. 182–3, for taking Lamentations 4.13–16 as referring to the priests, not exiles.

[55] Kaiser, *Klagelieder*, pp. 185–7.

[56] C. Mesters, *Die Botschaft des leidenden Volkes*, Neukirchen-Vluyn: Neukirchener Verlag, 1982, pp. 34–5, where other verses from other parts of Lamentations are also cited.

Attention will now be focused upon the most problematic, and at the same time most intriguing chapter of Lamentations, chapter 3. It consists of 66 verses, of which each three lines begin with successive letters of the Hebrew alphabet, i.e. verses 1 to 3 with the letter *aleph*, verses 4 to 6 with *beth* and so on. It is probably the latest of the five chapters to have been composed, and it was most likely placed as the central chapter, with its elaborate structure, in order to be of pivotal importance. It begins with words that imply that the poet has suffered personally from some sort of disaster.

> I am a man[57] who has experienced affliction
> through the rod of his anger.
> It is I whom he has led and driven
> into darkness, without light.
> Indeed, it is against me he has turned his hand[58]
> the whole day long.
> He has made my flesh and skin to waste away,
> and broken my bones.
> He has built walls and encircled me
> from head to toe.[59]
> He has made me dwell in dark places
> like those for ever dead.
> He has walled me in and I cannot get out,
> he has chained me with heavy chains.
> Even if I cry out and call for help,
> my prayer is useless.
> He has barred my way with blocks of stone,
> and diverted my paths from reaching their goal.

It will be noticed that these complaints are of a general nature and say nothing that connects the speaker with the destruction of Jerusalem. The contrast with chapter 5 is striking. The content may, of course, be affected by the constraints of the form – by the need to begin each set of three lines with a particular letter of the alphabet. But it is the insertion of the poem into its position in Lamentations that provides the contextual link with the catastrophe of 587.

The poem continues in this vein until verses 22–24.

---

[57] The normal translation is 'the man'; so most English versions, although NRSV has 'I am one', presumably to avoid the word 'man'. The translation here assumes that the Hebrew definite article is one of the cases where a definite person in the mind of the speaker should be rendered in English by the *indefinite* article. See A. B. Davidson, *Hebrew Syntax*, 3rd edn Edinburgh: T. & T. Clark, 1901, pp. 26–7.

[58] Omitting yahᵃfok, cf. BHK.

[59] Connecting Hebrew tᵉlāʾāh with Arabic talw heel.

YHWH's true love is indeed never ending,[60]
his mercies inexhaustible.
Each morning they are new;
his faithfulness is great.[61]
'YHWH is all I have,' I say,
therefore I will hope in him.

These remarkable verses have inspired at least three hymns: the 1541 composition of the reformer Johannes Zwick:

All Morgen ist ganz frisch und neu
des Herren Gnad und grosse Treu;
sie hat kein End den langen Tag,
drauf jeder sich verlassen mag;
[Each morning is fresh and new/the grace and faithfulness of the Lord./
    It lasts the whole day long; upon it may each rely].

and John Keble's 'New every morning is the love' and Thomas Chisholm's 'Great is thy faithfulness'. They lead into 15 verses of affirmation (vv. 25–39) beginning with the words

YHWH is good to those who wait for him,
to the one who seeks him.
It is good to wait patiently
for YHWH's deliverance.
It is good to bear a yoke
as in one's youth . . .
YHWH does not spurn his servants for ever.[62]
If he causes pain, he shows mercy
according to his great love.
It is not his will to afflict
or harm the human race.

These affirmations lead to a call for repentance, in verses 40–41:

Let us scrutinize our behaviour and examine it,
and turn back to YHWH.
Let us lift up our hearts and hands[63]
to God in heaven.

There follows in verses 42–66 a type of lament which, however, presents considerable problems to the interpreter.[64] The first difficulty is that of an

---

[60] Reading tammū, cf. BHK, Kaiser, *Klagelieder*, p. 151.
[61] Reading 'amūnatō to avoid the abrupt change to second person.
[62] Reading YHWH, cf. BHK, and adding 'avādāv for metrical reasons.
[63] Reading 'al instead of the first occurrence of 'el.
[64] They are well set out by Kaiser, *Klagelieder*, pp. 156–9.

abrupt change from the first-person-plural address to God in verses 42–47 to the first person singular in verses 48–66. Second, from verse 49 to the end, the poem assumes all the features of a psalm of lament of an individual who is being assailed not by a victorious foreign enemy but by his fellow countrymen. Kaiser, indeed, has drawn attention to verse 14, which, in the Hebrew reads,

> I have become a laughing-stock to all my people

– a sentiment that is common in psalms of lament, such as Psalm 22.6–7. This is how the verse was translated by the AV and RV as well as by Luther. However, modern versions such as the RSV, NEB (not NRSV) have read with some Hebrew manuscripts and the Peshitta the plural 'peoples', or 'nations' (*'ammîm*), thus making verse 14, at any rate, refer to oppression by the foreign victors, not by the poet's fellow citizens. A final difficulty is that in verses 48–66 the sentiments fluctuate between petition for help and affirmation that help has come. For example, verse 58 affirms:

> You have taken up my cause, Yнwн,[65]
> you have redeemed my life,

whereas verses 62 and 63 complain

> The words and machinations of my adversaries
> are against me all day long.
> Look at their sitting and rising up;
> I am the butt of their songs.

Of course, it depends on how the Hebrew verbs are translated. Kaiser, for example, makes many of the occurrences of the completed aspect into command forms, so that verse 58 reads:

> Führe, Herr, meine Streitfälle,
> erlöse mein Leben
> [Conduct my dispute, Lord;/deliver my life].

Perhaps this is a step too far towards consistency.

However these problems are tackled, what seems inescapable is the conclusion that whatever its origins, chapter 3 of Lamentations originally had nothing to do with the catastrophe of 587. It acquired that connection by being placed in the central position in the book. Its importance derives from this fact, something that must now be explored further.

If Lamentations is regarded as something composed entirely during the period 587 (or, as some would argue, 597) to 520, while the temple lay in

---

[65] Reading Yнwн, cf. BHK.

ruins, and was intended for liturgical use in the temple or among the community, then its main point seems to be to explain the reason for the catastrophe, and to call upon God to bring about a restoration. If, however, Lamentations reached its final form after the so-called period of the exile, even after the rebuilding of the temple, it assumes a quite different significance. Why should the work have been put together *after* the conditions that initiated it had been reversed?

The view taken here is that Lamentations was composed in order to remind the post-exilic community in its restored temple of aspects of the nature of God that it would have been easy to forget, in a situation in which all may have seemed comparatively well. While a passage such as 2.20–21 –

> Look, Yhwh, and consider,
> whom have you treated thus?
> Should women eat their offspring,
> children they have reared?
> Should priest and prophet be killed
> in Yhwh's sanctuary?[66]
> In the open spaces youth and elder
> lie upon the ground.
> My maidens and young men
> have fallen by the sword.
> In the day of your anger
> you have killed and slaughtered without mercy,

– might be intended to move God to compassion, it might also have been intended to describe to a later generation how things had once been – a reminder of those of a later generation of the actual horrors of war.

As someone who grew up in a heavily bombed part of South London during the Second World War and who, as a child, regularly saw bombed houses and injured people being brought out of them, I have a negative attitude to political leaders who believe today that international problems can be solved by air strikes, and who, by obscene linguistic coinages such as 'collateral damage', cover up the suffering that they cause to innocent people when they mean killing and injuring civilians. Texts such as Lamentations (and there are also plenty of modern harrowing descriptions of the effects of warfare) should be required reading for anyone who has the power to initiate warfare.

However, even if this was one of the reasons why Lamentations reached its final form after the catastrophe of 587 had been dealt with, that is, to keep alive some vivid memories of the catastrophe, there was also arguably

---

[66] Reading Yhwh.

a theological reason for its composition. I have mentioned above (p. 156) Kaiser's point that Lamentations enables the disaster of 587 to be seen not simply as a trick of fate, but as grounded in the moral character of Yhwh. Lamentations puts the blame fairly and squarely upon the wrongdoings of the people. If Yhwh did not punish his people for these wrongdoings, it would be an immoral world in which they were living. But Yhwh, and this is where chapter 3 is so important, is seen not only as a retributive judge, but as someone whose faithfulness can be praised and whose mercies are new every morning (Lamentations 3.22). The mercies without the judgement would amount to cheap grace, and would yield a view of God for whom respect could quickly evaporate. The strange fact about the destruction of Jerusalem in 587 BCE is that instead of leading the nation to give up faith in Yhwh altogether, it convinced some citizens of his freedom and his universal rule, and enabled them to hope in him. What should have led to a complete breakdown in communication led to a renewed relationship in which Yhwh could not again become a human tool in a one-way communication. Lamentations was a significant factor in this development.

Our post-Enlightenment and sanitized view of God makes the idea of divine punishment difficult to come to terms with. This is not helped by the fact that the idea of divine judgement has been hijacked by Christian and other sectarian groups who foresee an annihilating type of divine judgement for anyone who does not join them. Even mainstream evangelical churches profoundly misunderstand the notion of judgement, using it to convert what ought to be good news into a threat, thereby offering their members a false prospectus of salvation. In fact, judgement is something to be looked forward to by anyone who hopes for a better world, and who wishes to be a better person in that better world. The combination of judgement and mercy in Lamentations can be a source of inspiration in today's world. Divine judgement and punishment are not things from which people need to be saved; they are part of the process of salvation.

I move now to consider the hindrance to divine–human communication caused by the problem of the prosperity of the wicked and the suffering of those who try to be faithful to God. This adds a new dimension to the subject in the sense that the wicked, and those who are impressed by their prosperity, call into question the loyalty of God to those who are faithful to him. The latter then feel pressured into finding an answer to the prosperous wicked in order to justify God and their loyalty to him. This immediately introduces the danger that God ceases to be a participant in a communicative relationship and becomes an object in a quasi-philosophical discussion. This situation is more likely to arise in times of comparative peace and prosperity. Even the wicked may be inclined to reflect on their values if they find themselves facing ruin as a nation if threatened with disaster.

That so much space is devoted to this matter in the Old Testament is another indication of its realism. It is also an expression of values that have something to say to today's world. The psalmists who were oppressed by the prosperity of the wicked, and the injustice that they brazenly inflicted upon others, would be equally appalled at the corporate evils in today's developed world. They would be amazed at the fact that huge corporations can falsify their accounts, mislead their shareholders, deprive employees of their pension rights, and exploit indigenous peoples and their habitats in order to maximize profits. At the time of writing this chapter, governments and their central banks in the Western world are making huge sums of money available to prop up the banking system and the financial markets, because the greed of executives who earn in a year what others may earn in a lifetime if they are lucky, has brought the system to the point of collapse. It is amazing that this political will has suddenly manifested itself, while it cannot provide the very much smaller sums of money that would bring basic medical care to the millions of children who die before their fifth birthday, and also eliminate poverty and ignorance.

The most poignant expression of this problem is in Psalm 73, the first part of which reads as follows:

> Truly, God is good to Israel[67]
> to a people pure in heart.
> But as for me, I had almost stumbled,
> my steps had well-nigh slipped,
> because I was provoked to anger by the boastful
> and saw the prosperity of the wicked.
> They suffer no pain,
> their bodies are whole and fat.[68]
> They experience no misfortune as others do;
> they are not plagued like other men.
> Thus they wear pride like a necklace;
> they wrap themselves round with violence like a garment.
> Their eyes peer out from podgy faces;
> they obtain all their heart's desires.
> They mock, and speak maliciously;
> their speech, as from on high,
> works oppression.

---

[67] This rendering follows the MT and not the redivision of consonants yielding 'to the upright, God'.

[68] Reading lāmō tām, cf. BHK.

Their slander is directed against heaven,
and their tongues roam freely on earth.
Therefore people turn to them,
and regard them as fountains of knowledge.
They say, 'How can God know,
does the Most High have such knowledge?'
Such are the wicked;
they continually prosper, and increase their wealth.
Have I then kept my heart pure for nothing,
and washed my hands in innocency?
I have been afflicted all the day long,
and chastened every morning.

(Psalm 73.1–14)

In his perplexity the psalmist, either in, or on his way to, the temple, receives the reassurance that the wicked will, in fact, get their due reward.

You will put them in slippery places;
you will bring them down in ruin.

(v. 18)

Yet this, and in spite of the fact that the psalm ends with beautiful words which express the psalmist's hope and trust in God, is far from reassuring. If there is value in being loyal to God and in seeking to do what is right, this value cannot be justified by appealing to other factors, least of all the satisfaction of seeing those who deny these values being punished. By wanting to become an apologist for God's justice, the psalmist is moving the argument on to the grounds where the wicked are operating; and in the process God is being short-changed. Paul Tillich wrote that 'to argue that God exists is to deny him'.[69] By this he meant that it was demeaning to God to subsume him under the category of existence as defined by human understanding. The same can be said about any attempt to justify God in the face of innocent suffering or the prosperity of the wicked. It is a natural part of being human to want to understand everything and to find an explanation for it. When it comes to God, such attempts reduce God to a function of human reason. At this level of explanation, the view of the prosperous wicked, that 'God cannot know, and that the Most High has no such knowledge' is a strong argument.

This is not to say that it is wrong to try to find intellectual answers to these questions. Eberhard Jüngel has argued that any creative act necessarily

---

[69] P. Tillich, *Systematic Theology*, London: James Nisbet, 1953, vol. 1, p. 227; *Systematische Theologie*, Berlin: de Gruyter, 1987, vol. I/II, p. 239.

involves self-limitation on the part of the one doing the creating.[70] To beget and to raise children is to bring into the world people who will enjoy a freedom that may conflict with the interests and values of their parents. To create a work of art and to place it in the public domain involves relinquishing control over it. Conductors of a piece of music or directors of an opera or play may interpret or stage a piece in ways never envisaged by their composers or authors. They may even do so in ways that are fundamentally contrary to the intentions of the composers or authors. In the same way, Jüngel suggests, the creation of the world by God involves a freedom granted to its inhabitants that may bring them into conflict with the ideal will of the creator. This is very helpful but, as Jüngel would probably be the first to recognize, it is no more than a *human* attempt to justify God in a world in which so much seems to count against belief in him. Jüngel is specifically addressing the questions raised by Auschwitz.

This leads again to the book of Job, which has been mentioned elsewhere in the present work (p. 85). To the extent that the book revolves around arguments about the nature and reasons for the suffering of the innocent, it falls into the difficulty of being able to provide no more than human wisdom. This is true also of the heavenly scenes in the prologue. The satan is of the opinion that Job's pious behaviour is not altruistic, but a form of enlightened self-interest. He maintains that this will become clear if disaster overtakes Job. The satan is disappointed when Job maintains his uprightness in spite of the setbacks and sufferings that the satan is permitted to inflict upon Job. The argument of the three (later, four) so-called comforters, whose disputation with Job occupies much of the book, is that God rules a moral universe, that Job's suffering must be fully deserved, and that evildoers will be punished in due course. An implication of their arguments is that the ultimate reason for doing good is that it brings rewards, while those who are wicked are punished. As the satan puts it, 'Does Job fear God for nothing?' (Job 1.9). This comes to a head in chapter 42, when Job's possessions are restored to him with interest. The 'comforters' are shown to have been right in that the world is a moral universe in which good is ultimately rewarded. Even the satan is vindicated as God seems to reveal himself as someone who must, by such actions, justify the way the world is run, to those who criticize its apparent imperfections. The whole point of Job's arguments is undermined, and I used to set essays

---

[70] E. Jüngel, 'Gottes ursprüngliches Anfangen als schöpferische Selbstbegrenzung' in H. Deuser et al. (eds), *Gottes Zukunft – Zukunft der Welt: Festschrift für Jürgen Moltmann zum 60. Geburtstag*, Munich: Chr. Kaiser, 1986, pp. 265–75.

to my students in which they were asked to discuss whether the book of Job would be better off without its 'happy' ending!

All this, of course, leaves out of account chapters 38 to 41, in which YHWH speaks to Job out of a whirlwind. The divine 'answer' is no answer at all in the sense of an address to the questions that Job wishes to have answered. From a communicative point of view it is reminiscent of the evasive answers that politicians are trained to give. Job is reminded that he was not present when the world was made and that he has no idea how it functions. The divine speech touches upon lions, mountain goats, wild asses, the ostrich, the war horse and the hawk. It describes as the pinnacle of the works of God not the human race, but the crocodile![71] Yet the outcome of this apparently irrelevant parading of nature before Job is that Job says,

> I have spoken of great things I did not understand,[72]
> things too wonderful for me, that I could not know.
> I had heard of you by report only;
> now my eye sees you.
> Therefore I despise myself,
> and repent in dust and ashes.
>
> (Job 42.3b, 5–6)

In trying to get some sense of what this might be meant to convey, it is, perhaps, important to distinguish two questions: what did Job (assuming him to have been a person some of whose incidents in life are the basis for the book) experience? and, what did the writer(s) of the book of Job want to say to its presumed readers by way of this example? This is a distinction that more often than not has not been made in the commentaries. How-ever, although the second alternative will be adhered to here, namely, that of the communicative intention of the writer(s) rather than an attempted explanation of the experience of a putative Job, thoughts from those who follow the first alternative will also be utilized. Rudolf Otto, in *The Idea of the Holy*, argued that the divine speeches contained all the ingredients of his understanding of the 'holy' as a non-rational category. 'They . . . express in masterly fashion the downright stupendousness, the wellnigh daemonic and wholly incomprehensible character of the eternal creative power,' he wrote. However, that on its own would have struck Job utterly dumb, and Otto therefore qualifies this thought by suggesting that 'that of which we are conscious is rather an *intrinsic value*

---

[71] Taking the description of Behemoth in Job 40.15–24 to be the crocodile; cf. NEB and p. 50 above.

[72] Adding g⁽e⁾dōlōt, cf. BHK.

in the incomprehensible – a value inexpressible, positive, and "fascinating".' He adds that this is 'incommensurable with thoughts of rational human teleology and is not assimilated to them'.[73]

Another line of approach would be to invoke the notion of 'the sublime', a category (if that is what it is) that much exercised writers in the late eighteenth and early nineteenth centuries. Kant has a section on 'das Erhabenen' in the *Kritik der Urteilskraft*, and this was taken up by Schiller in his aesthetic writings.[74] As I understand them, Kant and Schiller were maintaining that the encounter with awesome and overwhelming phenomena in the world of nature worked upon human reason to produce a sense of the limits of human understanding, which at the same time contributed to a deeper awareness of human freedom. Kant and Schiller were criticized by Jean Paul Richter for concentrating upon quantitatively large phenomena as the occasions for experience of the sublime. He pointed out the importance of tiny phenomena in this process, a step approved by Jakob Friedrich Fries.[75] This correction would certainly bring us closer to the speeches in Job, which do not entirely concern themselves with quantitatively large animals or phenomena. Bloch's treatment in *Atheismus im Christentum* is, as would be expected, quite different. His thought-provoking and challenging assertion that 'Hiob eben ist fromm, indem er nicht glaubt'[76] is the basis for his conclusion that faced with the inexplicable, it is possible for humans to rise above it in hope, and to fashion a new existence.[77]

It is certainly not impossible that the writer(s) of Job had had experiences of large and small awesome phenomena in the natural world which

---

[73] R. Otto, *Das Heilige: Über das Irrationale in der Idee des Göttlichen und sein Verhältnis zum Rationalen*, Munich: C. H. Beck, 1936, pp. 100–1; ET (from which the above quotations are taken), *The Idea of the Holy: An Inquiry into the Non-rational Factor in the Idea of the Divine and its Relation to the Rational*, Harmondsworth: Penguin, 1959, pp. 95–6.

[74] I. Kant, 'Analytik des Erhabenen' in *Kritik der Urteilskraft, Kants Werke: Akademie Textausgabe*, Berlin: W. de Gruyter, 1968, vol. 5, pp. 244–64. F. Schiller, 'Vom Erhabenen' in *Sämtliche Werke*, vol. 5, Darmstadt: Wissenschaftliche Buchgesellschaft, 1993, pp. 489–512.

[75] J. P. Richter, 'Vorschule der Ästhetik', in *Sämtliche Werke*, vol. 1.5, Darmstadt: Wissenschaftliche Buchgesellschaft, 2000, pp. 106–7; J. F. Fries, *Neue Kritik der Vernunft*, Heidelberg: Mohr & Zimmer, 1807, vol. 3, pp. 319–20.

[76] E. Bloch, *Atheismus im Christentum*, Frankfurt am Main: Suhrkamp, 1968, p. 166. 'Job is pious in that he does not believe.'

[77] Bloch, *Atheismus*, p. 165. 'Die einfachste Art ist die, daß es in der Welt immer wieder einen Auszug gibt, der aus dem jeweiligen Status herausführt, und eine Hoffnung, die sich mit der Empörung verbindet, ja die in den konkret gegebenen Möglichkeiten eines neuen Seins fundiert ist' [The simplest way is that there is always in the world a way out which leads from the present state of things, and a hope that connects with indignation, which indeed is based on the concretely given possibilities of a new being].

convinced them of the limits of human understanding, and that they drew upon these experiences in their portrayal of Job.[78] There is also a certain fascination about Otto's notion of the 'intrinsic value of the incomprehensible'. Behind Bloch's interpretation lies the important question whether Job's experience resulted in a passive acceptance of the world as it was or whether it spurred him to hope and strive for a better world. It is this question that seems to me to be the most important one.

The sense of a breakdown in communication with God can be distressing for at least two reasons. It may disturb a private type of religion that affects few, if any persons, outside the circle of the one primarily involved. On the other hand, it may engender doubts about the rightness of someone's public commitment to religion that expresses itself through a church and/or other institution that is concerned to uphold and advance particular values in the world. In ancient Israel and Judah, of course, there were no churches to belong to. Religion was a commitment to Yhwh or some other deity, which took certain outward forms, especially those associated with communal or national celebrations or occasions. In view of this, it is likely that the issue at the heart of the texts that have been considered in this chapter was not the disturbance of what individuals did in their solitude or privacy, but the question of what values were to guide the community. It is no accident that in many of the psalms of lament the psalmist complains about the derision that is experienced at the hands of other members of the community who think that his religious commitments are at best valueless and pointless and at worst pernicious.

It can be argued that the same is true of the book of Job. It is easy for modern readers, with our privatized view of religion, to think of the character of Job as an individual with a personal problem. However, the portrayal of him as a man of wealth and substance would have conveyed to the presumed readers the sense of someone who was an important person in public affairs. While it is perhaps problematic to use the dialogue in chapters 3 to 37 to illumine the prologue and epilogue, the dialogue certainly portrays Job as someone occupying an important position in the community of his day. Chapter 29.7–25 speaks of how he was treated with great respect when he took his seat in the gate of the city; how he was relied upon by the fatherless and widows to give them justice; how, when he spoke to give an opinion or verdict, people waited expectantly for his verdict. Job 29.25a–b claims that

---

[78] See also the interesting essay by Otto on a description by John Ruskin of just such an experience, in R. Otto, *Aufsätze das Numinose betreffend*, Stuttgart and Gotha: Andreas Perthes, 1923, pp. 56–8.

I chose the way they should go,
I sat as their head,
dwelling like a king among his troops.

If we take back to Job the point that what is at issue in the book is not just the solution to an intellectual problem that is personal to an individual character, but a question that lies at the heart of the values that commit people to trying to create and maintain a certain type of society, the book can be read in a different way. In an earlier chapter (p. 87) it was pointed out that Job's 'comforters' accused him of corrupt and dishonest behaviour (Job 22.5–9). Job's desire for God to vindicate him must therefore have included a wish for a divine endorsement of how he had acted publicly. From this point of view, the confession of Job in chapter 42, however the writer(s) thought it may have been brought about, must not be seen as a humiliating acceptance of a total inability to understand the ways of God. Nor must it be understood in purely personal, pietistic, terms. While I do not agree with Bloch that Job does not believe in Yhwh, it seems to me that Bloch's portrayal of Job as a rebel against the values of the world in which he lives has much to contribute to the understanding of the book, including Job's confession. Part, at least, of the reconciliation that he experiences, is a reassurance that his life at the public and moral level has not been in vain.

The texts in the Old Testament that speak of apparent breakdowns in communication at the level of divine–human relationships do not require readers to become apologists for God. They invite them to reflect upon whether they seek to listen to God at all, and whether this listening process leads to an inner passive satisfaction, or the determination to hope and work for a better world.

6

What does it mean to be human?

Many years ago I suggested that the central question of Old Testament Theology was that posed by the psalmist in Psalm 8.4 [Hebrew 8.5], *mā 'ᵉnōš*, what does it mean to be human?[1] A return to this matter will occupy the final chapter in the present work. It is certainly a question that has a central importance in today's world.

An answer to the question that is implicit in modern political activity is that to be human is to be *homo economicus*. Government policies that affect schools and universities, and that devote large sums of money to the teaching of literacy, have as their goal the production of a skilled and competitive workforce that will enable Britain and the United States to compete in a global market economy, and generate the wealth that will ensure high standards of living. Zygmunt Bauman has recently commented on this kind of thinking by describing humanity in the so-called developed world as *homo eligens*, which he translates as 'man choosing'. He thereby tries to capture that imperative of global market capitalism, that nothing may remain what it is; that everything must constantly change. He quotes Richard Sennet, substituting certain key phrases of his own, in order to describe the plight that is the lot of *homo eligens*:

> Perfectly viable identities are gutted and abandoned, capable possessions and partners are set adrift rather than rewarded, simply because the self must prove to the market that it is capable of change.[2]

Not every political philosopher or sociologist is as pessimistic as Bauman, although his realism is an undoubted strength. Jürgen Habermas has attempted to define what it means to be human, ideally and counterfactually, in terms of communicative interaction. Humans are, or should be, willing to be persuaded against their interests by the force of the better argument in favour of justice and equality. He has devoted many pages to

---

[1] J. W. Rogerson, '"What does it Mean to be Human?" The Central Question of Old Testament Theology?' in D. J. A. Clines, S. E. Fowl and S. E. Porter (eds), *The Bible in Three Dimensions: Essays in Celebration of Forty Years of Biblical Studies in the University of Sheffield* (JSOTSS 87), Sheffield: Sheffield Academic Press, 1990, pp. 285–98.
[2] Z. Bauman, *Liquid Life*, Cambridge: Polity Press, 2005, p. 33.

analysing why, in practice, humans are not what they should be ideally. Luhmann, it is true, satirized Habermas's position as 'eine Idealisierung des Abwesenden' (an idealization of what is absent), but some theologians have found in Habermas's work a strongly salvific element.[3]

What can the Old Testament contribute to the discussion? At first sight the obvious answer is 'nothing'. Few, if any, of the circumstances that determine human life in today's so-called developed world were operative in ancient Israel. Charles Taylor, in his monumental *A Secular Age* has made a distinction between societies that belong to an 'ancien régime' and those that belong to modernity.[4] Among the differences between the two ideal types are that those in the 'ancien régime' are ordered hierarchically. Individuals gain their sense of identity by belonging to a stratum that is itself defined in relationship to other strata, from nobility, through clergy and bourgeoisie to peasants. Modern types are ordered horizontally. Citizenship does not depend upon membership of a particular order or place in society. A second difference is that types belonging to the 'ancient régime' perceive the world as enchanted, as inhabited by spiritual forces or agencies which can and do intervene in human affairs. The other type belongs to an increasingly disenchanted world.

Taylor's distinction suggests that there is an unbridgeable gulf between the Old Testament world and modern 'secular' society (he lays great stress on the ambiguity and complexity of the term 'secular'). This seems obvious from the very passage of the Old Testament that the quotation *mā ʾᵉnōš* comes. Psalm 8 reads as follows:

> YHWH our Lord,
> how glorious your name is in all the earth!
> Your honour is recounted[5] to highest heaven,
> from the mouth of infants and sucklings.
> You have established a bulwark because of your adversaries,
> to silence the enemy and avenger.
> When I look up at your heavens,
> the works of your fingers,
> the moon and stars that you have put in place,
> what is man that you call him to mind,
> or mortal man that you care for him?

---

[3] Luhmann, *Einführung*, p. 83; E. Arens (ed.), *Habermas und die Theologie: Beiträge zur theologischen Rezeption, kommunikativen Handelns*, Düsseldorf: Patmos Verlag, 1989; R. J. Siebert, *The Critical Theory of Religion: The Frankfurt School* (Religion and Reason 29), Berlin: Mouton, 1985.

[4] C. Taylor, *A Secular Age*, Cambridge, Mass.: Belknap Press of Harvard University Press, 2007, pp. 459–60.

[5] Reading tunnāh.

Yet you have made him only a little less than gods,
and crowned him with glory and honour.
You have made him master of the works of your hands,
putting everything under his feet.
All sheep and oxen, even the wild beasts;
birds of the air and fish of the sea,
all who traverse the ocean paths.
Yнwн our Lord,
how glorious your name is in all the earth!

The world-view implicit in this psalm is both that of an enchanted world, and a world that has an order in which humanity occupies a defined and fixed place. The supreme position is occupied by Yнwн, whose incomparability is reflected in the awesome night spectacle of the moon and stars. Yнwн does not dwell alone in the heavens; he is surrounded and served by beings called gods in the psalm. Humanity comes next, remarkably, placed only slightly lower than the gods who serve Yнwн. Then come the other inhabitants of the planet, in a relationship subordinate to that of humanity, and under the rule and governance of humanity. There can be no doubt that this is both a hierarchically ordered world, and an enchanted one. That Yнwн is not a kind of indifferent Deist architect of the universe, a Great Designer who leaves the world to its own devices, is indicated by verse 4 (Hebrew verse 3). The verb translated as 'care for' has the sense of exercising oversight and visiting. Yнwн is active in the affairs of humankind.

Taylor, of course, is not necessarily agreeing that what he describes as secularism (in one of its senses) represents reality. He makes clear his own Catholic commitment and the importance, to him, of the experiences and writings of people such as Teresa of Avila.[6] His book is an attempt to account sociologically and historically for changed attitudes to religious belief and practice among people in the West *generally* in the year 2000 as opposed to the situation in 1500. He is highly critical of the view that the change has come about simply because 'science' has made belief in God impossible. However, if Taylor's analysis is correct, something which the present work will take for granted, the question is raised of how the Old Testament could make any contribution to modern debate about how to define humanity. Can a set of texts that come from a world understood hierarchically and in terms of divine involvement inform a world that is understood horizontally and 'disenchantedly'?

One answer might be that the Old Testament, like the writings of St Teresa, articulates an understanding of reality that has been ignored

---

[6] Taylor, *A Secular Age*, p. 280.

by 'secularism' and that 'secularism' ought to take account of. Now I am certainly of the opinion that the Old Testament is a largely unknown work (even in the churches!) and that its content is often grossly misrepresented as being throughout barbaric and uncouth. One of the reasons for writing the present book is the hope that it might find its way into the hands of members of the general public and that they may come to a more positive appreciation of the Old Testament. However, I do not suppose that this book could have the effect of convincing people that the world is less 'disenchanted' than is popularly believed. The aim, therefore, will be a much more limited one. It will seek to demonstrate the thesis that the more humane humans become (whatever is meant by that), the closer they become to what the Old Testament calls the 'image of God' (Genesis 1.27) and, in what may seem a curious way, the more God and his purposes are realized in the world. That this is to convert theology into anthropology is a risk that is worth taking. It must also be pointed out that the task does not involve a kind of intellectual archaeology which tries to reconstruct beliefs and attitudes in ancient Israel and then apply them to today's world, although it is not possible to escape this kind of procedure entirely! What we have available are the texts that make up the Old Testament. They cannot be understood fully without the tools of modern biblical scholarship. However, with the help of scholarship, and a selectivity that derives from the modern standpoint from which the texts are being read, they can be brought to express insights that may resonate with the needs and concerns of readers both inside and outside the 'household of faith'.

The attempt to demonstrate the main thesis, that of approaching divinity via humanity, will come as the last task in this chapter. It will be preceded by an examination of texts that in different ways bear on the question of what it means to be human.

The first text to be considered is the poem at the beginning of chapter 3 of Ecclesiastes (or Qoheleth, as it is called in the Bible in Hebrew). It consists of 14 pairs of contrasted statements each half of which usually consists of two Hebrew words, the first of which is *'et*, 'time'. The introduction to the poem says that

> For everything there is a proper hour,
> for every matter a proper time, under the heavens.

Whether this adequately describes the scope of the poem that follows is unlikely.[7] The poem itself is most probably a compilation of sayings put together from various sources and, as such, expressing no overall plan or

---

[7] Rose, *Rien de nouveau*, p. 195.

theme.[8] However, in its context in Ecclesiastes it can be interpreted more or less coherently. It reads as follows:

> A time to be born, and a time to die.
> A time to plant, and a time to weed.[9]
> A time to kill, and a time to heal.
> A time to break down, and a time to build up.
> A time to weep, and a time to laugh.
> A time to mourn, and a time to dance.
> A time to throw stones, and a time to gather them.[10]
> A time to embrace, and a time to desist.[11]
> A time to seek, and a time to lose.
> A time to keep, and a time to discard.
> A time to rend, and a time to repair.
> A time to be silent, and a time to speak.
> A time to love, and a time to hate.
> A time for war, and a time for peace.

The poem answers the question 'What does it mean to be human?' in terms of the routines and events that define life in a subsistence agricultural society.[12] It is not an individual picture. The routines of planting, weeding, and reaping, of clearing the soil of stones and of building walls with them, of going to war and making peace, of mourning death and celebrating harvests, were communal activities. They were not gender-biased. Giving birth, and the rituals of mourning, and celebration, not to mention the agricultural routines, were as much the scene of women as of men. The poem also makes the point that in a subsistence agricultural society, human lives are regulated by imperatives of the world of nature over which humans have little or no control. When to plant, weed and harvest are not times arbitrarily chosen by farmers, but dependent on conditions in any given year. When to go to war was also dictated by agricultural necessity because armies had to live off the land. 2 Samuel 11.1 speaks of 'the turn (i.e. spring) of the year when kings go out (to war)'.[13] The routines essential to the practice of agriculture, such as clearing stones, and

---

[8] Fischer, *Skepsis*, pp. 221–2.

[9] Omitting nātūaʿ. For the rendering see K. Galling, 'Das Rätsel der Zeit im Urteil Kohelets (Koh. 3, 1–5)', *ZThK* 58 (1961), p. 6; Fischer, *Skepsis*, p. 220, note 168.

[10] See Galling, 'Das Rätsel', pp. 7–11 for a discussion of possible renderings.

[11] Omitting mēhabbēq.

[12] Rose, *Rien de nouveau*, p. 196, draws attention to the Gezer Calendar, for an exposition of which see O. Barowski, *Agriculture in Iron Age Israel*, Winona Lake: Eisenbrauns, 1987, pp. 32–8.

[13] Reading mᵉlākîm. Cf. S. R. Driver, *Notes on the Hebrew Text and the Topography of the Books of Samuel*, 2nd edn, Oxford: Clarendon Press, 1913, p. 289.

building and repairing walls and shelters, had to be fitted into a timetable whose main priority was planting and harvesting at the most advantageous times of the year. But the timetable defining human behaviour is biological as well as agricultural. Individuals have no control over when births or deaths occur, and the same is true of communities that celebrate births and mourn deaths as part of their corporate identity. Even marital intercourse (if this is indeed what is referred to in the verse about throwing and gathering stones) will be more effective at some times than others if it is to achieve the aim of producing offspring. There is also an interpersonal dimension in the poem if the words 'a time to be silent, and a time to speak' refer to the comforting of those in distress. Job 2.13 narrates that Job's friends sat with him for seven days and seven nights in silence, because they saw how great his suffering was. They waited for Job to speak first, before they said anything.

While the above explanation admittedly does not explain every clause in the poem, it is arguably sufficiently coherent for the question to be considered as to its view of what it means to be human. Does it paint a bleak view of a humanity enslaved by timetables imposed by the demands of nature and the inescapable facts of human biology?[14] Perhaps it does, and rightly so. In spite of all our attempts in today's Western world to defy our biological processes by hair colouring, skin lotions, cosmetic surgery, vitamin supplements, and the enormous financial resources devoted to health services, ageing and death cannot ultimately be avoided, and we may lead our lives less wisely than we might otherwise do, if we deceive ourselves into thinking that we might somehow live for ever. There may be something in the prayer in Psalm 90.12: 'Teach us so to count our days, that we may enter the gate of wisdom.'[15] We today (in the West) are not bound to the demands of an agricultural cycle in the way that ancient Israelites were, but this does not mean that we are free from routines that dominate our lives. What I notice, as a retired academic, is that I am no longer bound to an unforgiving timetable that began in mid-August with the publication of the examination results of those who had applied to study in my department, and then extended through the demands of teaching, examining and administration (with time having to be found for research and writing) until the graduation ceremonies in July. It was almost impossible for much of my working life to be away from the university from mid-May to the end of June because of the need to mark examination scripts in my own and other institutions. This kind of experience can no doubt be

---

[14] This is the general conclusion of Rose, *Rien de nouveau*, pp. 199–200.
[15] Reading hodiꜥēnū and vᵉnāvōꜛ lᵉvāv. Cf. BHK and Gunkel, *Die Psalmen*, p. 402. Cf. Also NEB.

easily paralleled in other walks of life. For example, parents can be caught up in a routine of delivering and collecting very young children from nursery care or schools, and/or taking older children to music lessons, sports activities or parties, to name only some such possible 'taxi' duties. Again, there are people in today's (Western) world for whom paid employment is an alienating and dehumanizing experience from which they seek relief by planning and taking holidays. If, with the writer of the poem in Ecclesiastes 3, we were to set out the external constraints of career and profession that define our lives, what would that tell us about what it means for us to be human? What space would there be for communal celebration of joy or participation in mourning; for spending time in silence with someone in distress who simply needed our presence?

If the world implied by the poem is compared with Bauman's picture of *homo eligens*, with its need for constant change in order for people to stay where they are, so to speak, the world presupposed in the poem is more stable and dependable than that inhabited by *homo eligens*. It is also a more intelligible world. The binary oppositions or antitheses of birth and death, planting and weeding, weeping and laughing, mourning and celebrating, helped to map out not just the course of individual lives, but the place of human life in the world generally. Within this map, times of mourning necessarily have their place alongside times of celebrations, just as do times of war (unfortunately, and as a consequence of human nature) alongside peace. Unlike some modern conceptions of life, the poem does not assume that the sole preoccupation of human living should be the pursuit of pleasure and happiness, with the interruptions to this quest that arise from bereavement, illness or accidents being considered as alien intrusions into the 'real purpose' of life.

Does the poem portray a humanity that has little or no freedom, a humanity whose existence is tied to an inexorable and unforgiving regime driven by human biology and external nature? The answer depends on how we define freedom and whether we think of it as the unlimited ability to do whatever we like, or as the possibility for creative and rewarding activity within an ordered framework. This, of course, is not the only way to define freedom, and some frameworks, for example those governing people in prison, allow for fewer creative possibilities than other frameworks. It is arguable that within the framework set out in the poem in Ecclesiastes 3 there are ample opportunities for creative action. Communal celebrations at harvest time, or when there was a birth or marriage, would not be identical in every region or village. The distinctive flavour of local life would be affected by leading families or by charismatic individuals in the community. The same would apply to the activities of individuals, especially in the ways that they responded to the emotional and financial needs of neighbours or relatives.

It will be useful at this point to refer to an essay by Charles Taylor entitled 'To Follow a Rule'.[16] The essay is an attack on an understanding of what it means to be human that Taylor considers to be intellectualist and individualist, and which he traces back to Descartes and Locke. It assumes that humans are called upon to become responsible, thinking minds, self-reliant in their judgements.[17] According to Taylor this notion has become part of modern thought and culture, and has moulded our contemporary sense of self. This 'stripped-down view of the [human] subject', as Taylor calls it,[18] has made deep inroads (he claims) into the social sciences, including rational-choice theory. The closeness of Taylor's unease about this development to Bauman's analysis of the human predicament as *homo eligens*, is striking. In Taylor's opinion, an alternative view of human intellectual activity can be deduced from the discussions in Wittgenstein's *Philosophical Investigations* about what it means to keep a rule.[19] He draws attention to views articulated especially in paragraphs 202 to 219 of the *Investigations* which appear to stress the shared assumptions involved in following a rule, and the fact that it may well become impossible to provide explanations for doing this so that one has to end up by saying that one follows the rule blindly.[20] This, according to Taylor, places the process of understanding in social space, and he develops this in the following way. If two people are observed sawing a log with a two-handled saw, or if they are seen dancing, they are participating in dialogical activities that imply the ability to draw upon and follow implicit rules. Taylor compares this ability with the ability to interiorize and follow the rules underlying language use, as in Saussure's distinction between *langue* (language system) and *parole* (language act, or use). Those rules are not consciously learned, but absorbed from the cultures in which people are embodied. For the

---

16 C. Taylor, 'To Follow a Rule' in idem, *Philosophical Arguments*, Cambridge, Mass.: Harvard University Press, 1995, pp. 165–80.

17 Taylor, 'To Follow a Rule', p. 169.

18 Taylor, 'To Follow a Rule', p. 169.

19 Taylor's essay was published before the appearance of the critical-genetic edition of the *Philosophische Untersuchungen*. See J. Schulte et al. (eds), Ludwig Wittgenstein, *Philosophische Untersuchungen: Kritisch-genetische Edition*, Frankfurt: Suhrkamp, 2001. The introductory essay by Schulte (pp. 12–47) describes the various stages of the genesis of the work and is critical of the edition published in 1953 by G. E. M. Anscombe and R. Rhees. The new edition prints all the extant versions.

20 Wittgenstein, *Philosophische Untersuchungen*, para. 219, p. 867. 'Wenn ich der Regel folge, wähle ich nicht. Ich folge der Regel blind' [When I follow the rule, I do not choose. I follow the rule blindly].

most part they are practised in an unreflected manner. Similarly the 'rules' that underlie human living in community are absorbed from that community and enable life to be negotiated and practised at various communal levels. Taylor notes that these common assumptions in a community are similar to what Bourdieu has called 'habitus';[21] and it should be added that there are also similarities with Luhmann's notion of 'symbolically generalized media of communication' (see above, p. 92). The analogy with Saussure is important because *langue* and *parole* have a mutual influence upon each other. Speech acts renew the language system and also alter it. From the point of view of the assumptions underlying, or the systems that make up, cultures, these too are both maintained and altered by what is done in practice.

Returning to the poem in Ecclesiastes 3 in the light of the above remarks, it will be seen at once how close the poem comes to what Taylor is arguing. The practices that are described in the poem are 'dialogical' and presume common acceptance of the 'rules' involved in producing food, maintaining buildings, defending the community, maintaining its social identity and cohesion through communal celebrations and rites of mourning, ensuring its continuance through marriage and the begetting of children. This is hardly a surprise in an ancient society long before the rise of the modern sense of individuality and individualism, but it is striking that a text from an ancient society can resonate with the arguments of a modern political philosopher who wants to question the assumption that modern Western society is exclusively individualistic.

Is the poem of Ecclesiastes 3 'hot' or 'cold' in the sense discussed in Chapter 2 (p. 25)? Does it describe something that resists change or is it a 'motor' that drives and adjusts to change? It could be the latter if, in the Marxist sense, it was composed for the purpose of 'conscientization': to seek to change a situation by making people aware of it. It could also be the latter if the intention of what immediately follows in Ecclesiastes 3 is to act as a kind of perspective or counterbalance to the poem.

In the traditional translations of the Old Testament, such as the RSV, Ecclesiastes 3.11 reads:

> He has made everything beautiful in its time; also he has put eternity into man's mind, yet so that he cannot find out what God has done from the beginning to the end.

---

[21] Taylor, 'To Follow a Rule', p. 174. See Bourdieu, *Outline of a Theory of Practice*, p. 214, note 1, where 'habitus' is defined in terms of 'disposition': 'it . . . designates a way of being, a habitual state (especially of the body) and, in particular, a predisposition, tendency, propensity, or inclination'.

If this is correct, we may have a statement to the effect that part of being human is to have senses or intimations of realities beyond the world of our immediate experience, intimations that make us embark upon intellectual or other journeys in a quest, perhaps unattainable, to discover the source or meaning of the feelings that are engendered. It would be natural to call to mind the famous opening of Augustine's *Confessions*:

> you have made us for yourself, and our heart is restless until it rests in you.[22]

The question is, is the traditional rendering correct?

There are three main problems with the rendering given in the RSV: the translation 'beautiful', the word 'eternity', and whether the Hebrew that has literally 'in their heart' can be satisfactorily rendered as 'into man's mind'. The easiest problem to solve is the first. The Hebrew *yāfeh*, taken with the immediately following *bᵉ'ittō*, 'in its time', cannot be expressing a sense of beauty in this context, but rather, appropriateness, suitability.[23] The NEB translation expresses this:

> He has made everything to suit its time.

The second problem has generated more scholarly literature than any other verse in Ecclesiastes.[24] It would be foolish to suppose that a solution could be proposed in the present work. The two main options appear to be either to take the Hebrew word *'ōlām* to mean something like 'duration' or to emend it to *'āmāl*, 'toil' by the transposition of the last two consonants. In the first case, a further move is necessary to make 'duration' mean 'a sense of duration', that is, an awareness of the passage of time, and this is what appears to be expressed in the NEB:

> he has given men a sense of time past and future.

If the emendation is made, the phrase can be rendered

> he has also put toil into their heart,[25]

although whether this makes any sense is arguable. The problem of the words 'in their heart' is whether the 'their' refers to humanity, as is presumed by many translations, or whether it refers to the antecedent, which is 'everything'. A case can be made for the antecedent being 'everything'

---

[22] Saint Augustine, *Confessions* (trans: H. Chadwick), Oxford: Oxford University Press, 1992, p. 3.
[23] See further Fischer, *Skepsis*, pp. 230–2.
[24] Fischer, *Skepsis*, p. 229.
[25] Fischer, *Skepsis*, p. 226, 'Auch die Mühe hat er ihnen ins Herz gegeben.'

(Hebrew *ʾet hakōl*) with the sense that God has put 'duration' or everlast-ingness into all that he has made. This has the advantage of avoiding both the emendation of *ʿōlām* and questionable renderings of it in relation to human hearts or minds.[26] If this solution is followed, and the temptation is avoided of reading into the text an Augustine-type expression of an apprehension of eternity, then the burden of the interpretation shifts to the latter part of the verse:

> yet so that he (humankind) cannot find out what God has done from the beginning to the end.

This gives the passage an openness. It leaves the human race in a kind of uncertainty – an uncertainty that is more 'hot' than 'cold' as it can be the trigger for a process of searching that is not content with a status quo. For the moment, the matter will be left here.

The next stage in the argument will be to develop in one direction the comparison made by Taylor between de Saussure's speech acts and lan-guage system, and the 'rules' that are implicit in the common assumptions that underlie communal action. In many societies attitudes and behaviour are directed towards the goal of physical perfection and beauty, together with an admiration for those of above average height, strength, beauty and prowess in sports, especially athletics. Whether it be Greek sculpture that sought to capture the essence of physical beauty, or modern competi-tions such as that to discover Miss World, not to mention the attempts of ordinary citizens to improve their looks or hone their bodies, there is widespread admiration for physical perfection and an abhorrence of defect or handicap. The Hebrew word for left-handedness, *ʾittēr* takes the form of the class of words that denote handicaps. The typical form is the vowel pattern *i–ē*, with a doubling of the middle consonant, or the lengthening of the first vowel if the middle consonant cannot be doubled. Other examples from biblical Hebrew include *gibbēn* (hump-backed), *ʿivvēr* (blind), *pissēah* (lame), *hērēš* (blind), *ʾillēm* (dumb). A longer list is given by Segal for 'later' Hebrew, including words meaning 'with large ears' and 'with small ears'![27] Left-handedness was considered to be sufficiently significant for it to be commented on in more than one Old Testament passage. The 'judge' Ehud is described as left-handed in Judges 3.15, although he is able to turn this to advantage when assassinating the Moabite oppressor of Israel, Eglon. Again, in Judges 20.16, there is the information that of the forces of the tribe of Benjamin that were ranged

---

26 See Lauha, *Kohelet*, p. 69.
27 Segal, *Grammar*, pp. 108–9.

against the Israelite tribes that had come to punish Benjamin for the murder of a Levite's concubine, there were 700 men who were left-handed. Against this, there is information that when Saul was chosen to be king of Israel 'he was taller than any of the people, from his shoulder upwards' (2 Samuel 10.23). This was clearly something in his favour! Similarly, when David was chosen from among his brothers to be anointed king by Samuel it was noted in the narrative that 'he was ruddy, a lad[28] with beautiful eyes and handsome appearance'.

The most extreme statement of the disadvantage of being less than physically perfect comes in Leviticus 21.16–20, where the following classes of people are excluded from priesthood:

> the blind, the lame, the disfigured, the deformed, whoever has a (permanently) broken foot or hand; the hump-backed, the dwarf; those with defective eyesight, with boils, or scabs, or crushed testicles.[29]

A note of warning is sounded, however, in the story of David. Samuel knows that he is to anoint only one of the sons of Jesse, and he does not know which one. When he sees Eliab, evidently a young man of striking physical presence, Samuel is sure that he is looking at God's chosen king. He is told, however,

> do not look at his appearance or the height of his stature; for God does not see as man sees.[30] Man looks at the appearance,[31] but YHWH looks on the heart.

This note of warning, that what counts as a striking example of perfection from a human angle is not necessarily the divine perspective, becomes significant in the description of the servant of YHWH in Isaiah 53.2–3, a passage familiar from Handel's *Messiah*, if not from the Bible.

> He grew up before our very eyes[32] like a young plant,
> as from a root in parched ground.
> He had no fine appearance,

---

[28] Reading 'elem. Cf. Driver, *Notes on Samuel*, p. 134.

[29] Extended discussion of the translation, and parallels from Qumran and other cultures, can be found in J. Milgrom, *Leviticus 17–22* (AB), New Haven: Yale University Press, 2000, pp. 1821–32, 1841–3. Milgrom makes the interesting comment that President F. D. Roosevelt's paralysed legs were successfully concealed from the American public during his long political career (p. 1842).

[30] Reading ka'ªšer yir'eh ha'ᵉlōhîm; cf. Driver, *Notes on Samuel*, p. 133.

[31] Reading lᵉmar'ēh 'ēnāîm; cf. Driver, *Notes on Samuel*, p. 133.

[32] Reading lᵉfānēnū, cf. BHK.

nothing striking, nothing attractive.[33]
He was despised, shunned by men,
one who suffered and was overcome by grief.
As one from whom men hide their faces,
he was despised, and we took no account of him.

Commentators who have understood the servant to be an individual rather than a personification of the Israelite nation, have been noticeably reluctant to draw the conclusion that the servant is described as in some way handicapped or disfigured from birth. This, of course, may not be what is implied by saying that he grew up as from a root in parched ground; but it is undeniable that the words 'as one from whom men hide their faces, he was despised . . .' implies something about the servant's appearance that was off-putting, to put the matter mildly. Those (surely now a small minority?) who prefer the corporate interpretation of the servant have no such difficulty. For them, the words refer to the small, exilic community in Babylon that can hardly expect to command any respect.[34] Returning to the individual interpretation, the question is that of the nature and extent of the disfigurements that made the servant's appearance off-putting. One view is that it could have nothing to do with the servant's natural appearance but that it was the 'result of mistreatment or illness'.[35] For North,[36] the servant's appearance was 'repulsive' but apparently the result of sorrow and disease. The 'disease' theory is a very old one, found as early as the Babylonian Talmud, *Sanhedrin* 98b. In a discussion of the names of the Messiah, Isaiah 53.4–5 is quoted as proof that one of the Messiah's names is 'the leper (lit. "white one") of the house of Rabbi'.[37] This, however, still does not grasp the nettle.

The view taken here is that the reluctance of Christian interpreters to see the servant as handicapped or disfigured from birth owes something to the traditional interpretation of the passage as a prophecy of the passion of Jesus. To see the disfigurement of the Servant in terms of suffering or illness rather than congenital handicap makes it easier to relate the passage to the New Testament. If, however, the servant was congenitally

---

[33] Omitting v^enir'ēhū and reading v^ehemdāh for v^enehm^edēhū. See C. R. North, *The Second Isaiah: Introduction, Translation and Commentary to Chapters XL–LV*, Oxford: Clarendon Press, 1964, p. 229.

[34] For a survey of the interpretations up to 1964 see H. H. Rowley, 'The Servant of the Lord in the Light of Three Decades of Criticism' in idem, *The Servant of the Lord and Other Essays on the Old Testament*, 2nd edn, Oxford: Basil Blackwell, 1964, pp. 3–60.

[35] J. L. McKenzie, *Second Isaiah* (AB), Garden City, NY: Doubleday, 1968, p. 131.

[36] North, *Second Isaiah*, pp. 234–5.

[37] For the translation see M. Jastrow, *A Dictionary of Talmud Babli, Yerushalmi, Midrashic Literature and Targumim*, New York: Pardes, 1950, vol. 1, p. 452.

handicapped, this goes right against the idea elsewhere in the Old Testament that physical perception was a sign of God's favour, and its opposite a sign of divine judgement. This would certainly be a much more powerful explanation for the rejection of the servant by his contemporaries, and would make more sense of the amazement expressed by those in the passage who use the word 'we', that the servant had indeed been the servant of Yhwh whose rejection had somehow brought about their reconciliation with God. If this interpretation is on the right lines, then Isaiah 53 is good news for handicapped people, especially if they have been told by no doubt well-meaning but misinformed Christians, that their handicap is in some way an outworking of divine disfavour. The Old Testament speaks with many voices and is invariably at its most interesting when it appears to contradict itself and to undermine commonly held views. Part of the answer to the question 'What does it mean to be human?' is that from God's perspective it does not entail outstanding physical appearance or perfection. God looks on the heart and, in the case of the servant, uses someone who has a physical handicap.

A further point that can be added is that one does not have to be an Israelite to be fully human. Reference has been made in an earlier chapter to the importance of the Moabite young woman, Ruth (p. 90), and to God's concern for the people and cattle of Nineveh in the book of Jonah (p. 58). God's concern for humanity, according to the Old Testament, is not properly understood if it is based upon a superficial reading of passages such as Psalm 147.20:

> he [Yhwh] has not acted thus for any other nation,
> nor taught them his ordinances.

The passage may imply a special relationship but not an exclusive one.

The passage in the Old Testament most pertinent to the question 'What does it mean to be human?' is Genesis 1.26–27.

> God said, 'Let us make man in our image, according to our likeness, and they shall have dominion over the fish of the sea, the birds of the air, the cattle, all the wild animals[38] and all creeping things that creep on the earth.'
> So God created man in his image,
> created him in the image of God,
> created them male and female.

The passage has generated an enormous amount of discussion and literature.[39] From the communicative point of view the most striking

---

[38] Adding hayyat: cf. Westermann, *Genesis*, p. 110.

[39] See G. A. Jónsson, *The Image of God: Genesis 1.26–28 in a Century of Old Testament Research* (CBOT 26), Stockholm: Almquist & Wiksell, 1988; also Westermann, *Genesis*, pp. 203–14.

interpretation is that of Westermann.[40] He rejects the approach that has influenced interpretation from the Church Fathers onwards, that the primary purpose of the passage is to say something about the *nature* of humanity. On the contrary, Westermann maintains, the passage is not about the nature and being of humanity, but concerns a divine act. If this is so, then the proper question concerns the purpose of the divine act, not the nature of humanity, nor even the role that humanity is to play in the world.[41] The question is answered by Westermann by saying that God creates humanity so that there can be a creature with whom he can communicate.[42] The same point is made, he argues, in Genesis 2, but in narrative form as opposed to the declarative form in Genesis 1.26–27. Noteworthy also is Westermann's observation that, for Genesis 1.26–27, the divine–human relationship and what it entails is not something additional to a somehow independent humanity; it is what makes humanity what it is.[43]

If this line of thought is followed, two questions arise: what 'happens' between God and humanity, and what is its purpose? In trying to answer the first question it is possible to rule out the answer that was given by the Christian churches for most of their history, and which would still be held by churches in many parts of the two-thirds world. This would be that there is a revelatory communication from God that was effected by a kind of dictation of Holy Scripture to inspired individuals, such as Moses. This idea is captured by portrayals in mediaeval illustrations of biblical writers being spoken to by the Holy Spirit in the form of a dove. A more refined version of this is that God communicated to and through prophets by triggering associations of ideas through everyday experiences. Two examples that are often cited come from Jeremiah 1, where an almond tree (Hebrew *šāqēd*) reminds Jeremiah of the verb 'keeping watch' (Hebrew *šōqēd*), and a boiling pot tilted to the south leads him to foresee danger from the north (Jeremiah 1.11–12, 13–14). McKane comments that

> The prophet has a premonition of impending judgement which arises out of an ordinary experience. He had been looking at a pot resting on a fire and had noticed that it was tilted, that the contents were threatening to lap over

---

[40] Westermann, *Genesis*, pp. 214–17.

[41] That the role (Aufgabe) is the important point is maintained by von Rad, *Genesis*, p. 39.

[42] Westermann, Genesis, p. 217: 'damit etwas zwischen Gott und seinem Geschöpf geschehe' [so that something can happen between God and what he has created].

[43] Westermann, Genesis, p. 218. 'Die Gottesbeziehung ist nicht etwas zum Menschen Hinzukommendes, der Mensch ist vielmehr so geschaffen, daß sein Menschsein in der Beziehung zu Gott gemeint ist' [The relationship with God is not something that comes additionally; man is rather so created, that his humanity is determined by his relationship with God].

one side and that there would be a spillage in that direction when the pot boiled. This ordinary observation took on the character of revelatory experience for one who was absorbed in his prophetic calling and devoured by a concern to discharge his responsibility . . . The almond branch by an association with another sound and its meaning is mysteriously transmuted into a word of Yahweh.[44]

Helpful though this is, at its best it can only account for the prophetic literature of the Old Testament, and at its worst for only a handful of incidents, the few other instances including, perhaps, Jeremiah 18.1–11, and Amos 8.1–3.

In the nineteenth and twentieth centuries it was the category of history that became central to attempts to account for what 'happened' between God and humanity. History was seen as a process in which God had led the Israelite nation through successive stages of instruction, and the idea that God was essentially an educator was reflected in the titles of various works. The opening essay by F. Temple in *Essays and Reviews* was entitled 'The Education of the World'.[45] How this approach was carried through varied considerably. At one extreme, J. C. K. von Hofmann believed that because biblical history was *Heilsgeschichte*, the history of God's interventions or activities in the world, it could not be subjected to the critical rigours of historical research.[46] At the other extreme, a scholar such as W. R. Smith could assert that Israelite history as reconstructed by the modern critical research of his day – a reconstruction that differed fundamentally from what was recounted in the Old Testament itself – was nonetheless a history of God's self-disclosure.[47] One thing that von Hofmann and Smith had in common was their belief that what God communicated through 'history' was not merely information about himself, but a relationship with his people.

As I have made clear in an earlier chapter, this is not an approach that I can follow precisely in this way, because I believe that history is not a 'thing' but rather, a set of narratives about the past (see pp. 16–19). These narratives embody cultural memory. Yet it is precisely in this sense that their value lies. Cultural memory is bound up with identity, and the

[44] McKane, *Jeremiah*, vol. 1, pp. 17–18.
[45] F. Temple, 'The Education of the World' in *Essays and Reviews*, London: Longman, Green, Longman, and Roberts, 1861, pp. 1–49.
[46] J. C. K. von Hofmann, *Weissagung und Erfüllung im alten und im neuen Testament*, 2 vols, Nördlingen: Verlag der C. H. Beck'schen Buchhandlung, 1841–4; see the discussion in Rogerson, *Old Testament Criticism*, pp. 104–11.
[47] See J. W. Rogerson, *The Bible and Criticism in Victorian Britain: Profiles of F. D. Maurice and William Robertson Smith* (JSOTSS 201), Sheffield: Sheffield Academic Press, 1995.

cultural memories in the Old Testament define the people of Israel, understood as a religious community, in terms of a relationship with Yhwh. We may say, in relation to Genesis 1.26–27, that just as for the human race as a whole, to be human means to be such that things can 'happen' between God and humanity, so to be the (religious) people of Israel is to be such that things 'happen' between that community and Yhwh. The avowed purpose of this, according to passages such as Genesis 12.3, is so that all nations (i.e. the whole human race) may receive blessing. The Old Testament, we might say, is the account of a project, as understood by its writers/editors, but bearing in mind that it speaks with many voices rather than one voice. What is this project, and how would the nations (i.e. humanity) benefit? An answer is given in the vision of the end times that is found in both Isaiah 2.2–4 and Micah 4.1–4, in almost identical language. Part of it, indeed, has to do with information about God. The nations that will go up to the eschatological temple in Jerusalem will go in order to learn God's way and laws (Micah 4.2). But there will also be fundamental implications for interhuman relationships. The nations will 'hammer their swords into plough blades and their spears into pruning knives; nation will not lift up the sword against nation; no longer will they study warfare' (Micah 4.3b–c). There cannot be a divorce between greater knowledge of Yhwh's laws and a greater achievement of humane human behaviour. The two are bound inextricably together. To have the one, for example greater knowledge of God's ways, without the other, that is, greater practice of humane behaviour, would be to make a mockery of whichever of the pair was being ignored. To be human therefore also involves becoming increasingly humane. If this principle is applied to the Old Testament, it has to be admitted that many narratives fail the test that this imposes upon them, especially those which describe or advocate violence to non-Israelites. It may well be that such passages are more rhetorical than real, but this does not alter their narrative content or, indeed, their potentially negative impact upon readers.

However, there is another strand – and it is far from inconsiderable – that is constantly critical of the nation and its leaders and practices. Indeed, it is one of the remarkable features of the Old Testament, and the point that will now be argued is that this strand, by drawing attention to Israel's failures, is to be understood in terms of the project – the creation of a humane humanity. The logic is that if Israel fails to be what it is, then there is no hope that humanity at large can be or become what is intended in the project of creation.

It is natural for people to be proud of, and loyal to, the group and groups from which they derive their identity. This is certainly true of parts of the Old Testament. The portrait of Solomon in 1 Kings 3—10 is one that celebrates his achievements. This is especially true of chapter 10, which records the visit of the Queen of Sheba, who says to Solomon,

> the report that I heard in my country about your affairs and your wisdom is true; and I did not believe the reports until I came and saw with my own eyes, and indeed I had heard only the half of it. (1 Kings 10.6–7)

Even in the case of kings disapproved of by the biblical writers/editors, there are references to their achievements: to the might (*gᵉvūrāh*) of Omri (1 Kings 16.27), the building projects of Ahab (1 Kings 22.19), the recovery of Damascus (and Hamath?) to Israel by Jeroboam II (2 Kings 14.28). But the criticisms are far more severe.

A pivotal place is occupied by the story of the making of the Golden Calf in Exodus 32. Whatever the origins of this narrative (possibly an attempt to discredit Bethel, which had taken the place of Jerusalem after the latter's destruction in 587),[48] it can be read according to the argument that is being advanced here. If Israel (as a religious community) is defined in relation to YHWH, then its apostasy amounts to a refusal to be what it is. This is not simply an intellectual matter of choice, rather as we today can think of the religious allegiances of people or their rejection of any such allegiances, as part of what the market offers intellectually by way of choice. It is fundamental to the nature and destiny of humanity, if the argument is accepted that Israel's vocation is to become ever more humane for the benefit of the whole human race. At a deeper level the narrative poses the question whether the human race can become more humane simply by its own efforts. The Golden Calf is the work of the Israelites' own hands.

This way of approaching the text can be applied to all the narratives that are concerned with religious loyalty in the Old Testament, in particular to the deuteronomistic framework of the book of Judges and the books of Kings. It has to be admitted that this framework in Judges repels by its artificiality, and its crude equation of loyalty to YHWH with political and material success, and unfaithfulness to YHWH with disaster and foreign domination. It can also be read as an admittedly artificial attempt to express something that was noted in an earlier chapter (p. 41), that YHWH does not give up his project. The people may indeed decide to opt out of the project; this does not bring it to an end. F. D. Maurice caught something of this when he described the Old Testament as the story of

---

[48] See Davies, *Origins of Biblical Israel*, pp. 161–71.

'a government of voluntary creatures to teach them subjection: – an education of voluntary creatures to make them free'.[49]

The deuteronomistic verdict on the kings of Judah and Israel in the books of Kings can similarly be written off in simplistic terms. All the kings of the northern kingdom, Israel, are condemned because Jeroboam had set up Bethel and Dan as rival cult centres to Jerusalem (1 Kings 12.25–33). Kings of the southern kingdom, Judah, are praised if they suppressed sanctuaries in Judah other than Jerusalem, and condemned if they allowed or encouraged worship at the 'high places'. From a modern point of view this seems to be an intolerant attitude to the principle of the freedom of worship. From the point of view of what is being argued here, worship other than at Jerusalem, and assuming (probably against what was actually the case) that only there could true loyalty to YHWH be demonstrated, was a rejection of Israel's (the religious community's) identity and therefore a denial of God's project.

But the strand that is being identified in the Old Testament is not only to be found in the deuteronomic literature. In the so-called Book of the Covenant, the following passage occurs in Exodus 22.21–27 [Hebrew 22.20–26].

> You may not oppress a stranger [50] nor coerce him; for you were strangers in the land of Egypt. You may not afflict any widow or orphan. If you afflict them[51] and they[52] cry fervently to me I will certainly hear their[53] cry. My anger will burn and I will kill you with the sword. Your wives will become widows, your sons orphans.
>
> If you lend money to any one of my people with you who is poor, you shall not do so as a creditor; you shall not charge him interest. If ever you take as a pledge your neighbour's cloak you must return it to him before the sun goes down. It is his only form of covering, the cloak for his body. What else can he sleep in? If he cries out to me I shall hear, because I am full of compassion.

---

[49] F. D. Maurice, *The Patriarchs and Lawgivers of the Old Testament*, London: MacMillan & Co., 1892, p. 63.

[50] Hebrew gēr, which is taken here to mean anyone, Israelite or non-Israelite, living away from their kin group. For a discussion of the term see C. Bultmann, *Der Fremde im antiken Juda: Eine Untersuchung zum sozialen Typenbegriff 'ger' und seinem Bedeutungswandel in der alttestamentlichen Gesetzgebung* (FRLANT 153), Göttingen: Vandenhoeck & Ruprecht, 1992, who would not necessarily accept the above definition. For his discussion of Exodus 22.21 [Hebrew 22.20], see pp. 168–70.

[51] Hebrew 'him', but the versions have the plural. See BHK.

[52] Hebrew 'he'.

[53] Hebrew 'his'.

This is the kind of passage that is often cited as evidence that the Old Testament is replete with offensive contents. It is easy to fasten upon verse 24 [Hebrew verse 23] with its threats of divine vengeance and to overlook what is likely to provoke it. At the simplest level, the passage is about the need for social justice, and the threat of divine retribution serves to underline the point that social justice is not a trivial matter. The reference to 'any one of my people' also makes clear that injustice done to the poor (and by implication the others mentioned in the passage) is also injustice done to God. The poor (and the others) are not just anybody, they are 'My (God's) people'. A special bond exists between them and God, one that is also implied in Genesis 1.26–27, that humans are created in the divine image. It is necessary, however, to go deeper, and say that the passage is not merely about social justice as a human category, although it is certainly also that. In the whole context of Exodus 21—23, and whatever the origins of the material in the passage and the editorial processes of the enlargement to which it has undoubtedly been subjected,[54] the passage is about how Israel (as a religious community) is to be defined in terms of the obligations implied in the special relationship with YHWH. That special relationship is abused if the stranger, the widow, the orphan, and the poor are abused; and if the special relationship is abused, so is the divine project directed towards the whole of humanity, which is the reason for the special relationship.

Another instance of the strand that is being followed here – a strand either explicitly or implicitly critical of Israel (as a religious community) – is the so-called Court Chronicle of David in 2 Samuel 9—20. Although it will be treated here as a literary whole, its growth to its present literary form was undoubtedly protracted and complex.[55] Its remarkable feature in its final form is its frank portrayal of David as an adulterer, in effect a murderer, a weak and vacillating parent, and a far-from-convincing ruler. Its content does not need to be set out in detail. The highlights are David's seduction of Bathsheba while her husband, Uriah, is absent on military service; David's attempts to cover up the fact that he has made Bathsheba pregnant, by recalling Uriah and expecting him to sleep with Bathsheba; and David's instruction to Joab to arrange for Uriah to be killed in battle when Uriah, abstaining from sexual relationships while on active service, refuses all sexual contact with his wife. The sequel is that God punishes David by means of rape and fratricide among his children, and two revolts

---

[54] See Bultmann, *Der Fremde*, p. 168.
[55] See Kratz, *Komposition*, pp. 187–91; W. Dietrich, *Die frühe Königszeit in Israel: 10. Jahrhundert v. Chr.* (BE 3), Stuttgart: Kohlhammer, 1997, pp. 203–20.

against his rule, one led by his son Absalom. This is not only remarkable in itself as a piece of literature, but astonishing, given the respect accorded to David in other parts of the Old Testament. In 1 Samuel 13.14 David is described as a man after God's own heart, and in 1 Kings 3.14 Solomon is promised a long and prosperous life if he keeps God's statutes and commandments as his father David did. The highest compliment paid to Hezekiah in 2 Kings 18.3 is that he did what was right in the sight of Yₕwₕ, according to all that David had done. Later tradition identified David with the composition of a good number of the psalms in the book of Psalms, thus portraying him as a man of prayer and faith. Future hopes for the restoration of the nation rested in part upon the raising up of a leader from the dynasty of David, who could even be described as 'my servant David' (Ezekiel 34.23).

Given the outstanding respect accorded to David in various parts of the Old Testament, why was his character portrayed with such brutal frankness in 2 Samuel 9—20? An answer could be given, of course, in terms of the presence in the material of the views of different interest groups, pro- and anti- the monarchy in general and David in particular. There is probably some truth in this. The question remains, however, why the inconsistency survived; why no attempt was made to remove sentiments that were at variance with ideas that were so important for the future hopes of Israel.

Kratz makes the interesting observation that, directly or indirectly, the adoption of the first commandment, that Yₕwₕ alone was to be the God of Israel, had an effect upon the final redaction processes of the books of Samuel and Kings and their incorporation within the larger literary complex of Genesis to 2 Kings.[56] He argues that the acceptance that Yₕwₕ alone should be king over Israel both placed the whole institution of kingship in ancient Israel and Judah under judgement, and at the same time opened the future to the hope that Yₕwₕ's kingship, expressed through a renewed davidic dynasty, would restore the nation to what Yₕwₕ intended it to be.[57] This is not too far removed from what is being argued in the present chapter, with the difference that it is Genesis 1.26–27 that is the decisive reference point rather than the first of the Ten Commandments. From this point of view it can be said that the unflattering portrayal of David points to a breakdown at a decisive point in God's project for the human race through Israel. The failure of the king 'after God's own heart' is not only an offence against morality and an abuse of

[56] Kratz, *Komposition*, pp. 166, 173, 190.
[57] Kratz, *Komposition*, p. 190.

the privileges enjoyed by David (whether as historical personage or as a character in the narrative). It is also a betrayal of what is implied in the creation of the human race in the divine image.

I have been following Westermann's interpretation of Genesis 1.26–27, which puts the stress upon the *reason* for the creation of humanity in the divine image, and which argues that it is so that something can happen between God and humanity. I have suggested that this can be seen as a process of *becoming*, a project undertaken by God through the medium of Israel. I now want to develop this in a different direction. In the history of the Christian interpretation of the passage, the divine image has often been seen as a kind of property or endowment which has been bestowed upon humanity by God.[58] There has been much discussion about whether some, or all, of what was endowed has been destroyed or distorted by the 'fall', and different theological answers have been given to this question by different theological traditions. I want to argue that being made in the divine image is essentially an 'empty' concept, one which has to be filled with meaning in the light of human history and what can be learned from it. There are two reasons for this.

In his *Die Entdeckung der Person*, Theo Kobusch has drawn attention to the considerable difference between the concept of 'person' in the United Nations 'Universal Declaration of Human Rights' of 10 December 1948, and how 'personhood' was viewed in the ancient world.[59] He makes the claim that 'the discovery of the person . . . is not yet complete. In reality it is a process which extends over centuries.'[60] If this is accepted, it must be of importance for the question 'What does it mean to be human?' and it is one of the main reasons for my view that being made in the divine image is an 'empty' concept that has to be filled with meaning.

In December 1998 a symposium was held in Sheffield on the subject of the 'image of God' at which the contributions included talks from handi-capped, gay and lesbian, feminist and womanist, and black persons. They spoke of their experience of being, in some cases, regarded as dubious or aberrant instances of people made in the divine image. They insisted that they were made in the divine image and that they had a part to play in filling the concept with content and meaning.[61] In terms of what has been

---

[58] See the account in Westermann, *Genesis*, pp. 204–6.

[59] T. Kobusch, *Die Entdeckung der Person: Metaphysik der Freiheit und modernes Menschenbild*, Darmstadt: Wissenschaftliche Buchgesellschaft, 1997. See also Kather, *Person*.

[60] Kobusch, *Entdeckung*, p. 11. 'Die Entdeckung der Person . . . ist noch nicht abgeschlossen. In Wirklichkeit ist sie nämlich ein Prozeß, der sich über Jahrhunderte hinzieht.'

[61] The contributions can be found in J. Mayland (ed.), *Growing into God: Exploring Our Call to Grow into God's Image and Likeness*, London: Church House Publishing, 2003.

argued in this chapter, it can be said that the acceptance that handicapped, gay and lesbian, feminist and womanist, and black people are made in God's image is something that is happening between God and humanity by means of humanity developing a greater sensitivity to groups that have previously been legally, socially or economically excluded from full recognition. It is also a way of saying that being made in the divine image is not an individualistic matter. We become more truly human the more that we accept others as being truly human. There is an interesting dialectic here. Adorno, in his *Negative Dialectics*, stresses the importance of the uniqueness of individuals, and develops a view of society that is sharply critical of all social and economic processes that rob individuals of their uniqueness. Genocide is the ultimate form of integration, and he proposes a 'categorical imperative' in terms of the prevention of a recurrence of Auschwitz.[62] Simon Jarvis has summarized Adorno's project in the striking phrase 'the coercionless synthesis of the manifold', a phrase which expresses very well the point being made here.[63] To be created in the divine image is to be recognized as a unique individual, yet that individuality only becomes meaningful in communal life that is a 'coercionless synthesis' of the unique individualities. It is only within such a whole that the creative potentials of the individuals can be expressed in such a way as to enrich the whole; and in this whole process it is not only humanity that is discovering and developing its humanity. There is, so to speak, an enrichment and enlargement of the divine itself.

This vision requires an appropriate term, and I want to suggest that something of the sort is provided by Seyla Benhabib's distinction between the 'politics of fulfilment' and the 'politics of transfiguration'.[64] Her definition is as follows:

> The politics of fulfillment [*sic*] envisages that the society of the future attains more adequately what present society has left unaccomplished. It is the culmination of the implicit logic of the present. The politics of transfiguration emphasizes the emergence of qualitatively new needs, social relations, and modes of association, which burst open the utopian potential within the old.[65]

I would maintain that the Old Testament throughout is concerned with the 'politics of transfiguration'. This is expressed in the tension between

---

[62] T. W. Adorno, *Negative Dialektik* in *Gesammelte Schriften*, vol. 6, p. 355, 'Der Völkermord ist die absolute Integration'; ET *Negative Dialectics* (trans. E. B. Ashton), London: Routledge, 1973, p. 362.

[63] S. Jarvis, *Adorno: A Critical Introduction*, Cambridge: Polity Press, 1998, p. 32.

[64] S. Benhabib, *Critique, Norm and Utopia: A Study of the Foundations of Critical Theory*, New York: Columbia University Press, 1986.

[65] Benhabib, *Critique*, p. 13.

Genesis 1 and Genesis 9 – the world of our experience (Genesis 9) and the world conceived ideally (Genesis 1; p. 45 and the whole of Chapter 2 on creation narratives). It is also implicit in the moral imperatives that are derived from the story of the Exodus, even while it has to be acknowledged that aspects of that story, such as the killing of first-born Egyptians and the destruction of the Egyptian army at the Red Sea, are problematic for modern readers. The main point in the narrative concerns the transfiguration of an enslaved people into a liberated people, albeit a liberated people that finds its freedom difficult to cope with (see pp. 34–8). However, the story also contains transfiguring potential, as has been pointed out above in the chapter on social relationships. What I have called 'structures of grace' – social arrangements whose aim is to make possible the practical application and expression of graciousness – could also be called the 'politics of transfiguration'. It corresponds to Benhabib's language about 'the emergence of qualitatively new needs, social relations and modes of association'.

Along with its visions of a politics of transfiguration, the Old Testament is realistic about the stumbling-blocks to the realization of the vision, and a good deal of space has been devoted in the present work to a discussion of these stumbling-blocks. There are passages in the prophetic literature that combine the ideal and the actual by envisaging a future transformation of human reality. Ezekiel 36.24–27 reads,

> I will take you from the nations and gather you from all the lands, and I shall bring you into your own land. I will sprinkle upon you clear water, and you will be clean. I will cleanse you from all your defilements and all your idolatries. I will give you a new heart and put a new spirit within you. I will take away the heart of stone from your body, and give you a heart of flesh. I will put my spirit within you, and bring it about that you walk in my statutes and observe my laws.

It should not be overlooked that this passage is a promise of the restoration of Judah and Israel from their places of exile, and the reconstruction of the people of God in their own land. The temptation should also be resisted to see the passage fulfilled in the giving of the Holy Spirit to the Church following the death and exaltation of Jesus. Christians are as much in need of a heart of flesh instead of a heart of stone, as anyone else. An important point is how verse 27 is to be translated. What is found in the English versions, as represented by the RSV –

> I will . . . cause you to walk in my statutes (NEB 'make you conform to my statutes')

– can easily create the impression that what is envisaged is the denial of human freedom, and the creation of a race of robots. The use of the Hebrew *ʿāsāh* has the sense of 'bring it about that'.[66] NIV sees the difficulty and has 'move you to follow my decrees'. What is being spoken of in the promise of a 'new spirit' is the creation of a new set of conditions in which, without coercion, humanity will observe God's statutes because of a desire to do so and because they are seen as the greatest good after which one should strive. In this new order, of course, the divine statutes and laws cannot be the same as the old ones. Those are designed for a humanity with a heart of stone.[67] There is, then, a paradox. The text sets before readers something that cannot be attained by humanity. In effect, it says that ultimately, God's project of creating humanity in the divine image is bound to fail. Yet the purpose of the passage is not to create despair but hope. One way in which it does this is to speak of possibilities which belong fully to a different world but which may be available in this world – divine forgiveness, divine love and divine grace. These are properties which become most apparent at the point when humans recognize their limitations and weaknesses. Even in an imperfect world they can bring hope and transfiguration.

The introduction of concepts such as divine forgiveness, love and grace move the discussion into an area where dialogue between the Old Testament and modern thinkers wrestling with the question 'What does it mean to be human?' probably cannot be continued. Seyla Benhabib finds the utopian potential of a politics of transfiguration in the communicative ethics of Jürgen Habermas, and I have a good deal of sympathy for her point of view. But whatever else it is, the Old Testament is a set of religious texts – a witness to faith. Ultimately, to treat it as anything different is to deny the witness, and what caused the texts to be written. However, the present work has been written in the hope that the Old Testament can also be read with profit by people who are uncertain about religious faith and yet who entertain a desire to live in a better world, and to be better people as part of that world. If this 'communicative theology' commends itself to any such readers, and also rescues the Old Testament from the ignorant contempt in which it is often held, then it will have been worth the effort to write it.

---

[66] See BDB, p. 795.

[67] See further on Ezekiel 36.27, B. Maarsingh, *Ezechiël III* (De Predeking van het Oude Testament), Nijkerk: G. F. Callenbach, 1991, pp. 71–2; also the Excurson on *ruach* in W. Zimmerli, *Ezechiel* (BKAT 13), Neukirchen-Vluyn: Neukirchener Verlag, 1969, pp. 1262–5. P. Joyce, *Ezekiel: A Commentary*, London: T. & T. Clark International, 2007, pp. 204–6.

Bibliography

Adorno, T. W., *Minima Moralia* in *Gesammelte Schriften*, Darmstadt: Wissenschaftliche Buchgesellschaft, 1998, vol. 4, ET *Minima Moralia, Reflections from Damaged Life* (trans. E. F. N. Jephcott), London: Verso, 1978

Adorno, T. W., *Negative Dialektik* in *Gesammelte Schriften*, vol. 6, ET *Negative Dialectics* (trans. E. B. Ashton), London: Routledge, 1973

Adorno, T. W., *Philosophie der neuen Musik*, in *Gesammelte Schriften*, vol. 12

Adorno, T. W., 'Geschichtsphilosophischer Exkurs zur Odyssee' in R. Tiedemann (ed.), *Frankfurter Adorno Blätter*, Munich: Edition Text and Kritik, (V) 1998, pp. 37–88

Adorno, T. W. and Horkheimer, M., *Dialektik der Aufklärung* in Adorno, *Gesammelte Schriften*, vol. 3, ET *Dialectic of Enlightenment* (trans. J. Cumming), London and New York: Verso and NLB, 1979

Albertz, R., *Religionsgeschichte Israels in alttestamentlicher Zeit*, 2 vols (ATD Ergänzungsreihe 8), Göttingen: Vandenhoeck & Ruprecht, 1992

Albertz, R., 'Jobeljahr' in M. Görg and B. Lang, *Neues Bibel-Lexikon* (*NBL*), Zurich: Benzinger Verlag, 1998, vol. 2, pp. 346–7

Albertz, R., 'Sabbatjahr' in *NBL*, vol. 3, pp. 394–5

Alt, A., 'Der Anteil des Königtums an der sozialen Entwicklung in den Reichen Israel und Juda' in idem, *Kleine Schriften zur Geschichte des Volkes Israel*, Munich: C. H. Beck, 1968, vol. 3, pp. 349–72

Alter, R., *The Art of Biblical Narration*, London: George Allen & Unwin, 1981

Amitov, Y., 'Ts'on' in *Enziklopedia HaMiqrait* (Hebrew), vol. 6, Jerusalem: Bialik Institute, 1971, pp. 645–9

Anderson, A. A., *Psalms* (NCB), 2 vols, London: Oliphants, 1972

Anderson, B. W. (ed.), *Creation in the Old Testament*, London: SPCK, 1984

Anderson, G. W. (ed.), *Tradition and Interpretation: Essays by Members of the Society for Old Testament Study*, Oxford: Clarendon Press, 1979

Arens, E. (ed.), *Habermas und die Theologie: Beiträge zur theologischen Rezeption, kommunikativen Handelns*, Düsseldorf: Patmos Verlag, 1989

Aristotle, *The Nichomachean Ethics* (ed. H. Rackham), Loeb Classical Library, London and Cambridge, Mass.: Heinemann and Harvard University Press, 1956

Assmann, J., *Das kulturelle Gedächtnis: Schrift, Erinnerung und politische Identität in frühen Hochkulturen*, Munich: C. H. Beck, 1999

Assmann, J., *Religion und kulturelles Gedächtnis*, Munich: C. H. Beck, 2000

Augustine, *The City of God against Pagans* (Loeb Classical Library; trans. E. M. Sanford and W. M. Green), London and Cambridge, Mass.: Heinemann and Harvard University Press, 1965

Augustine, *Confessions* (trans. H. Chadwick), Oxford: Oxford University Press, 1992

Barclay, O., 'The Nature of Christian Morality' in B. N. Kaye and G. J. Wenham (eds), *Law, Morality and the Bible*, Leicester: Intervarsity Press, 1978, pp. 125–50

Barowski, O., *Agriculture in Iron Age Israel*, Winona Lake: Eisenbrauns, 1987

Bartelmus, R., *Theologische Klangrede: Studien zur musikalischen Gestaltung und Vertiefung theologischer Gedanken durch J. S. Bach, G. F. Händel, F. Mendelssohn, J. Brahms und E. Pepping*, Zurich: Pano Verlag, 1998

Barton, G. A., *Ecclesiastes* (ICC), Edinburgh: T. & T. Clark, 1908

Bauman, Z., *Liquid Life*, Cambridge: Polity Press, 2005

Baumann, G., '"Zukunft feministischer Spiritualität" oder "Werbefigur des Patriarchats"? Die Bedeutung der Weisheitsgestalt in Prov 1—9 für die feministisch-theologische Diskussion' in L. Schottroff and M.-T. Wacker (eds), *Von der Wurzel getragen: Christlich-feministische Exegese in Auseinandersetzung mit Antijudaismus*, Leiden: Brill, 1996, pp. 135–52

Baumgarten, H. M., *Kontinuität und Geschichte: Zur Kritik und Metakritik der historischen Vernunft*, Frankfurt a.M.: Suhrkamp, 1972

Baumgarten-Crusius, L. F. O., *Grundzüge der biblischen Theologie*, Jena, 1828

Baxter, R., *A Christian Directory* in *The Practical Works of Richard Baxter*, vol. 1, Morgan, Pa.: Soli Deo Gloria Publications, 2000

Beauchamp, P., 'Création et fondation de la loi en Gn 1,1–2,4' in F. Blanquart (ed.), *La Création dans l'orient ancien* (Lectio Divina 127), Paris: Cerf, 1987, pp. 139–82

Benhabib, S., *Critique, Norm and Utopia: A Study of the Foundations of Critical Theory*, New York: Columbia University Press, 1986

Benjamin, W., *Das Passagen-Werk* in *Gesammelte Schriften V*, Frankfurt a.M.: Suhrkamp, 1982, ET *The Arcades Project* (trans. H. Eiland and K. McLaughlin), Cambridge, Mass.: Harvard University Press, 1999

Benjamin, W., *Über den Begriff der Geschichte* in *Gesammelte Schriften* I.2, Frankfurt a.M.: Suhrkamp, 1991, pp. 691–704

Benjamin, W., 'Eduard Fuchs, der Sammler und der Historiker' in *Gesammelte Schriften* II.2, pp. 465–505

Bewer, J. A., *Jonah* (ICC), Edinburgh: T. & T. Clark, 1912

Blanquart, F. (ed.), *La Création dans l'orient ancien* (Lectio Divina 127), Paris: Cerf, 1987

Bloch, E., *Atheismus im Christentum*, Frankfurt a.M.: Suhrkamp, 1968

Bloch, E., *Das Prinzip Hoffnung*, Frankfurt a.M.: Suhrkamp, 1973

Blum, E., *Die Komposition der Vätergeschichte* (WMANT 57), Neukirchen-Vluyn: Neukirchener Verlag, 1984

Bourdieu, P., *Outline of a Theory of Practice*, Cambridge: Cambridge University Press, 1977

Braulik, G., *Deuteronomium II* (NEB), Würzburg: Echter Verlag, 1992

Brett, M., *Biblical Criticism in Crisis? The Impact of the Canonical Approach on Old Testament Studies*, Cambridge: Cambridge University Press, 1991

Bright, J., *A History of Israel* (OTL), London: SCM Press, 1960

Brock, B., *Singing the Ethos of God: On the Place of Christian Ethics in Scripture*, Grand Rapids: Eerdmans, 2007

Brodbeck, K.-H., *Die Herrschaft des Geldes: Geschichte und Systematik*, Darmstadt: Wissenschaftliche Buchgesellschaft, 2009

Bruce, F. F., 'The Theology and Interpretation of the Old Testament' in G. W. Anderson (ed.), *Tradition and Interpretation: Essays by Members of the Society for Old Testament Study*, Oxford: Clarendon Press, 1979, pp. 390–3

Bultmann, C., *Der Fremde im antiken Juda: Eine Untersuchung zum sozialen Typenbegriff 'ger' und seinem Bedeutungswandel in der alttestamentlichen Gesetzgebung* (FRLANT 153), Göttingen: Vandenhoeck & Ruprecht, 1992

Bultmann, C., Dietrich, W., and Levin, C. (eds), *Vergegenwärtigung des Alten Testaments: Beiträge zur biblischen Hermeneutik: Festschrift für Rudolf Smend zum 70. Geburtstag*, Göttingen: Vandenhoeck & Ruprecht, 2002

Bultmann, R., *Theologie des Neuen Testaments*, 9th edn, Tübingen: J. C. B. Mohr (Paul Siebeck), 1984

Burney, C. F., *Notes on the Hebrew Text of the Books of Kings*, Oxford: Clarendon Press, 1903

Calvin, J., *Genesis* (trans. J. King), Edinburgh: Banner of Truth, 1965

Chalcraft, D. J. (ed.), *Social-Scientific Old Testament Criticism: A Sheffield Reader*, Sheffield: Sheffield Academic Press, 1997

Childs, B. S., *Introduction to the Old Testament as Scripture*, London: SCM Press, 1979

Clines, D. J. A., Fowl, S. E., and Porter, S. E. (eds), *The Bible in Three Dimensions: Essays in Celebration of Forty Years of Biblical Studies in the University of Sheffield* (JSOTSS 87), Sheffield: Sheffield Academic Press, 1990

Cohen, A., *The Psalms*, Hindhead: Soncino Press, 1945

Crüsemann, F., *Der Widerstand gegen das Königtum: Die antiköniglichen Texte des Alten Testaments und der Kampf um den frühen israelitischen Stadt* (WMANT 49), Neukirchen-Vluyn: Neukirchener Verlag, 1978

Crüsemann, F., *Die Tora: Theologie und Sozialgeschichte des alttestamentlichen Gesetzes*, 2nd edn, Gütersloh: Chr. Kaiser/Gütersloher Verlagshaus, 1997

Danto, A. C., *Analytical Philosophy of History*, Cambridge: Cambridge University Press, 1965

Davidson, A. B., *Hebrew Syntax*, 3rd edn, Edinburgh: T. & T. Clark, 1901

Davidson, R., *The Courage to Doubt: Exploring an Old Testament Theme*, London: SCM Press, 1983

Davies, P. R., *In Search of 'Ancient Israel'* (JSOTSS 148), Sheffield: Sheffield Academic Press, 1992

Davies, P. R., *The Origins of Biblical Israel*, London: T. & T. Clark International, 2007

Deuser, H., et al. (eds), *Gottes Zukunft – Zukunft der Welt: Festschrift für Jürgen Moltmann zum 60. Geburtstag*, Munich: Chr. Kaiser Verlag, 1986

Dever, W. G., *Who Were the Early Israelites and Where Did They Come From?*, Grand Rapids: Eerdmans, 2003

Diamond, A. R. P., 'Jeremiah' in J. D. G. Dunn and J. W. Rogerson (eds), *Eerdmans Commentary on the Bible*, Grand Rapids: Eerdmans, 2003, pp. 534–48

Dietrich, W., *Die frühe Königszeit in Israel: 10. Jahrhundert v. Chr.* (BE 3), Stuttgart: Kohlhammer Verlag, 1997

Dietrich, W., *'Theopolitik': Studien zur Theologie und Ethik des Alten Testaments*, Neukirchen-Vluyn: Neukirchener Verlag, 2002

Diller, C., *Zwischen JHWH-Tag und neuer Hoffnung: Eine Exegese von Klagelieder 1* (ATSAT 82), St Ottilien: EOS Verlag, 2007

Dostoyevsky, F., *The Brothers Karamazov* (trans. David Magarshak), London: Penguin, 1982

Driver, S. R., *The Parallel Psalter*, Oxford: Clarendon Press, 1898

Driver, S. R., *Deuteronomy* (ICC), Edinburgh: T. & T. Clark, 1902

Driver, S. R., *The Book of Genesis* (Westminster Commentaries), London: Methuen, 1904

Driver, S. R., *Notes on the Hebrew Text and the Topography of the Books of Samuel*, 2nd edn, Oxford: Clarendon Press, 1913

Driver, S. R., and Gray, G. B., *The Book of Job together with a New Translation* (ICC), Edinburgh: T. & T. Clark, 1921

Duchrow, U., '"Eigentum verplichtet" – zur Verschuldung anderer: Kritische Anmerkungen zur Eigentumstheorie von Gunner Heinsohn und Otto Steiger aus biblisch-theologischer Perspektive' in R. Kessler and E. Loos (eds), *Eigentum, Freiheit und Fluch. Ökonomische und biblische Einwürfe*, Gütersloh: Kaiser, 2000, pp. 14–42

Dunn, J. D. G. and Rogerson, J. W. (eds), *Eerdmans Commentary on the Bible*, Grand Rapids: Eerdmans, 2003

Ebeling, G., *Dogmatik des christlichen Glaubens*, Tübingen: J. C. B. Mohr (Paul Siebeck), 1979

Eichrodt, W., *Theology of the Old Testament*, vol. 1, London: SCM Press, 1961

Elliger, K., 'Der Jakobskampf am Jabbok: Gen. 32,23ff als hermeneutisches Problem', *ZThK* 48 (1951), pp. 1–31

Emerton, J., 'The Hebrew Language' in A. D. H. Mayes (ed.), *Text in Context: Essays by Members of the Society for Old Testament Study*, Oxford: Oxford University Press, 2000, pp. 171–99

Ewald, H., *Geschichte des Volkes Israel*, vol. 1, Göttingen, 1843, p. 9, ET *History of Israel*, vol. 1, London, 1876

Fischer, A. A., *Skepsis oder Furcht Gottes? Studien zur Komposition und Theologie des Buches Kohelet* (BZAW 247), Berlin: de Gruyter, 1997

Floss, J. P., 'Form, Source and Redaction Criticism' in J. W. Rogerson and J. M. Lieu (eds), *The Oxford Handbook of Biblical Studies*, Oxford: Oxford University Press, 2006, pp. 591–614

Fries, J. F., *Neue Kritik der Vernunft*, Heidelberg: Mohr & Zimmer, 1807

Fritz, V., *Das Buch Josua* (HAT 1.7), Tübingen: Mohr Siebeck, 1994

Fromm, E., *Man for Himself: An Inquiry into the Psychology of Ethics*, London: Routledge, 2003

Galling, K., 'Das Rätsel der Zeit im Urteil Kohelets (Koh. 3, 1–5)', *ZThK* 58 (1961), pp. 1–15

Gerstenberger, E., *Das dritte Buch Mose. Leviticus* (ATD 6), Göttingen: Vandenhoeck & Ruprecht, 1993

Gerstenberger, E., *Theologien im Alten Testament: Pluralität und Synkretismus alttestamentlichen Glaubens*, Stuttgart: Kohlhammer, 2001

Gottwald, N. K., *The Tribes of Yahweh: A Sociology of the Religion of Liberated Israel 1250 to 1050 B.C.E.*, New York: Orbis, 1979

Grabbe, L. L., *A History of the Jews and Judaism in the Second Temple Period*, vol. 1: *A History of the Persian Province of Judah*, London: T. & T. Clark International, 2004

Gunkel, H., *Das Märchen im Alten Testament*, Tübingen: J. C. B. Mohr (Paul Siebeck), 1921, ET *The Folktale in the Old Testament*, Sheffield: Almond Press, 1987

Gunkel, H., *Genesis* (GHAT), 7th edn, Göttingen: Vandenhoeck & Ruprecht, 1966

Gunkel, H., *Die Psalmen* (GHAT), 5th edn, Göttingen: Vandenhoeck & Ruprecht, 1968

Gunn, D., 'Jonah' in J. D. G. Dunn and J. W. Rogerson (eds), *Eerdmans Commentary on the Bible*, Grand Rapids: Eerdmans, 2003, pp. 699–702

Habermas, J., *Theorie des kommunikativen Handelns*, 2 vols, Frankfurt a.M.: Suhrkamp, 1981

Habermas, J., 'Religion in der Öffentlichkeit' in *Zwischen Naturalismus und Religion: Philosophische Aufsätze*, Frankfurt a.M.: Suhrkamp, 2005

Halbe, J., '"Altorientalisches Weltordnungsdenken" und alttestamentliche Theologie: Zur Kritik eines Ideologems am Beispiel des israelitischen Rechts', *ZThK* 76 (1979), pp. 382–418

Hardmeier, C., *Erzähldiskurs und Redepragmatik im Alten Testament* (FAT 46), Tübingen: Mohr Siebeck, 2005

Häring, H., *Das Böse in der Welt: Gottes Macht oder Ohnmacht*, Darmstadt: Wissenschaftliche Buchgesellschaft, 1999

Hayes, J. H., and Miller, J. M., *Israelite and Judaean History* (OTL), London: SCM Press, 1977

Heschel, A. J., *The Prophets*, New York: Harper & Row, 1962

Hofmann, J. C. K. von, *Weissagung und Erfüllung im alten und im neuen Testament*, 2 vols, Nördlingen: Verlag der C. H. Beck'schen Buchhandlung, 1841–4

Hopkins, D. C., *The Highlands of Canaan: Agricultural Life in the Early Iron Age* (SWBA 3), Sheffield: Almond Press, 1985

Horne, T. H., *An Introduction to the Critical Study and Knowledge of the Holy Scriptures*, 5th edn, London, 1825

Horst, F., 'Brachjahr und Schuldverhältnisse: 15,1–18' in idem, *Das Privilegrecht Jahwes: Rechtsgeschichtliche Untersuchungen zum Deuteronomum* (FRLANT 45 [NF 28]), Göttingen: Vandenhoeck & Ruprecht, 1930, reprinted in idem, *Gottes Recht*, pp. 79–103

Horst, F., 'Das Eigentum nach dem Alten Testament' in idem, *Gottes Recht: Studien zum Recht im Alten Testament* (TB 12), Munich: Chr. Kaiser Verlag, 1961, pp. 208–12

Howard, A., *Basil Hume: The Monk Cardinal*, London: Headline, 2005

Ibn Ezra, Abraham, *'Al HaTorah*, Jerusalem: Mossad Harav Kook, 1976

Jacquet, L., *Les Psaumes et le coeur de l'homme: Étude textuelle, littéraire et doctrinale*, vol. 2, n.p.: Duculot, 1977

Janowski, B., *Konfliktgespräche mit Gott: Eine Anthropologie der Psalmen*, Neukirchen-Vluyn: Neukirchener Verlag, 2003

Jarick, J. (ed.), *Sacred Conjectures: The Context and Legacy of Robert Lowth and Jean Astruc*, London: T. & T. Clark International, 2007

Jarvis, S., *Adorno: A Critical Introduction*, Cambridge: Polity Press, 1998

Jastrow, M., *A Dictionary of Talmud Babli, Yerushalmi, Midrashic Literature and Targumim*, New York: Pardes, 1950

Jeremias, J., *Die Propheten Joel, Obadja, Jona, Micha* (ATD 24.3), Göttingen: Vandenhoeck & Ruprecht, 2007

Jónsson, G. A., *The Image of God: Genesis 1.26–28 in a Century of Old Testament Research* (CBOT 26) Stockholm: Almquist & Wiksell, 1988

Joyce, P., *Ezekiel: A Commentary*, London: T. & T. Clark International, 2007

Jüngel, E., 'Gottes ursprüngliches Anfangen als schöpferische Selbstbegrenzung' in H. Deuser et al. (eds), *Gottes Zukunft – Zukunft der Welt: Festschrift für Jürgen Moltmann zum 60. Geburtstag*, Munich: Kaiser, 1986, pp. 265–75

Jüngel, E., *Das Evangelium von der Rechtfertigung des Gottlosen als Zentrum des christlichen Glaubens*, Tübingen: Mohr Siebeck, 1998

Kaiser, O., *Klagelieder* (ATD 16/2) in H.-P. Müller, O. Kaiser and J. A. Loader, *Das Hohelied, Klagelieder, Das Buch Ester*, Göttingen: Vandenhoeck & Ruprecht, 1992

Kaiser, O., 'Die Botschaft des Buches Kohelet' and 'Beiträge zur Kohelet-Forschung' in idem, *Gottes und der Menschen Weisheit* (BZAW 261), Berlin: de Gruyter, 1998, pp. 126–200

Kant, I., 'Analytik des Erhabenen' in idem, *Kritik der Urteilskraft, Kants Werke: Akademie Textausgabe*, Berlin: W. de Gruyter, 1968, vol. 5, pp. 244–64

Kaplan, E. K., and Dresner, S. H., *Abraham Joshua Heschel: Prophetic Witness*, New Haven: Yale University Press, 1998

Kather, R., *Person: Die Begründung menschlicher Identität*, Darmstadt: Wissenschaftliche Buchgesellschaft, 2007

Kaye, B. N., and Wenham, G. J. (eds), *Law, Morality and the Bible*, Leicester: Inter-Varsity Press, 1978

Kertész, I., *Kaddish for a Child Not Born* (trans. C. W. and K. A. Wilson), Evanston, Ill.: Northwestern University Press, 1997

Kessler, R., *Staat und Gesellschaft im vorexilischen Juda vom 8. Jahrhundert bis zum Exil* (SVT 47), Leiden: E. J. Brill, 1992

Kessler, R., 'Arbeit, Eigentum und Freiheit: Die Frage des Grundeigentums in der Endgestalt der Profetenbücher' in R. Kessler and E. Loos (eds), *Eigentum, Freiheit und Fluch: Ökonomische und biblische Einwürfe*, Gütersloh: Kaiser, 2000, pp. 64–88

Kessler, R., and Loos, E. (eds), *Eigentum, Freiheit und Fluch: Ökonomische und biblische Einwürfe*, Gütersloh: Kaiser, 2000

Kierkegaard, S., *Training in Christianity* (trans. W. Lowrie), London: Oxford University Press, 1941

Kippenberg, H. G., *Seminar: Die Entstehung der antiken Klassengesellschaft*, Frankfurt a.M.: Suhrkamp, 1977

Kobusch, T., *Die Entdeckung der Person: Metaphysik der Freiheit und modernes Menschenbild*, Darmstadt: Wissenschaftliche Buchgesellschaft, 1997

Kratz, R. G., *Die Komposition der erzählenden Bücher des Alten Testaments*, Göttingen: Vandenhoeck & Ruprecht, 2000

Kraus, H.-J., *Psalmen*, 2nd edn (BKAT 15.1), Neukirchen-Vluyn: Neukirchener Verlag, 1961

Kraus, H.-J., *Klagelieder*, 4th edn (BKAT 20), Neukirchen-Vluyn: Neukirchener Verlag, 1983

Laato, A., and Moor, J. C. de (eds), *Theodicy in the World of the Bible*, Leiden: E. J. Brill, 2003

Lauer, S., 'Leiden II' in *TRE*, vol. 20, pp. 672–6

Lauha, A., *Kohelet* (BKAT 19), Neukirchen-Vluyn: Neukirchener Verlag, 1978

Lemaire, A., 'The Tel Dan Stela as a Piece of Royal Historiography', *JSOT* 81 (1998), pp. 3–14

Leutzsch, M., 'Das biblische Zinsverbot' in R. Kessler and E. Loos (eds), *Eigentum, Freiheit und Fluch: Ökonomische und biblische Einwürfe*, Gütersloh: Kaiser, 2000, pp. 108–10

Lévi-Strauss, C., *The Savage Mind*, London: Weidenfeld and Nicolson, 1966

Lindsay, A. D., *The Two Moralities: Our Duty to God and to Society*, London: Eyre & Spottiswoode, 1940

Loades, A. L., and McLain, M. (eds), *Hermeneutics, the Bible and Literary Criticism*, London: Macmillan, 1992

Loretz, O., 'Die prophetische Kritik des Rentenkapitalismus: Grundlagen-Probleme der Prophetenforschung' *UF* 7 (1975), pp. 271–8

Luhmann, N., *Soziale Systeme: Grundriß einer allgemeinen Theorie*, Frankfurt a.M.: Suhrkamp, 1987

Luhmann, N., *Einführung in die Theorie der Gesellschaft*, Darmstadt: Wissenschaftliche Buchgesellschaft, 2005

Luhmann, N., *Die Moral der Gesellschaft*, Frankfurt a.M.: Suhrkamp, 2008

Maarsingh, B., *Ezechiël III* (De Predeking van het Oude Testament), Nijkerk: G. F. Callenbach, 1991

McCalla, A., *The Creationist Debate: The Encounter between the Bible and the Historical Mind*, London: T. & T. Clark International, 2006

McKane, W., *Jeremiah* (ICC), Edinburgh: T. & T. Clark, vol. 1, 1986, vol. 2, 1996

McKenzie, J. L., *Second Isaiah* (AB), Garden City, NY: Doubleday, 1968

Marx, K., 'Theses on Feuerbach XI' in K. Marx and F. Engels, *The German Ideology*, London: Lawrence & Wishart, 1970, pp. 121–3

Mason, R., *Preaching the Tradition: Homily and Hermeneutics after the Exile*, Cambridge: Cambridge University Press, 1990

Maurice, F. D., *The Patriarchs and Lawgivers of the Old Testament*, London: MacMillan, 1892

Mayes, A. D. H. (ed.), *Text in Context. Essays by Members of the Society for Old Testament Study*, Oxford: Oxford University Press, 2000

Mayland, J. (ed.), *Growing into God: Exploring our Call to Grow into God's Image and Likeness*, London: Church House Publishing, 2003

Mesters, C., *Die Botschaft des leidenden Volkes*, Neukirchen-Vluyn: Neukirchener Verlag, 1982

Milgrom, J., *Leviticus 17–22* (AB), New Haven: Yale University Press, 2000

Millard, A., 'Authors, Books, and Readers in the Ancient World' in J. W. Rogerson and J. M. Lieu (eds), *The Oxford Handbook of Biblical Studies*, pp. 544–64

Müller, A., *Proverbien 1—9: Der Weisheit neue Kleider* (BZAW 291), Berlin: de Gruyter, 2000

Neumann-Gorsolke, U., *Herrschen in den Grenzen der Schöpfung: Ein Beitrag zur alttestamentlichen Anthropologie am Beispiel von Psalm 8, Genesis 1 und verwandten Texten* (WMANT 101), Neukirchen-Vluyn: Neukirchener Verlag, 2004

Niebuhr, B. G., *Römische Geschichte*, 1–2, Berlin: Reimer, 1811–12, ET by J. C. Hare and C. Thirlwall, *The History of Rome*, 4th edn, London: Taylor & Walton, 1847

Nietzsche, F., *Jenseits von Gut und Böse* in Friedrich Nietzsche, *Sämtliche Werke: Kritische Studienausgabe*, vol. 5 (ed. G. Colli and M. Montinari), Munich: Deutscher Taschenbuchverlag; Berlin: W. de Gruyter, 1980, pp. 9–243, ET *Beyond Good and Evil*, London: Penguin, 1990

Nietzsche, F., *Die Umwertung aller Werte* exists in a number of references in Nietzsche's posthumous papers. See *Sämtliche Werke*, vol. 15, p. 336 for details.

Nietzsche, F., *Zur Genealogie der Moral: Eine Streitschrift* in *Sämtliche Werke*, vol. 5, pp. 247–412

North, C. R., *The Second Isaiah: Introduction, Translation and Commentary to Chapters XL–LV*, Oxford: Clarendon Press, 1964

Notes and Queries in Anthropology, 6th edn, London: Routledge & Kegan Paul, 1951

Noth, M., *Überlieferungsgeschichte des Pentateuch*, Stuttgart: Kohlhammer Verlag, 1948; ET *A History of Pentateuchal Traditions*, Englewood Cliffs: Prentice Hall, 1972

Noth, M., *The History of Israel*, London: A. & C. Black, 1958, translated from *Geschichte Israels*, 2nd edn, Göttingen: Vandenhoeck & Ruprecht, 1955

Noth, M., *Das vierte Buch Mose* (ATD 7), Göttingen: Vandenhoeck & Ruprecht, 1966

Oesterley, W. O. E. and Robinson, T. H., *A History of Israel*, 2 vols, Oxford: Clarendon Press, 1932

Otto, E., *Theologische Ethik des Alten Testaments*, Stuttgart: Kohlhammer, 1994

Otto, E., *Krieg und Frieden in der Hebräischen Bibel und im Alten Orient: Aspekte für eine Friedensordnung in der Moderne*, Stuttgart: Kohlhammer, 1999

Otto, R., *Aufsätze das Numinose betreffend*, Stuttgart and Gotha: Andreas Perthes, 1923

Otto, R., *Das Heilige: Über das Irrationale in der Idee des Göttlichen und sein Verhältnis zum Rationalen*, Munich: C. H. Beck, 1936, ET *The Idea of the Holy: An Inquiry into the Non-rational Factor in the Idea of the Divine and its Relation to the Rational*, Harmondsworth: Penguin, 1959

Parker, D., 'The New Testament' in J. W. Rogerson (ed.), *The Oxford Illustrated History of the Bible*, Oxford: Oxford University Press, 2001, pp. 110–33

Poole, M., *A Commentary on the Holy Bible* (1685), Edinburgh: Banner of Truth Trust, 1962

Premnath, D. N., 'Latifundialization and Isaiah 6.8–10', *JSOT* (40) (1988), pp. 47–60

Preuss, H. D., *Theologie des Alten Testaments*, vol. 2: *Israels Weg mit JHWH*, Stuttgart: Kohlhammer Verlag, 1992

Prideaux, H., *The Old and New Testament Connected in the History of the Jews and Neighbouring Nations*, London, 1716–18

Pritchard, J. B., *Ancient Near Eastern Texts relating to the Old Testament*, 2nd edn, Princeton: Princeton University Press, 1955

Pury, A. de, and Römer, T. (eds), *Die sogenannte Thronfolgegeschichte Davids: Neue Einsichten und Anfragen* (OBO 176), Freiburg Schweiz: Universitätsverlag; Göttingen: Vandenhoeck & Ruprecht, 2000

Qimhi, D., *Haperush Hashalem al Tehillim*, Jerusalem: Massad Harav Kook, 1971

Rad, G. von, 'Das theologische Problem des alttestamentlichen Schöpfungsglaubens' in idem, *Gesammelte Studien zum Alten Testament* (TB 8), Munich: Chr. Kaiser Verlag, 1961, pp. 136–47, ET 'The Theological Problem of the Old Testament Doctrine of Creation' in B. W. Anderson (ed.), *Creation in the Old Testament*, London: SPCK, 1984, pp. 53–64

Rad, G. von, *Das fünfte Buch Mose* (ATD 8), Göttingen: Vandenhoeck & Ruprecht, 1964

Rad, G. von, *Genesis* (ATD) Göttingen: Vandenhoeck & Ruprecht, 1972

Renkema, J., 'Theodicy in Lamentations?' in A. Laato and J. C. de Moor (eds), *Theodicy in the World of the Bible*, Leiden: Brill, 2000, pp. 410–28

Rich, F., *The Greatest Story ever Sold: The Decline and Fall of Truth from 9/11 to Katrina*, New York: Penguin, 2006

Richter, J. P., 'Vorschule der Ästhetik', in idem, *Sämtliche Werke*, vol. 1.5, Darmstadt: Wissenschaftliche Buchgesellschaft, 2000

Richter, W., *Exegese als Literaturwissenschaft: Entwurf einer alttestamentlichen Literaturtheorie und Methodologie*, Göttingen: Vandenhoeck & Ruprecht, 1971

Richter, W. (ed.), *Biblia Hebraica transcripta* (ATSAT 33.1–33.13), St Ottilien: Eos Verlag, 1991–3

Riesener, B. I., 'Rut' in *NBL*, vol. 3, pp. 384–6

Robinson, N. H. G., *The Groundwork of Christian Ethics*, London: Collins, 1971

Rogerson, J. W., *Myth in Old Testament Interpretation* (BZAW 134), Berlin: de Gruyter, 1974

Rogerson, J. W., 'Progressive Revelation: Its History and its Value as a Key to Old Testament Interpretation' (the A. S. Peake Memorial Lecture 1981), *Epworth Review* 9 (1982), pp. 73–86

Rogerson, J. W., *Old Testament Criticism in the Nineteenth Century: England and Germany*, London: SPCK, 1984

Rogerson, J. W., 'Was Early Israel a Segmentary Society?' *JSOT* 36 (1986), pp. 17–26

Rogerson, J. W., '"What does it Mean to be Human?" The Central Question of Old Testament Theology?' in D. J. A. Clines, S. E. Fowl and S. E. Porter (eds), *The Bible in Three Dimensions: Essays in Celebration of Forty Years of Biblical Studies in the University of Sheffield*, Sheffield: Sheffield Academic Press, 1990, pp. 285–98

Rogerson, J. W. *Genesis 1–11* (OTG), Sheffield: JSOT Press, 1991

Rogerson, J. W., 'What is Religion? The Challenge of Wilhelm Vatke's *Biblische Theologie*' in C. Bultmann, W. Dietrich and C. Levin (eds), *Vergegenwärtigung des Alten Testaments: Beiträge zur biblischen Hermeneutik: Festschrift für Rudolf Smend zum 70. Geburtstag*, Göttingen: Vandenhoeck & Ruprecht, 2002, pp. 272–84

Rogerson, J. W., *W. M. L. de Wette, Founder of Modern Biblical Criticism: An Intellectual Biography* (JSOTSS 126), Sheffield: Sheffield Academic Press, 1992

Rogerson, J. W., 'Wrestling with the Angel: A Study in Historical and Literary Interpretation' in A. L. Loades and M. McLain (eds), *Hermeneutics, the Bible and Literary Criticism*, London: Macmillan, 1992, pp. 131–44

Rogerson, J. W., *The Bible and Criticism in Victorian Britain: Profiles of F. D. Maurice and William Robertson Smith* (JSOTSS 201), Sheffield: Sheffield Academic Press, 1995

Rogerson, J. W., *Chronicle of the Old Testament Kings: The Reign-by-Reign Record of the Rulers of Ancient Israel*, London: Thames & Hudson, 1999

Rogerson, J. W. (ed.), *The Oxford Illustrated History of the Bible*, Oxford: Oxford University Press, 2001

Rogerson, J. W., *The Psalms in Daily Life*, London: SPCK, 2001

Rogerson, J. W., 'Additions to Daniel' in J. D. G. Dunn and J. W. Rogerson (eds), *Eerdmans Commentary on the Bible*, Grand Rapids: Eerdmans, 2003, pp. 804–5

Rogerson, J. W., 'Israel to the End of the Persian Period: History, Social, Political and Economic Background' in J. W. Rogerson and J. M. Lieu (eds), *The Oxford Handbook of Biblical Studies*, Oxford: Oxford University Press, 2006, pp. 271–3

Rogerson, J. W., *According to the Scriptures? The Challenge of Using the Bible in Social, Moral and Political Questions*, London: Equinox, 2007

Rogerson, J. W., 'Charles-François Houbigant: His Background, Work and Importance for Lowth' in J. Jarick (ed.), *Sacred Conjectures: The Context and Legacy of Robert Lowth and Jean Astruc*, London: T. & T. Clark International, 2007, pp. 83–92

Rogerson, J. W., 'Die Neubesinnung auf die Identität Israels in der exilischen Epoche' in H. Irsigler (ed.), *Die Identität Israels: Entwicklungen und Kontroversen in alttestamentlicher Zeit* (Herders Biblische Studien 56), Freiburg: Herder Verlag, 2009, pp. 101–9

Rogerson, J. W. and Davies, P. R., *The Old Testament World*, 2nd edn, London: T. & T. Clark International, 2005

Rogerson, J. W. and Lieu, J. M. (eds), *The Oxford Handbook of Biblical Studies*, Oxford: Oxford University Press, 2006

Rose, M., *Rien de nouveau: Nouvelles approches du livre de Qohéleth: Avec une bibliographie (1988–1998) élaborée par Béatrice Perregaux Allisson* (OBO 168), Fribourg: Edition Universitaires Suisses; Göttingen: Vandenhoeck & Ruprecht, 1999

Rowley, H. H., 'The Servant of the Lord in the Light of Three Decades of Criticism' in idem, *The Servant of the Lord and Other Essays on the Old Testament*, 2nd edn, Oxford: Basil Blackwell, 1964, pp. 3–60

Rütersworden, U., *Die Beamten der israelitischen Königszeit: Eine Studie zu śr und vergleichbaren Begriffen* (BWANT 117), Stuttgart: Kohlhammer Verlag, 1985

Sarot, M., 'Theodicy and Modernity' in A. Laato and J. C. de Moor (eds) *Theodicy in the World of the Bible*, Leiden: Brill, 2003, pp. 1–26

Sarot, M., 'Apathie' in *RGG*, vol. 1, pp. 582–3

Schiller, F., *Wallensteins Lager* in F. Schiller, *Sämtliche Werke*, vol. 2, Darmstadt: Wissenschaftliche Buchgesellschaft, 1981, pp. 275–311

Schiller, F., *Geschichte des Dreißigjährigen Kriegs* in *Sämtliche Werke*, vol. 4, pp. 363–745

Schiller, F., 'Vom Erhabenen' in *Sämtliche Werke*, vol. 5, pp. 489–512

Schiller, H.-E., *Bloch-Konstellationen: Utopien der Philosophie*, Lüneburg: zu Klampen, 1991

Schmid, H. H., 'Schöpfung, Gerechtigkeit und Heil: "Schöpfungstheologie" als Gesamthorizont biblischer Theologie', *ZThK* 70 (1973), pp. 1–19, ET 'Creation, Righteousness and Salvation: "Creation Theology" as the Broad Horizon of Biblical Theology' in B. W. Anderson (ed.), *Creation in the Old Testament*, London: SPCK, 1984, pp. 102–17

Schmidt, L., *'De Deo': Studien zur Literarkritik und Theologie des Buches Jona, des Gesprächs zwischen Abraham und Jahwe in Gen 18.22ff. und von Hi 1* (BZAW 143), Berlin: de Gruyter, 1976

Scholder, K., *Ursprünge und Probleme der Bibelkritik im 17. Jahrhundert* (FGLP 10/33), Munich: Kaiser, 1966

Schottroff, L., and Wacker, M.-T. (eds), *Von der Wurzel getragen: Christlich-feministische Exegese in Auseinandersetzung mit Antijudaismus*, Leiden: E. J. Brill, 1996

Schroer, S., 'Terafim' in *NBL*, vol. 3, pp. 816–17

Schulte, J., et al. (eds), Ludwig Wittgenstein, *Philosophische Untersuchungen: Kritisch-genetische Edition*, Frankfurt: Suhrkamp, 2001

Schunk, K.-D., *Nehemiah* (BKAT 23), Neukirchen-Vluyn: Neukirchener Verlag, 2008

Seebass, H., 'Über den Beitrag des A. T. zu einer theologischen Anthropologie', *KuD* 22 (1976), pp. 41–63

Segal, M. H., *A Grammar of Mishnaic Hebrew*, Oxford: Clarendon Press, 1927

Siebert, R. J., *The Critical Theory of Religion: The Frankfurt School* (Religion and Reason 29), Berlin: Mouton, 1985

Skinner, J., *Genesis* (ICC), Edinburgh: T. & T. Clark, 1910

Smend, R., *Deutsche Alttestamentler in drei Jahrhunderten*, Göttingen: Vandenhoeck & Ruprecht, 1989

Smend, R., 'Gerhard von Rad' in idem, *From Astruc to Zimmerli: Old Testament Scholarship in Three Centuries* (trans. M. Kohl), Tübingen: Mohr Siebeck, 2007, pp. 170–97

Smith, W. R., *The Old Testament in the Jewish Church*, Edinburgh, 1881

Smith, W. R., *Kinship and Marriage in Early Arabia*, 2nd edn, London: A. & C. Black, 1907

Steudel, J. C. F., *Vorlesungen über die Theologie des Alten Testaments*, Berlin: Reimer, 1840

Taylor, C., *Sources of the Self: The Making of the Modern Identity*, Cambridge: Cambridge University Press, 1989

Taylor, C., 'To Follow a Rule' in idem, *Philosophical Arguments*, Cambridge, Mass.: Harvard University Press, 1995, pp. 165–80

Taylor, C., *A Secular Age*, Cambridge, Mass.: Belknap Press of Harvard University Press, 2007

Temple, F., 'The Education of the World' in *Essays and Reviews*, London: Longman, Green, Longman, and Roberts, 1861, pp. 1–49

Thompson, S., *Motif-Index of Folk Literature*, Bloomington: Indiana University Press, 1966

Tillich, P., *Systematic Theology*, London: James Nisbet, 1953; *Systematische Theologie*, Berlin: de Gruyter, 1987

Utzschneider, H., *Gottes Vorstellung: Untersuchungen zur literarischen Ästhetik und ästhetischen Theologie des Alten Testaments* (BWANT 9.15), Stuttgart: Kohlhammer, 2007

Veerkamp, T., *Die Vernichtung des Baal: Auslegung der Königsbücher (1.17–2.11)*, Stuttgart: Alektor-Verlag, 1983

Wellhausen, J., *Prolegomena zur Geschichte Israels*, Berlin: Reimer, 1883

Westermann, C., *Das Buch Jesaja. Kap. 40-66* (ATD 19), Göttingen: Vandenhoeck & Ruprecht, 1966

Westermann, C., *Genesis* (BKAT 1), Neukirchen-Vluyn: Neukirchener Verlag, 1968

Wette, W. M. L. de, *Beiträge zur Einleitung in das Alte Testament*, vol. 1: *Kritischer Versuch über die Glaubwürdigkeit der Bücher der Chronik mit Hinsicht auf die Geschichte der Mosaischen Bücher und Gesetzgebung*, Halle: Schimmelpfennig & Compagnie, 1806, reprint Darmstadt: Wissenschaftliche Buchgesellschaft, 1971

Wette, W. M. L. de, 'Beytrag zur Charakteristik des Hebräismus' in *Studien*, vol. 3.2 (ed. C. Daub and F. Creuzer), Heidelberg, 1807, pp. 241–31

Whybray, R. N., 'Ecclesiastes 1.5–7 and the Wonders of Nature', *JSOT* 41 (1988), pp. 105–12

Whybray, R. N., *Ecclesiastes* (OTG), Sheffield: Sheffield Academic Press, 1989

Wildberger, H., *Jesaja* (BKAT 10.1), Neukirchen-Vluyn: Neukirchener Verlag, 1972

Witte, M., *Die biblische Urgeschichte: Redaktions- und theologiegeschichtliche Beobachtungen zu Genesis 1,1–11,26* (BZAW 265), Berlin: W. de Gruyter, 1998

Wolff, H. W., *Hosea*, 2nd edn (BKAT 14.1), Neukirchen-Vluyn: Neukirchener Verlag, 1963

Wolff, H. W., *Jona* (BKAT 14.3), Neukirchen-Vluyn: Neukirchener Verlag, 1977

Wolff, H. W., *Micha* (BKAT 14), Neukirchen-Vluyn: Neukirchener Verlag, 1980

Wright, G. E., *God Who Acts: Biblical Theology as Recital* (SBT 8), London: SCM Press, 1952

Wright, G. E., *Biblical Archaeology*, revised and expanded edition, Philadelphia: Westminster Press, 1962

Zenger, E., *Gottes Bogen in den Wolken: Untersuchungen zu Komposition und Theologie der priesterlichen Urgeschichte* (SBS 112), Stuttgart: Verlag Katholisches Bibelwerk, 1983

Zimmerli, W., *Ezechiel* (BKAT 13), Neukirchen-Vluyn: Neukirchener Verlag, 1969

Zohary, M., *Plants of the Bible*, Cambridge: Cambridge University Press, 1982

Index of references to the Bible and ancient Jewish texts

Index of names

Index of subjects

213